AF883184

UNCOMMON SOLDIER

For Tanya

UNCOMMON SOLDIER

Brave, compassionate and tough, the making of Australia's modern diggers

CHRIS MASTERS

ALLEN&UNWIN

Australian Government

Australia Council for the Arts

This project has been assisted by the Australian Government through the Australia Council for the Arts, its funding advisory body.

First published in Australia in 2012
This paperback edition published in 2013

Copyright © Chris Masters 2012

All rights reserved. No part of this book may be reproduced or transmitted in any form or by any means, electronic or mechanical, including photocopying, recording or by any information storage and retrieval system, without prior permission in writing from the publisher. The Australian *Copyright Act 1968* (the Act) allows a maximum of one chapter or 10 per cent of this book, whichever is the greater, to be photocopied by any educational institution for its educational purposes provided that the educational institution (or body that administers it) has given a remuneration notice to Copyright Agency Limited (CAL) under the Act.

Allen & Unwin
83 Alexander Street
Crows Nest NSW 2065
Australia
Phone: (61 2) 8425 0100
Fax: (61 2) 9906 2218
Email: info@allenandunwin.com
Web: www.allenandunwin.com

Cataloguing-in-Publication details are available from the National Library of Australia www.trove.nla.gov.au

ISBN 978 1 74331 732 7

Typeset in 12/16pt Adobe Caslon by Midland Typesetters, Australia
Printed and bound in Australia by Pegasus Media & Logictics

MIX
Paper | Supporting responsible forestry
FSC www.fsc.org
FSC® C008194

The paper in this book is FSC® certified. FSC® promotes environmentally responsible, socially beneficial and economically viable management of the world's forests.

25 24 23 22 21

CONTENTS

A QUARREL WITH MYSELF

The question of what is special about the Australian soldier settled into my consciousness from the time I could think and read. I grew up after World War II in the period of silence that followed the thunder, one among a vast crowd standing beyond the hunched circle of experience. Grandparents and parents exhausted by two wars were sick of talking about it; they were counselled not to, they were brutalised, ashamed, haunted and proud. The frosted glass door the war generations slammed on the subject compelled in me a sharpening of concentration and interest.

Some of my first reading included yellowing copies of wartime yearbooks found in Australian homes of that era: *Khaki and Green*, *Jungle Warfare* and the like. Gathered down from the bookshelf and carried to a patch of sunlight on the verandah, I would soak in the images of lean, tough, sun-tanned soldiers who as far as I could tell could not be mistaken for anything but Australian. Sometimes these men would be bearing weapons and a look of serious business. Sometimes they would be laughing, and even showing tenderness if, for example, they were photographed with a wounded mate.

I searched those images for the missing narrative and a keener sense of what really happened. Where was the enemy? What was the joke? How was that soldier wounded? A childish eagerness took on the first rubbings of patriotism.

It was hard to avoid. On the way to school, along the road to the December holiday, I passed the monuments—they were everywhere. I could not miss the inscriptions, which pressed a deeper groove. A sense of pride formed up alongside nascent notions of service and sacrifice.

I knew the Australian soldiers were volunteers. Like the surf lifesavers who dashed without hesitation to the rescue, the soldiers would return to civilian dress when the job was done. On Anzac Day, when suits were pulled from cupboards, medals pinned and corned beef and pickle sandwiches cut into small triangles, I lined up for more morsels of meaning. If there was boasting I did not hear it. Big noting was not Australian.

By my teenage years I began to hear traces of dissent. George Johnston's book *My Brother Jack* released some of the ghosts of war. My own uncle Dave, rarely spoken of, had returned from New Guinea a troubled man, a drinker. Alan Seymour's play 'The One Day of the Year' challenged the spiritual purity of Anzac; the Vietnam War challenged much more. There was noisy, generational opposition. Australian soldiers were no longer all volunteers. They were again fighting someone else's war, and civilians who were supposed to be protected were being maimed and killed. There was argument that we were not just *on* the wrong side, we *were* the wrong side.

I was eligible for the Vietnam draft and would have gone with other conscripts had my number come up. My mother, who worked as a local newspaper reporter, was appalled when I told her. When visiting her I scanned the inevitable 'home towners', the press releases and photographs sent by the government to local newspapers. They were stories of other local boys, now in uniform, whose exploits had earned a ribbon and a brush with fame. It seems Mum's own propaganda had worked wonders.

My number did not come up but I would see war nevertheless, ironically because of Mum's influence. By the time I was a young adult it was clear there was no other job for me but journalism, and for me no better place to practise it than the ABC's *Four Corners.*

At *Four Corners* a foreign story was often set in a distant war zone, where I would see plenty of soldiers going about their business. It was not always pretty: in Vietnam decades of violence delivered hunger and poverty; in Cambodia the cities were shattered and the country a graveyard; in the former Yugoslavia I saw soldiers on the rampage. Blood and brain tissue on a wall where civilians were slaughtered, ammunition abandoned by the roadside to make space for the looting. In Africa there was starvation born of violence; I watched children die. In Rwanda the bodies were piled higher than the roof of our vehicle. I passed stricken faces and felt I was in hell.

For 25 years I saw cruelty. I saw madness. I saw war. And it made me wonder whether it makes us much the same. Humans will be brave and cowardly; they will use their uniform to protect, and they will use their uniform to pillage. Perhaps soldiers the world over are much the same. The experience of war imposes common characteristics, comradeship (or, as we say, mateship) predominant and also routine, banal expressions of evil.

While I saw plenty that shocked and demoralised me, I can't say the accumulating experience made me a pacifist. Of course it made me anti war, but I am also anti plague and pestilence. There is too much danger out there, too many guns and dark hearts for us to be anything but sensible about protecting ourselves.

But in that quarter century I also saw something else that challenged notions of modern soldiering—the battlefield had changed. Ground wars were not so often being fought in abandoned farmland and deserts, through defined trench lines and barbed wire. Instead, the battlefield was all around us in remote villages, neighbourhoods, nightclubs and multiple-storey office buildings.

Newly trained soldiers would be forced to make split second decisions about whether the person approaching was an innocent pregnant woman or a suicide bomber. Critical decisions on the battlefield that might tell on a nation's appetite to commit forces were as likely to be made by the soldier on the ground as by the general back at headquarters.

A mass of intelligence gathered by eyes watching from on the ground to deep space meant that the primary target could now be the commander secreted in a remote bunker rather than the conscript in the front line. But that commander may well have chosen refuge in a village rather than a headquarters bunker, and the young soldier watching that village from his Forward Observation Post had the capacity to call in thunderous destruction: helicopter gunships, long-range artillery, strike fighters, drones and long range bombers.

That soldiers with the power to rain death on entire communities faced no equivalent enemy—Al Qaeda does not have a navy or an air force. However, the good side of the story is that this well-trained soldier in the Forward Observation Post was less likely to decide to destroy the village. It is easier to make decisions like that sitting in front of a bank of monitors a continent away or from 20,000 feet.

A new term was formed to describe the devolving responsibility, and soon the strategic corporal became the strategic private. The notion that soldiering was the province of dumb grunts was under severe challenge. The modern Australian soldier required a range of skills: driver, signaller, medic, rifleman.

In the course of my work I saw those skills in action. In 1999 at Batugade in East Timor, close to the West Timor border, I joined Australian soldiers. There had been some skirmishes with Indonesian-backed militia, but despite the provocation restraint was the notable order of the day.

At stand down, as the sun dipped and the likelihood of attack increased, I marvelled at the professional discipline of young Australian soldiers who vanished with the night. They stayed awake, sometimes with the help of a bayonet positioned beneath their chin. The only sound that night from the Australian side was the reporter's snoring.

I spoke to East Timorese civilians who also marvelled at the concept of the soldier transformed from oppressor to protector. During Indonesian rule civilians had become used to hiding from soldiers, and I heard over and over stories of taxi drivers whose vehicles were hijacked by Indonesian soldiers and of mothers hiding their daughters.

Having seen soldiers use their uniform to tax and violate civilians, I was heartened by evidence to the contrary. I became fascinated with the idea of the civilised soldier tempted by the possibility that Australians had qualities well suited to peace keeping operations, where not fighting can be every bit as important as fighting. No doubt some of these ideas folded into childhood impressions of the noble digger and the Anzac legend.

You would have to say the reality of the digger story stood in bold contrast to reports constantly uncovered at home of boorish, brutish misogynist behaviour that instigated inquiry after inquiry into Defence culture. While the battlefield abroad was changing, so too was pressure increasing at home for cultural reform.

The world can be a grim place, and investigative reporting a grim business. Periodically, for the sake of my soul, I had taken to making the odd program that would inspire more than it would depress. I began to develop a preference for those battlefields where people no longer shoot at you.

For the 1988 Bicentennial I was asked to make a program on Gallipoli. *The Fatal Shore* is still watched many times every day at the backpacker hostels that line the shores of Cannakale.

More documentaries followed on the battlefields of Greece and Crete, Kokoda, the Western Front and so on. I saw little reason to quarrel with a favourite Australian proposition that by the end of both world wars Australians were among the best soldiers; the hometown boast that General John Monash was the most creative and effective commander of World War I still endures. Monash spoke of characteristics that made the Australian soldier special: 'The democratic institutions under which he was reared, the advanced system of education by which he was trained—teaching him to think for himself and to apply what he had been taught to practical ends—the instinct of sport and adventure which is his national heritage, his pride in his young country, and the opportunity which came to him of creating a great national tradition, were all factors which made him what he was.'[1]

Monash's character portrait survived the many new renderings of the Anzac legend in the decades that followed. The key elements of courage, mateship, initiative, egalitarianism and decency held firm under fire. But as I made those documentaries I was more and more exposed to stories of soldiers of other nations in whom identical virtues were similarly enshrined.

British historians in particular saw nothing self-effacing in the Australian story. To them Monash was just one of many able commanders, and they could cite British units that fought as effectively and bravely as the Australians. Other allies such as the Canadians and New Zealanders laid claim to even greater prowess.

When I looked further I saw the blemishes that march well from the front of the legend. Australians had the highest desertion rate among allied forces in World War I. British officers reported incidents of Australians troops robbing and murdering German prisoners. When listening to interviews with British veterans at the Imperial War Museum, I heard some speak of Australian soldiers winning the respect of their officers partly because their officers feared they would kill them if they overstepped the mark. In general, the allies respected and admired the Australians but with serious reservations, mostly to do with ill discipline and boastfulness.

When I made a documentary on the 1942 fall of Singapore I heard much worse. Accusations of hubris persisted alongside accounts of Australian desertion, looting and rape. The Australian commander General Gordon Bennett *did* abandon his men. The notion that Australians were natural soldiers and leaders does not sit easily with the stories of reinforcements deserting as the Japanese waded through the mangroves of Singapore Island while General Gordon Bennett prepared to quietly slip away.

The catastrophic Singapore and Malaya campaign did not seem to receive the same level of attention as the fighting that ended in glory. While Australia's 8th Division fought tough and spirited battles, the story of the fighting became eclipsed in popular memory by the later accounts of soldier sacrifice and survival while prisoners of the Japanese.

When I reported on the famed Kokoda campaign I noticed again that the ill-trained and ill-equipped 39th Battalion's brave and stubborn resistance at Isurava was better known than the story of the 53rd Battalion by their side. Also ill-led, many of the 53rd dropped their weapons and ran.

I also noticed that positive attributes of Australians at war were more evident with the accumulation of training and experience. At the beginning of World War I Australian soldiers were hardly at their best. In April 1915, propelled more by the spirit of adventure than a sober appreciation of the task at hand, they threw themselves into the strategic folly of Gallipoli, galloping up the slopes with reckless abandon.

The steep learning curve of the Gallipoli campaign meant months of suffering before the lack of planning and leadership was redeemed. It would take years of fighting to learn how to die and win rather than die and lose.

In August 1918 Australians scaled the heights of Mount St Quentin in France, overwhelming the German defenders with grim efficiency. The British General Rawlinson called it the most outstanding feat of arms of the war. The reputation for tough fighting took its place alongside the 60,000 marked and unmarked graves.

World War II saw a similar pattern of over extension, of battling to catch up to the legend. The 6th Division, thrown into an unwinnable conflict in Greece and Crete, was almost lost. And in the islands to Australia's north, the 8th Division was lost.

However, as the war progressed, Australian soldiers in New Guinea, Bougainville and Borneo were again routing the enemy from their foxholes. American historian Eric Bergerud wrote: 'When brought up to strength, and given the flexibility and firepower that modern sea and airpower provided, the invincible Australian killing machine of 1943 developed smoothly from the AIF of late 1942. Few armies in modern times have combined steadiness, savvy and ferocity the way the Australians did. It was an extraordinary performance.'[2]

For decades now I have had this quarrel with myself; an adolescent temptation to see the Aussie digger as principled and heroic endured alongside a questioning of the evidence and concern about a stretching of the truth.

When I watched the swelling ranks of pilgrims to Gallipoli, respect for sacrifice merged with apprehension about symbolism. When asked to explain why they had crossed the globe, the young tourists can be muddled and mawkish and in a way shell shocked, having stepped into a no man's land separating myth and reality. I have my doubts about the visit representing closure, as I have doubts about the worth of continuing to exhume and identify remains.

I found young Australian soldiers similarly awkward and proud, as if when hoisting their backpack they test the weight of the burden. Soldiers are famously suspicious of bullshit; they know they are not ten foot tall and bulletproof, they know that hubris kills. Former Chief of Army General Peter Leahy rejects the warrior label embraced by United States Marines. And unlike the Americans, young Australian soldiers rarely invoke patriotism as a motivation for risking their lives.

Soldiers have never been able to share the experience of war with civilian cousins, nor do they seek to. This is their magnificent gift to us, and it ought not be presumed to be our due. In Afghanistan

I was surprised by the trace of anger I heard when soldiers spoke of a failure to understand what they are doing back at home.

When I returned from a reporting assignment in Afghanistan in 2007 with another idea in mind I turned to this project. What I saw persuaded me that the best measure of the Anzac legacy is found in the present. Also deserving of attention is the modern battlefield and the training that prepares the soldiers. What they are taught matters as well as what they have inherited.

When I spoke to remarkably focused and capable young soldiers on patrol in a maddeningly complex battle space, I was often surprised by how new they were to Army life. They had learned a lot in little time, as sometimes the process from civilian to combat soldier was not much more than a year.

This book is about that process, the fascinating transformation from civilian to soldier. The objective is to bring us closer, to help us better know the modern digger.

My job of doing just that proved more difficult than first anticipated. I have never been a soldier, and at first that did not seem a problem; some of the best chroniclers of soldiers have been journalists. Charles Bean, the author of *Anzac to Amiens*, carried a pen and typewriter. And journalists are used to knowing nothing much more than how to tell a story.

While Bean's mission took a lifetime, the modern news cycle is not so generous. When assignments are more often measured in hours and minutes, it is not easy for an outsider to gain the trust and co-operation of those within a necessarily insular subculture. Over time, in exasperation, Australian journalists sent to cover the Iraq and Afghanistan conflicts took to working with soldiers of other nations, notably Americans, because of a range of barriers to the Australian story.

One obstacle is historic. The Australian Defence Force's default position in its dealings with media is caution. Another explanation is cultural. Australians, unlike Americans in particular, don't perform on cue. The amount of time, effort and expense involved in breaking down those barriers post 2001 saw the Australian news industry turning away from the soldier's story. Despite a significant commitment to Afghanistan, there was no permanent correspondent. A decade-long conflict saw only ad hoc coverage.

From my point of view there was no use blaming the soldier. Extra effort was required to win trust and to deal with the investigative reporter's eternal problem of continuing to discover and deal with more and more of what you don't know.

A benefit of the outsider looking in is useful objectivity; you tend to ask the questions the public would ask. In the last six years I undertook hundreds of interviews with serving soldiers, former soldiers and their families. The questions I am drawn to are these: How is it that the digger stands tall yet disconnected? And why is there such a chasm between political and public support for the Afghanistan mission?

Although Australians have been deployed on a range of peacekeeping missions, the focus in this book is on Afghanistan. The story told is mostly from the soldiers' perspective, and it is far from complete. The government does not hand over its files for an ongoing operation, so I can write only about episodes where I have personally gathered knowledge. While what has been uncovered is significantly to the credit of the soldiers, the exercise of bringing it to light has proved as difficult as for any subject I have ever undertaken.

In the end, after all those interviews and a lifetime's deliberation, are they uncommon soldiers? Yes, without a doubt.

HELPING OUT

There is ongoing need for assistance to families of deceased soldiers as well as for injured and disabled personnel. The following organisations are deserving of our support.

The Australian Defence Force Assistance Trust
PO Box 1983
West Perth BC6872

Commando Welfare Trust
Locked Bag 1405
Dandenong South, Victoria 3164
0418 314 940
www.commandotrust.com
info@commandotrust.com

Legacy
Locked Bag 8

Queen Victoria Building, NSW 1230
1800 Legacy (534 229)
www.legacy.com.au
enquiries@legacy.com.au

SAS Resources Fund
PO Box 633
Nedlands, WA 6909
08 9269 8079
www.sartrust.org.au
sartrust@bigpond.com

Soldier On
Suite 202A, Belconnen Churches Centre
Benjamin Way,
Belconnen, ACT 2617
0478 589 132
www.soldieron.org.au
admin@soldieron.org.au

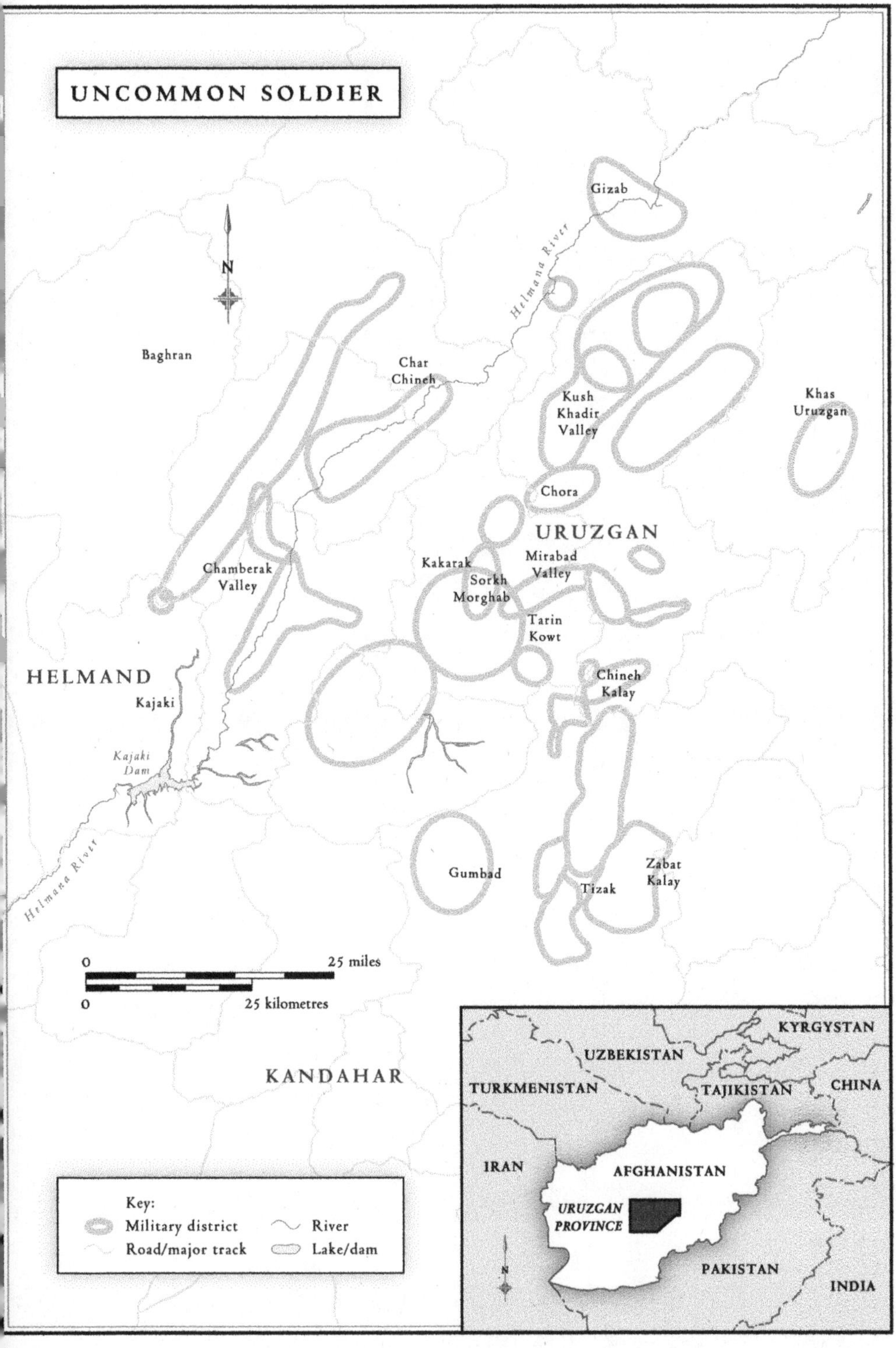

UNCOMMON SOLDIER
N
Gizab
Helmand River
Baghran
Char
Chineh
Kush
Khadir
Valley
Khas
Uruzgan
Chora
URUZGAN
Kakarak
Mirabad
Valley
Chamberak
Valley
Sorkh
Morghab
Tarin
Kowt
HELMAND
Chineh
Kalay
Kajaki
Kajaki
Dam
Helmand River
Gumbad
Zabat
Kalay
Tizak
0
25 miles
0
25 kilometres
KANDAHAR
Key:
Military district
River
Road/major track
Lake/dam
KYRGYSTAN
UZBEKISTAN
TURKMENISTAN
TAJIKISTAN
CHINA
IRAN
AFGHANISTAN
URUZGAN
PROVINCE
N
PAKISTAN
INDIA

CHAPTER 1
CORPORAL DAN

In the course of researching this book, I often heard of a type of soldier with special skills, someone physically brave and practically intelligent; someone who led and was followed without a voice raised or ego challenged. In my imaginings I conjured the picture of the super athlete from my schooldays, the kid who captained cricket and football, now grown up to exchange his footy jumper for a uniform. While sometimes the image conformed, when I met these special soldiers most at first appeared unexceptional.

If, for example, you spotted Corporal Dan on a bus in 'civvies', I doubt you would identify him as an elite soldier. He is healthy and tanned but unremarkably so, with none of the 'look at me', personal trainer-type fitness and not a trace of aggression in his bearing. If you bothered to wonder, you might think him an IT specialist out of his dust jacket, or maybe a teacher keen to get home. By that standard Dan seems to qualify as an uncommon soldier.

If on that bus you came to ask directions and converse with Dan, you would not at first learn a lot. He would more likely ask about you. He would volunteer little, and you would part company recognising an understated, courteous and even gentle persona.

So consider this: the very same Dan, on 1 November 2007, then 24 years old, is a Commando, the last man in an assault team on a ten hour climb towards the snow-covered ridgelines of the Kush Khadir Valley. The team is 84 kilometres north-west of its main base at Tarin Kowt, in the Uruzgan province of Afghanistan.

Dan is a member of Rotation V. This deployment is the Australian Special Operation Task Group's fifth since the war began in 2001. At this stage the principal rationale for going to war was to obliterate the mountain sanctuaries of Al Qaeda.

Dan's section is climbing towards a ridge top where, in support of a wider operation, a planned observation post will keep eyes on the valley below. They have climbed with little pause since dusk and are near exhausted as dawn approaches. They do not follow defined paths, instead they 'cross grain' the escarpment to avoid being caught silhouetted against the night sky.

Dan is fighting to maintain concentration as well as contain fatigue when, above his breathing, he picks up a soft warning tongue clicking from the soldier ahead. He looks to see the soldier giving a thumb down, 'danger close' signal.

The next sound is a voice calling 'Hoi'. And, as if with the flick of a switch, Dan's exhaustion vanishes. Through his night-vision goggles he sees a man slipping out of the shadows about 10 metres ahead and above. Peering into the gloom, the man at first identifies the approaching figure as one of his own. The foreigners are not expected to climb so high.

The man, about 30 years of age, wearing a full beard and in

white robes, raises his rifle. It is a folding stock Kalashnikov variant, an AK74, the weapon of a Taliban commander.

From that moment, as soldiers will often say, 'the training kicks in'. As they will also say, it is as if subsequent actions proceed in a kind of choreographed slow motion. Eyes lock. 'The windows of the soul,' says Dan, the slow-motion image now forever freeze framed in his mind.

The Taliban commander is closer to the soldier ahead of Dan, whose yell, 'Shoot the cunt', will be recalled by everyone else in the section other than Dan. As he shouts, Dan raises his Colt M4, the standard issue Special Forces assault rifle much admired for its balance, reliability and all-important feel.

Dan and the Taliban commander fire together. The Australian Commando feels the heat of the rounds from the AK74 as they tear through his trousers, smashing a water bottle in one of his pockets, discharging the warm liquid. 'Here we go,' thinks Dan. But it is the Taliban commander who is hit. His body contorts with shock, falling and rolling against Dan's legs. There is no time for further reflection. 'One dead enemy,' he yells. A Taliban with a rocket-propelled grenade (RPG) is seen sprinting and ducking. 'Ten metres full right, two enemy.'

The battle is on; weapons from both sides open up. The Australians can see they are below a cave mouth. An enemy PKM machine gun opens up from another ridgeline about 300 metres distant. The Australians have bumped a nest of insurgents; the cave is their command post.

The PKM is spewing fire, every fourth round a red tracer. From the cave mouth the Australians can hear a commander directing the attack. They treat the area with 40 mm grenades fired from an attachment on their M4s. Dan's weapon has a stoppage.

He unhooks his 66 mm rocket launcher. 'Such a bugger to carry,' he says. 'You might as well use it.'

Rounds from the PKM are crashing into the rocks around him. It is too dark to aim properly. Dan estimates the trajectory in the way he did with an orange toy gun as a boy. The high explosive round lights up the ridge and the PKM is heard no more. More 40 mm fire is poured into the cave, collapsing the walls. The shouting from inside ceases but from the surrounding area it intensifies, as does increasingly accurate enfilade fire.

They have been fighting for about 10 minutes and the sun is beginning to colour the horizon. As soon as it cracks the Australians will be unmasked. 'On me, on me, on me.' Dan counts the men out as they withdraw past his position. Co-ordinates are radioed. 'Danger close' and friendly mortar rounds whistle overhead and crash like a roaring freight train into the rock face above. The Australians pull back and are hundreds of metres further down the mountain when the close air support arrives and more high explosive bursts burn brighter than the now-rising sun.

Dan's section later passes through the Kush Khadir village, at the foot of the valley, where word of the conflict has already reached. Support for the Taliban tends to vary from village to village, in keeping with a patchwork of tribal allegiances and enmities; here they are hated. The locals cheer and shake Dan's hand.

Later, back in Australia, something similar if less demonstrative occurs when Corporal Dan from 4th Battalion (Commando), the Royal Australian Regiment is presented with a Commendation for Gallantry.

*

Now this. Four years further on and Dan is back in another valley, this time in the west of Uruzgan, close to Helmand province. It is Rotation XVI, and the more things change the more they stay the same. The Australian Area of Operations has extended, with many small patrol bases scattered through the valleys. An age-old 'ink blot' approach has been applied, the foreigners' presence gradually soaking up more local support as they ever so slowly gain trust.

Dan is literally what has come to be called a 'strategic corporal'. The nature of counter-insurgency warfare is such that junior soldiers are required to bear immense responsibility. A general in a distant compound can't have 'eyes on' to the same degree where he can expertly judge whether a missile is to be released or a sniper round discharged. More often it is the younger soldier who is entrusted with the split second call. And it is a call that could have serious strategic consequences if the target turns out to be a local mayor and ally on a mission to negotiate peace, or when the compounds high-value targets are seen entering double as class-rooms for religious instruction of children. If the junior soldier makes the wrong call, the repercussions will impact not only upon the battle, but the war itself.

August will be a busy month. Fighting tends to intensify after the snowmelt and in the weeks before Ramadan. The insurgents' 'ratlines', the communication channels to the east in and out of Pakistan, are more navigable. And in the valleys, the irrigated crops have grown dense enough to enable further freedom of movement.

The Coalition has by now a far more dominant presence, but it does not control the ground. The International Security Assistance Force (ISAF) is able to identify the areas where local trust has grown, but it can't ignore the reality that danger is everywhere.

The Taliban's evolved stratagem of using minimum force to maximum effect has made every Coalition gain that much harder to measure.

Even so, Dan's confidence has grown. The *dascht*, the desert zone and green zone, the narrow strip of farmland alongside the rivers, is now far more familiar to the 28-year-old strategic corporal. The Australians have acquired 'greater fidelity of how the enemy operates'. Dan no longer needs to wait for an intelligence report to predict enemy movements. Like many a good soldier, he has learned to think in the way of his adversary.

Dan has sought permission to briefly deploy the sniper team he now leads to Patrol Base Tycz near the village of Saraw. After the Dutch withdrawal from Uruzgan in 2010, the Americans took over. Dan likes the Americans, an attitude that is widely shared among the Australians and is clearly reciprocated.

Australia's strategic alliance with the United States was and remains a central reason for being in Afghanistan. Not so much understood is how well it works on the ground. There were virtues to the alliance with the Dutch, but it was never a comfortable cultural fit. And although the US relationship is not perfect, there is obvious synergy in combining Australian expertise with American muscle movement.

Dan has proposed siting an observation post near the village of Shahid-e Hasas. His sniper team is part of Bravo Company of the 2 Commando Regiment, which was formed in 2009 from the former 4th Battalion. Dan's team of six would work with American snipers from Operational Detachment Alpha, the Army Green Berets. The Americans and Australians, as it happens, are united in headwear as well: 2 Commando Regiment is as intensely proud of its own Sherwood green beret.

A 1 kilometre stretch of road had twice been mined in the preceding week, and the road was about to be patrolled by the Americans and a unit of Australia's Mentoring Task Force (MTF). The MTF, drawn from the broader Australian Defence Force, attends to the new focus of training the Afghan National Security Forces until the 2014 takeover. A further role of the mentors is one of persuading often-illiterate villagers that the soldiers are there to protect rather than oppress them.

The MTF works alongside Dan's Special Operations Task Group (SOTG), having drawn what many consider the shorter straw—the 'Hold' component of the 'Clear, Hold, Build' counter-insurgency doctrine. This means feet or wheels on the ground, ensuring a visible presence to spread comfort within the local population and distance them from the Taliban.

A difficulty of the valuable ground patrolling is that the active Taliban spotter networks can see patrols coming and, more to the point, can make a pretty good stab at figuring where they are likely to return. While the Australian soldiers know well the virtues of cautious route selection, in the narrow Uruzgan valleys the options are sometimes limited.

A routine for the MTF is key leadership engagement, whereby they get to know village elders through *shura*s, or meetings. There is a required constancy to this type of engagement as trust isn't built through a single meeting, but an obvious problem for the Australian soldiers cum diplomats is that in setting up the *shura*s they surrender concealment and surprise. MTF soldiers are known to sometimes describe themselves as tethered goats.

Before dawn Dan's team makes its way to the observation post. As a member of Special Forces he is assigned more of the 'Clear' responsibility; that is, to do what soldiers are best known for—to fight, to close with, and to kill the enemy. But often the SOTG does what Dan is now doing: watching. The best soldiers know when not to fight. Most of the time in the field is spent 'ground truthing', soaking in every detail of the environment and observing patterns of movement.

Once in position the sniper teams are practised at maintaining concealment. Shrouded in shaggy 'ghillie' suits, or the Australian 'yowie' derivative, they fold into the landscape. Dan is well practised at waiting, not bothering to eat or sleep. Years of training have conditioned him to do without. There is no point in waking to find your weighted body sliding down an incline. While outwardly there is no sign of movement, inside he is alive with concentration, turning over scenarios and constantly asking 'what if, what if?'

After dawn he watches the armoured Bushmasters roll through, figuring an ideal choke point to lay a roadside bomb is at the edge of a village and within his range of fire. He further predicts that if the column is attacked, it will more likely occur on the return journey.

Since 2007 roadside bombs have become the insurgents' principal weapon of choice. A crude device—a small plastic tub of homemade explosives mixed with scrap metal shrapnel and wired to a simple battery pack—even more crudely delivers astonishing 'bang for buck'. Beyond tearing life and limb from Coalition soldiers and even greater numbers of Afghans, in a blinding flash the improvised explosive device (IED) can convert a million dollar armoured vehicle to twisted and smoking junk. The Taliban, seeing the carnage delivered by IEDs, has increased their use by 400 per cent.

By this day, 15 August 2011, more than half the growing list of casualties were a consequence of IEDs, with many of Dan's

Coalition comrades dying in thin-skinned vehicles. These have now been largely withdrawn from the battlefield, progressively replaced by heavier armoured mine-resistant vehicles, the Coalition forced to increase spending by billions to counter a weapon produced for a few dollars.

At 0630 Dan sees a local on a motorbike emerge from the village. He is a fighting age male, who appears to be scouting the 1 kilometre stretch of road at the mouth of the valley, the very location the snipers have targeted.

At 0930, as if on cue, two men move towards the location on another motorbike. In broad daylight they carry an improvised bomb, having no idea they are under observation. Through his spotting scope, just 400 metres away, Dan sees the older man dismount. The magnification is such he is able to watch the man's teeth in close up stripping the detonation wires, and his fingers as he splices them together.

Taliban bomb makers are known within their community as 'scientists'. The one now seen in close up paring the wires is about 50 years of age. He will prove to be a veteran of this agonising war, intelligence tracking his existence to as far back as 2001.

On this occasion the scientist is activating a bomb more commonly seen in Iraq than Afghanistan: a direction fragmentation charge shaped in the form of a large tube. Unlike the majority of the smaller conventional IEDs laid by the insurgents, this one has devastating power.

The eight-man team on the hill 400 metres away watches the scientist's assistant lay and conceal a battery pack at the other end of the wire. The insurgents' labour is practised and unhurried; they clearly know what they are doing.

So do the snipers. Dan corrects the sighting on his marksman rifle, a Heckler and Koch 417. A US Green Beret marksman alongside does the same. Two in the team act as spotters; the other six will simultaneously fire. A synchronised volley will make it hard to know where the shots have come from, and impossible to know how many weapons have fired.

Dan calls the shot. The older man drops straight away. The other is hit but manages to move. Another man carrying a rifle appears from the village, as if to reinforce. Within seconds he is also hit, but not fatally, managing to take cover. Not for the first time, Dan marvels at the capacity of humans to withstand the catastrophic impact of a high velocity 7.62 bullet.

Like many of the 'troops in contact' incidents in Afghanistan, this one sees the roar of battle pass as swiftly as it began. The eight-man team on the hill, unusually, has time to undertake a battle damage assessment. It moves down to the site of the planned detonation. The scientist lays dead, shot once through the chin. A pink frothy blood trail indicates the other man has been hit in the lungs. The two men who had been winged are later found dead in a cave 600 metres away.

At this point the patch of ground where the bomb was to be laid turns into a crime scene. Evidence recovered through biometric analysis will help link the scientist to a string of bombings. His body is moved out of the way; villagers will later attend to the burial. After the charge is examined and photographed, it is detonated. The savage blast gives Dan pause to think about the headlines that would have been made in Australia if the attack on the returning column of Bushmasters had gone as planned.

*

Soldiers always say that despite the danger they prefer to be out in the field. In August 2011 Dan gets plenty, perhaps too much of what he wished for. Eight days later he is on another all-night climb to another overwatch position above the village of Ashre Kalay, in Khas Uruzgan. In mid-summer and at 2600 metres elevation, even at night you risk entering a hypoxic state.

In the valley below the heat is such that locals have taken to working the fields late in the evening, when the temperature is bearably cooler. The Commando sniper team is above an abandoned Afghan National Police checkpoint.

When daylight arrives it sees a group of males gathering 800 metres away. Four men are carrying AK47s. The sniper team can see one giving orders, and watch as the men begin to conceal the weapons in their robes. The four gun carriers are within a larger group who do not appear to be carrying weapons.

Under the Australian rules of engagement, the men with weapons constitute legitimate targets. They are within range, particularly of the 50 calibre Barrett sniper rifle. The sniper team calls in on the radio what it sees and is told to engage.

The sniper co-ord is again called—'Call signs on, standby, fire'—and the six Australians commence engagement. Two insurgents are winged, spun by the power of the bullets. One ducks behind a wall. Another runs and is hit, dropping instantly in an aqueduct. Through binoculars the Commandos see men crawling to recover the man who fell dead. They watch as the two who have been winged are carried to safety. The Australians do not shoot. 'We know they are bad but we also know our rules. They have no weapons.'

From his position 800 metres away Dan can feel the village atmospherics change. The air is suddenly full of menace; a barrage of fire rains in on them. Many insurgents that were unobserved by the snipers are close by. The insurgents are 'drake shooting'—targeting likely firing positions. Bullets travelling at 830 metres per second begin to 'crack/thud' in close, sustained fire. The practised ear can discern from the two sounds, the sonic boom and the strike, roughly how far the shooter is away. This one is uncomfortably close. A PKM ranges in on them and the single shot marksman begins to find his mark. 'When that happens it starts to feel very personal.'

The Australians are now under heavy fire; RPGs air burst above them. Over the roar Dan can hear the enemy yelling. Although he can't see them, the sound perspective puts them very close. And they are. When he throws a hand grenade in the insurgents' direction he hears the Taliban shout a warning: '*Las Bam*.' Having done a stint at the Army's School of Languages, Dan knows this translates as 'hand bomb'—and he knows they are metres away.

Dan runs for better cover, falling winded and corking his leg. Another Commando thinks he has been hit. On the ground, he pulls out a map and begins to read out the co-ordinates over the radio. Effective mortar fire begins to strike the enemy positions. A joint terminal attack controller with a laptop computer strapped to his webbing calls in an air strike. Somewhere beyond the naked eye an American B1 bomber releases a joint direct attack munition, a guided bomb, that follows the path prescribed by a young soldier on the ground whose fingertips have the power to summon the fires of hell.

There is soon more company in the air. American Apache helicopter gunships have heard the numbers of the call signs in contact over the radio. 'We know when the Americans hear our call sign they will support us.' An Apache strafes the area; RPGs arc back in its direction. Dan looks up, clearly discerning the face of the pilot sitting in the centre of the cockpit as if on a bar stool, giving him the thumbs up. It is a powerful moment. 'Brilliant,' says Dan. Heavily outnumbered, the six Australians and their Afghan interpreter have pulled off a narrow escape.

By bookending these two incidents, from November 2007 and August 2011, a telling snapshot of the war is revealed. In 2007, when Dan fought the Taliban in the mountain eyrie, encounters were more random. The enemy operated in larger groups and seemed more prepared to stay and fight protracted actions. By 2011, however, the Australians could claim many more areas where the Taliban's grip had been weakened. But as Dan has now seen, the gains had not extinguished the enemy's capability. The insurgents encountered on the hills above Ashre Kalay were well trained, probably in Pakistan. 'If they think they can win they will still have a crack.'

The insurgents' use of IEDs was an even more effective way to pin down the Coalition's massive and expensive war machine. Two days before the Ashre Kalay action, Private Matthew Lambert succumbed to wounds after a roadside bomb detonated. He became the 28th Australian soldier killed since the war began.

At the time of the first action described in 2007, three Australian lives had been lost. In 2002 Sergeant Andrew Russell died of wounds after his long-range patrol vehicle clipped a mine in a neighbouring province. He became the first Australian killed in action since the Vietnam War. Camp Russell, the Special Forces base in Uruzgan, bears his name.

Five years later another life was claimed. In October 2007 Trooper 'Poppy' Pearce was killed when the Australian light armoured vehicle he was driving triggered an IED in the

Chora Valley, 6 kilometres out of Tarin Kowt. All who visit 'Poppies', the recreation centre at the main Australian base, have cause to remember the popular 41 year old.

In the same month Sergeant Matthew Locke, a Special Air Service Regiment trooper who had won a Medal for Gallantry for an action in the preceding year, was shot and killed. Sergeant Locke was struck in the chest by a machine gun bullet in the midst of heavy battle. The fighting in the Chora Valley was part of the same campaign as Corporal Dan's mountaintop action.

In the 2007 rotation alone, Australian Special Forces killed and identified 400 Taliban. They knew they were seriously thinning the ranks of the enemy. The swarm attacks would soon abate, and mid- to high-level commanders would avoid entering the Australian area of operations, the Uruzgan province.

The Australians drew no attention to the body counts. Boasting about the death toll of Afghans and their allies is hardly likely to play well in Afghanistan. And back home in Australia it would seem just as bloodthirsty. In contrast, the Australian public became well acquainted with our own body count. It is not hard to understand why a sense of Australians as more victim than victor had formed.

While militarily the Australians had made significant progress, the battle for public opinion was nothing short of carnage wherever you looked, even though in Uruzgan local Afghans more often died at the hands of the Taliban than the foreigners. Further, while the foreigners exercised unequal power within a framework of humanitarian rules, the Taliban in turn operated to a standard of calculated inhumanity. The way the locals saw it, the violence would not be so extreme if the foreigners were not around. The foreigners could not expect to be excused because they could not overturn ordinary Afghan logic.

Ordinary Australians also grasped logic that was equally hard to defeat. Why were Australian lives being lost in this remote and pitiless graveyard? How could these robed mountain bandits represent a threat to citizens of a far distant continent? By 2007 the proposition that Afghanistan remained an Al Qaeda sanctuary was beginning to lose conviction.

However, another form of conviction was commensurately growing. The Australian soldiers could see the progress they were achieving much more clearly than did those back at home. And every new casualty, whether for good or bad, was increasing their commitment.

In November 2007 this personal stake in the war was driven home within Bravo Company and Dan's small and tight band of brothers. Three weeks after the mountain assault at Kush Khadir, Dan was again hiking into battle. This time his team was heading towards two 'compounds of interest' at Musa Kalay, east of Charmestan, in the upper reaches of the Mirabad Valley. Six soldiers from the Afghan National Army accompanied the Australian patrol.

The area was a known enemy staging post at the junction of three Taliban ratlines. At this stage intelligence-gathering techniques were not so developed, but reliable information suggested medium-value targets were likely to be on location. The target was 30 kilometres from the Tarin Kowt Camp Russell base. Dan's team's vehicle drop off point on the night of 22–23 November would be 8 kilometres short of the target.

Each soldier carries around half his body weight in kit, a range of weaponry, ammunition, water, medical supplies, communication devices and body armour, which means hefty ballistics plates front and rear. At this stage Coalition forces favoured night attacks. The night offers obvious cover and the standard issue night-vision equipment conferred a clear advantage.

Dan was in a rear cordon. Another team would make a Level One clearance, or a soft knock approach, rather than the Level Two blowing in of the door. The first man through the door is Dan's friend and a well-respected member of the Commando Regiment, Private Luke Worsley.

Dan had known Luke since they did their initial employment training at Singleton back in 2002. The 26-year-old bearded private is a powerful yet gentle spirit. 'A top bloke, dedicated, fit . . . a big man with a big heart.'

In the way of many a mission, detailed planning immediately goes awry. As they approach the mud brick compound, a sentry with an RPK machine gun has spotted them and is seen scaling down a rooftop to warn his comrades. He is immediately engaged and killed, but the gunfire has sounded the warning. And so too does Luke Worsley, who calls out in Pashto as he goes through the door. The Commando, vulnerable in the narrow doorway the Australians call the 'fatal funnel', fires a short burst that is met from 18 metres away by a PKM machine gun and from 10 metres away by an AK47.

One round from the PKM strikes Luke Worsley's lighter Special Forces attack helmet, entering his temple above the left eye. Another Commando, Corporal Cam, goes forward, pushing through the fire fight and regaining the initiative. He kills the assailants in one determined sweep with his M4 and hand grenades.[1] Special Forces training drills encourage decisive action; dealing with the shock of a lost comrade is for later.

Gun battles break out elsewhere. Dan has heard over the coms that Bravo Company has suffered a killed in action. In his rear cordon they fire a nine-banger distraction grenade to confuse other Taliban fighters whose weapons are lighting up at different points of the compounds. A young woman picks up an AK47 dropped by her presumed fallen husband and begins firing at the Australians. She is also killed. Children are heard crying. Cam sees another member of his team 'manoeuvre through the fire fight to get to a newborn baby and manoeuvre that baby out of the fire fight to ensure its safety'. All of the Taliban within the compound are killed but so too are civilians, and not for the first or last time. One is a teenage girl.

The incident is telling of a disconnection between the reality of this type of war and its comprehension at home. The soldiers fight in a human space: there are no defined trench lines, flanks or neutral territory. Too often when the guns begin to roar, somewhere in between can be heard the wailing of women and children.

The Taliban well understand and frequently exploit the defensive cover of a civilian environment. And Coalition forces, including Australians, find it difficult to discriminate between civilian and combatant when, as on this occasion, fighting erupts in the close quarter living space of a village compound.

The Australians know that even though there is no clear line defining the battlespace, somehow they must make every effort to ensure it is not crossed.

A formal inquiry into the deaths of Luke Worsley and civilians at Musa Kalay was undertaken. The inquiry officer, another soldier, found the Commandos had acted with discipline in keeping with training drills, noting that without the effective control and co-ordination demonstrated there would have been more casualties, 'both friendly and non-combatant'.[2] According to the team leader, Sergeant 'Chook': 'Through the fire fight there were civilian casualties taken, but saying that, we didn't just go in there and go crazy. It is very difficult but it's just the way they fight.'

While the report of the inquiry is published on a government website, the story of how the war is truly fought is not well communicated. This is partly because journalists see very little of the action, partly because of the high security blanket that shrouds Special Forces operations, and probably because explaining civilian deaths is beyond the ability of just about everyone.

At dawn the Australians troop out of Musa Kalay, and it is fair to say the grief they carry with them is mostly for their comrade. Dan says it is eerie. 'Buggered and tearful' is how he puts it. Luke is the first close mate to be killed. The loss, which will not be the last, reaches deep into the tight Army family. The raw recognition that it could have been one of them becomes clearer to each of the Commandos slogging their way out. It will soon come home as well to every wife and mother.

Bravo Company calls for a helicopter evacuation, but it is not available. They carry their 110 kilogram comrade on a stretcher, taking turns, while also shepherding the persons under control who have been detained. The 8 kilometre journey is the company's most difficult. However, rather than reduce commitment to an uncertain objective of delivering security to this wild country, it increases resolve. The experience will not stop

Dan coming back to Afghanistan, but it will give rise to something new.

All soldiers yearn to be outside on operations practising everything they have trained for. They will, of course, feel moments of acute fear. The threat of being torn to pieces by an IED or struck by a bullet that won't be deflected by either fate or body armour is ever present, but they still prefer to be out there. The main fear now for Dan is seeing another of his mates killed.

Corporal Dan will see a lot more action. He is that kind of soldier. Every unit has one, someone who is like a magnet for battle. In 2011 I spent some time with his company, watching them come in and out of action. I listened hard as they reported their experiences. You can't help noticing that when it comes to describing the killing of an enemy they have a way of lapsing into abstract, using phrases such as 'I reduced him'.

It is soon clear to me that this shy and understated soldier has killed many men, so I asked him an awful question, the kind journalists are known for: 'How many?'

'I don't know. We are not like some of the Americans, who give you that sixteen confirmed . . . all that shit. No . . . I don't keep a count.'

'How do you live with it?'

'No problems . . . sleep well. Don't dwell on it.' Dan is a professional soldier: his job is to kill, to live with it and get on with the next mission. What is striking about him is what you see in many of these soldiers—that their strength is less external and specific as it is internal and general. They absorb a range of characteristics from every corner of the world: the army, their mates and society.

*

On a return visit to his home town on the Murray River, Dan is in a pub talking to some mates. He sees a group of Afghan fruit pickers and wanders over, conversing with them in Pashto. They are surprised. So, too, are his old school mates.

I ask him what he tells people when they strike up a conversation on a bus or a plane.

'I tell them I am a fire fighter.'

CHAPTER 2
'I DON'T KNOW HOW TO EXPLAIN IT BUT IT'S REALLY COOL'

They snap off the date as if responding to an order. It is enshrined in personal history alongside birthdays and anniversaries. 'Thirteen November 2001,' says Dan. They all seem to know their first day. Tony Gilchrist, who would rise to the rank of Major and be decorated for his bomb disposal work in Iraq, barks: 'The 6th of May 1987.'

Inside the gate at Kapooka in southern New South Wales is a sign: 'Soldiering Begins Here'. They wheel past it twice a week, on buses from Sydney and Melbourne that generally manage to arrive within 10 minutes of each other. Before then people of every caste have been flown in from every corner of the continent. Keeping an eye on them aboard the bus is a draft conducting officer. 'On the bus everyone was nice to you, until you got there,' the then seventeen-year-old recruit Gilchrist recalls.

It is a fascinating process, this transformation of men and women from civilian to soldier. In the next eleven weeks a nation is buttoned into uniform. They are mostly young, not long out of school. The age limit used to be 35, but some time ago that went out the window, so among the anxious faces there are some worry lines already forming.

When they spill from the buses in the late afternoon, crisp and businesslike instructors await. The 'jubies', as they are known, for being soft-centred like sweets, will soon learn you can't go far in the Army without saluting a nickname and acronym. The old world is no more. They are about to be swallowed whole by the ARTC, the Army Recruit Training Centre.

Future Warrant Officer Nichol Anderson remembers it as 'the scariest place I had ever been. Mum said when she put me on the bus she would see me in a week because I was not the kid who liked being told what to do.'

The gathering ranks shuffling to order do not look like the First XI. Indeed, some don't even look like the Tenth XI. All shapes and sizes, the bald and the not so beautiful form up. There is no height limit. The Army has surprising confidence in its ability to resize. What we see are human casings yet for reassembly.

The recruits already have some idea that signing on to defend freedom means giving it up. There are rules for everything. There are rules about rules. Arriving by private vehicle is not allowed, and cameras are to be left at home. The recruits are permitted one suitcase only, containing clothing and personal papers. The process of forging the team begins with four recruits assigned to unload the baggage.

The waiting instructors expect some surprises. Sergeant George Griffin spots a kid with a toy model of a C130 aircraft, telling me, 'At least we don't see them bringing their golf clubs any more.' Soon to be an Afghanistan veteran, then seventeen-year-old Josh Dowsing recalls 'getting into trouble within the first ten minutes for calling a corporal mate three times in a row'.

The sight of the wide-eyed arrivals tempts many a waiting instructor to a quiet punt on survival rates, Sergeant Adam West forming 'a fair idea who was not going to make it. Not that you've got the knives out. A single mother would come off the bus and generally be missing the kids after three days and she'd be home. That wasn't always the case. We were not always right, which was good because some would turn it on you and say bugger you, I'm going to pass.'

Corporal Rachel Ingram agrees. 'There was a bit of a game around first impressions. He won't make it, no, yes. We were often proven very wrong.'

Kapooka, on the southern outskirts of Wagga Wagga in rural New South Wales, was established on grazing land in 1942. Also known as 'Blamey Barracks', it formally honours the nation's only Australian-born Field Marshal, whose birthplace is nearby. The story of this 1800 hectare soldier farm is amazing. Many generations have learned things here that cannot be recorded. Over the decades, through an ever-reducing scale of trial and error, the Australian Army in its own distinctive way has honed a black art. An instructor in 2007, Corporal Anthony Purdy told me while later undertaking officer training: 'I wish I could write down what they have in their tool box and try and bottle it.'

Although there are many books about officer training, notably at the Royal Military College Duntroon, there has never been a book about Kapooka. Maybe one reason is that the recruits are only there for 80 days and their instructors for perhaps a year or two, so corporate memory is retained less by the ebb and flow of graduates and their teachers as the place itself. The lessons seem to soak into the red brick walls and yellow green pastures.

Lieutenant Colonel Blue Mawson is one of the few with a longer view. He first saw Kapooka as a young captain in the 1970s. Having returned as an instructor many times in a period when the Army did little else but train, he came to settle in the area, in retirement taking on the job of safety officer. Blue sees the modern digger as nothing like the ones who went over the top to certain death at Gallipoli. 'Over time soldiering has required a need for greater brainpower. We change attitudes—that is the key. Young men and women become part of this larger family.'

Bram Connolly enlisted from South Australia aged seventeen in February 1991. A father's friend had been a forward scout during the Vietnam War. 'He had some great stories about how to stay silent in the jungle and use your watch to tell the direction you were heading. From an early age I aspired to have those same experiences and learn those same skills.'

Also from South Australia, and joining in the same year, Troy Simmonds might at first have been something very different. At Flinders University and making student films, he was on his way to becoming another Peter Weir. Connolly and Simmonds would both end up in Special Forces, Connolly fighting the dramatic action that ends this book and Simmonds in another akin to the final scene in Peter Weir's film *Gallipoli*, which almost ended his life.

To get this far the recruits have undergone a trial more stringent than many realise. Having found their way to Defence Force recruitment offices around the nation, they have filled out forms and undertaken physical examinations and aptitude tests, as well as sat through interviews and psychological screening.

Private Andrew, another of the young soldiers who would go on to join the ranks of Special Forces, remembers being asked at the Parramatta office 'four hundred questions that were weird. Do you ever have an urge to jump from a tall building? What kind of fruit do you like?'

It is at this first stage that risk assessment filters are applied to screen out the unsuitable. 'Recruitment judgment is based on negative selection,' explains Colonel Peter Murphy, who served as the Army's former Director of Psychology. 'Even if they pass some tests with flying colours, a history as a social misfit, lack of stable employment, record of conflict etc. makes them too much of a risk to themselves as well as the organisation.' In all, around 17 per cent are rejected after applying to the Australian Regular Army, and 5 per cent for the Reserves.

This screening can be a big surprise to the fitness fanatics who read *Soldier of Fortune* and can identify all forms of military weaponry. Murphy says: 'I would be very surprised if a gun collector got in. A hint of romantic motivation will attract questions to gauge a level of maturity.'

Organisational psychologist Lieutenant Colonel David Schmidtchen, author of *The Rise of the Strategic Private*, says: 'We need to put weapons in the hands of stable, sensible people who can make good judgments, otherwise we are asking for trouble.'

'We are not looking for muscle-bound idiots,' says Brigadier Simone Wilkie, a former commandant at Kapooka. For her, psychology reports are more important than the aptitude tests. 'We don't automatically take the nine out of ten who are bright but might not have the social skills and are not as resilient, flexible and adaptable.'

Schmidtchen puts it this way: 'Some really smart people might look the goods on paper, but have never been under pressure in their life. It is hard to know. Some step up and adapt. Others don't.'

Not that they are looking for the sublime average either. A minor criminal record is not a certain barrier to entry. Nor is evidence of tattoos and body piercing, which are assessed on a case-by-case basis and, by most accounts, are better acquired later.

Peter Murphy agrees with Blue Mawson's view that the modern cohort is smarter. 'The dumb grunt is a cliché. Soldiers now going into Infantry generally have the mental aptitude to get them into officer training. Good soldiers are not necessarily the types you want to take home to Mother, either. We are not mind readers, so how they perform on operations is too far down the track to predict, but we know we need an ethical as well as capable soldier for the demanding work ahead.'

The first important step is getting this disparate bunch geared up and standardised. At the quartermaster store, dress and equipment preparation see them outfitted with a full kit packed in a large green bag. Tailor and mother of three, Bub Noack has watched the levelling process for over twenty years. 'It's like Christmas for some. They pull out everything, three T-shirts, pyjamas, the lot, while others are barely bothered.'

The dirt brown T-shirts are each stenciled with the recruit's surname. In the blur of the first three days, confusion overwhelms. Listening and concentration skills are yet to develop. Nervous recruits will incorrectly spell their own names, print their first name instead of the last, or put it on the wrong side of the shirt. The very sight of Bub Noack standing beyond the bewilderment can trigger yearnings for home and tears. 'A Reservist on Saturday said, "I should not be here" and burst into tears. They say, "Dad made me join". They miss their mothers. We used to ask underpants size and they would say, "I don't know, Mum buys them".'

Tony Gilchrist, who returned as an instructor, remembers tears in the barracks at night and while collecting gear. 'Too nervous to ask to change them, they had taken clothing that was twice the proper size.' At an outfitting session I ask one of the newly arrived recruits what it feels like and am told, 'It is a blur, like stepping into a different country.'

Pay and entitlements are explained. For the first week they receive $100 cash, followed by fortnightly payments of around $1200, with additional allowances for married soldiers. Once they have signed on and pledged their oath of allegiance they are expected to serve for between three and six years, although not all make it to the required minimum.[1]

Accommodation is four to five per room, males and females separated, the latter in rooms closest to the office. Some of the young women can find the transition hard. No more make-up, high heels, no giggling when told to stand to attention. Of Nichol Anderson's original female platoon of 33, only 22 would march out. 'You could tell in the first three weeks whether it was for you.'

Furnishing is sparse, consisting of bunk beds, lockers, small desks, chairs and an ironing board. One of the most telling decisions of all, who you share with, is left to fate or, more specifically, the alphabet. Michael Whitely, who joined in 2005, told me: 'Mum had made my bed until the day I joined the Army. I had to learn about making a hospital corner on a bed sheet.'

The early morning is the biggest shock. In the more distant past the bashing of garbage tin lids at 6 am would see recruits gathered bleary eyed in the corridors with sheets over their shoulders. They now do without the garbage tins.

Recruits are given 15 minutes to shower and dress. The narrow timeframe enforces co-operation. Dan calls it 'cyclone training'.

It is about time management. The sense of urgency applied to the morning routine will become a habit. They talk to each other and share the load. Someone in the group will know how to mop a floor or iron a shirt. You can't get it all done unless you organise to have one corner the bed sheets while a mate polishes brass, as another irons, as someone else showers and shaves. For many the shave will be their first. One of Tony Gilchrist's roomies, with neither equipment nor experience, was handed an old razor and emerged 'looking like his face had been hit with a whipper snipper'.

Ensuring the rest of the body is in good enough shape to begin training is the next important step. While the application process is pitiless, the training phase is a little more gentle. 'The objective is to train in rather than train out,' explained Commanding Officer Lieutenant Colonel Max McIntyre on one of my visits to Kapooka.

The first fitness assessment tests are nothing like the crucible of old. In runners, shorts and T-shirts, they line up to undertake a series of short sprints governed by an instructor and an electronic beeper. The shuttle run, or beep test, of around 1100 metres is to be completed in 6.5 minutes. In addition, all Army recruits have to show they can manage 45 sit-ups. Males must be able to complete 15 push-ups, the females eight.

For this squad of 98 recruits, only two don't make it. Instructors do notice a variation through the year. The November arrivals not long from school can be better motivated than March arrivals, who might have drifted for a time before recognising the perfect alternative was not going to find them. Instructor Rachel Ingram would occasionally wonder how some had made it this far. 'We had kids who could not physically adopt a push-up position, not having the body strength to hold their own weight.'

Kapooka swiftly proves to be not the place for someone with a secret motive to beat a drug or alcohol problem, or get slim for summer. For this early training stage recruits can leave upon request. Most who drop out do so in the first two weeks, rarely because of the physical demands, but more likely because they find they are not used to sharing a bedroom and don't take to the early mornings and lack of freedom.

The softer initiation is at variance to the make or break days when even fit soldiers could succumb to the demands of basic discipline, group co-ordination and personal grooming. Blue Mawson recalls past discharge rates as high as 21 per cent, compared to a current constant of around 10 per cent. He speaks with grudging regard for a Platoon Commander in the 1970s who would 'line up a whole platoon from smallest to biggest. Then he gave the smallest a clip on the head and the biggest a smack in the mouth. He would tell them, "Right, I have handled the biggest and the smallest. Anyone want to have a go?" And he produced champion platoon after platoon.'

When Tony Gilchrist joined in the 1980s this *Lord of the Flies* approach still lingered. 'They had a Queen song, "Another One Bites the Dust", which they would play when we returned to barracks. If your trunk was packed at the end of the bed you knew you were gone. It was a tool they used. You did not want to be the one. They would pick on one to make sure that the other three in the room got the message.'

'You don't complain looking back. It weeded out the unfit,' a soldier from the old school explained. 'If you crack under stress of being yelled at you don't belong in a job where you are getting shot at. It is harsh, but there is a point to it. Being given ridiculous jobs to do initiates respect for command. You don't look at a job as good or bad, you do it.'

Now it is different. 'There have been numerous studies evolving the training model,' says Max McIntyre. 'We are now much more sensitive to health, injuries and the need for rest and good nutrition. They come in with a variety of fitness levels. We can't make them super soldiers in eleven weeks. But they do develop a physical robustness. We don't push them too fast and we take more time than most employers.'

Not that you can easily kill the 'we were tougher in my day' bias. Older instructors continue to lament the warm and cuddly approach applied to the generations not so used to walking to school and playing team sport. Platoon Commanders joke about asking the jubies what sport they play, and being told 'footy'; asking where they played and hearing 'Nintendo'.

Travis Robinson, who joined in 1997 and got out in 2003, told me: 'There was this one stage when we were just getting soldiers marching into the battalion that were absolutely pathetic and would just whinge about sleeping in the mud or things that infantrymen have to do. As a soldier you just grin and bear it. But these people, they were just a massive pack of whingers.'[2]

By the 1990s it was clear the new intakes were not robust enough. 'We were breaking too many. Initially we had them doing route marches totalling 58 kilometres in three months and causing a lot of stress fractures,' says Blue Mawson, who sees the change as about being smart rather than soft.

For the first of the eleven week Regular Army course recruits are known for their attempts to escape into the camouflage of the uniform; they call it going 'grey'. Dan, standing at this junction of the teenage and adult world, remembers trying to dissolve into the background, to be a 'grey man', someone who is not noticed.

A 'gobby', a term borrowed from the British Army, is the reverse. The watchful begin to notice someone who 'gobs off', who by making their opinions known might not be fitting in quite so well. When one person stuffs up the entire group is punished. By the first three weeks the pull of the group has its effect.

Sergeant George Griffin sees the 'peer group pressure as positive rather than negative. At school what is cool is the opposite in the Army.' Josh Dowsing remembers: 'You have to play the game. Yes sir, no sir. If you stand out a lot you get a lot of attention. So you try to be a grey man and you think you are not getting noticed but you are.' Matt Lines, a later Medal for Gallantry winner, took his dad's advice: 'Big ears, big eyes. Small mouth.'

The power of the group will push as well as pull. Friendships form, competition wells, and those who choose to stay soon find they do not want to be left behind. This is when Dan began to step up.

But even the willing can suffer setbacks. While Kapooka is not as tough as it used to be, it is no holiday camp either. Hard physical training means that in the first weeks there are many injuries: hamstrings pulled, bones broken, hips fractured.

Some recruits will also beat a path to the psychologist. In her time as an instructor, Rachel Ingram particularly recalls a bulky young man destined for the Infantry, who on day five when he went to the armoury 'would not put his hand on the weapon. We had three discharges like that, all males. They know before we know they are not suited.' Dan remembers 'a guy trying to suicide in the first two days'.

The Digger James Platoon, named after a former Director General of Army Health, is designed to cater for those who are held back. While no shame is meant to attach to those assigned to the platoon, it can be hard watching new mates carry on while enduring remedial treatment to overcome an injury. Platoon Commander Lieutenant Penny Snoodyk empathises: 'Injured recruits could see society regarding them as failures. They can't march out with the same people they marched in with. But they make new friends and at the end they can be a good soldier.'

On many a digger's website you can find less diplomatic posts about drop-outs or 'lingers', short for malinger. 'On the first night this bloke jumped into bed. It was short sheeted. He was too scared to move so he slept all gimped up, woke with a back injury and was sent to DJs' . . . One bloke in his late twenties was an accountant. Every time we put webbing in his hands he shook uncontrollably . . . All the girls in my platoon were lingers, except the lesbian. She was good value.'[3]

'Linger' is a term the modern army would like to kill. Penny Snoodyk says: 'We don't use the word. We are about equity and diversity. We try to shift the culture of the blame game.'

When the Australian Army nominates its nine core values, which include courage, leadership, initiative and toughness, compassion makes the list. This value is clearly seen in the Weary Dunlop platoon, named after the Australian soldier famous for humanity in the face of inhuman treatment by the Japanese, for recruits who transit out. When I visit, a dejected young man waiting with his bag packed tells me he's leaving because of an allergy to bee stings discovered the hard way.

Platoon Commander Sergeant Rob Stanford says the determination that a recruit does not have soldierly qualities tends to be gradually rather than dramatically realised. 'They think it might be like school but the discipline is a culture shock. They are not used to getting out of bed. Some don't make friends. Some pester us to get out as quick as they can and some try to stay as long as they can.'

For the larger herd on this soldier farm there is no time to look back, Kapooka being perennially busier than spring muster. To the visitor, the grounds are at first deceptive. The 'Home of the Soldier' appears empty and more conspicuous for a lack of action, tumble-weeds lazily moving with the wind and kangaroos sheltering in patches of shade. But then from across at the range comes the crash of gunfire and through the shadows you see groups moving or more specifically marching, the newer ones more distinctive for their unpolished gait. The 900 recruits who are there at any one time are out and about, engaged in weapons training and drill or consumed by lectures on topics such as 'Note Taking', 'Listening' and the 'Requirement for Soldierly Conduct'.

It can be harder on the older recruits who have forgotten the art of remaining patient while enduring the mundane. Sam Drake joined at the age of 37. 'There was no war when I was eighteen,' he explained. 'I would look at the EXIT sign and try to enter a happy space, thinking, I'll get out one day.'

The recruits' 0600 start stretches through to 2100, fifteen hour days for seven days a week. They get in at night, ensure gear is ready for the next day and flop. Meals are shovelled down. They have 20 minutes, which leaves little room for conversation. The food is plentiful, 'like Sizzlers every day', says one excited recruit. When he joined in the mid 1990s, Adam West from Keith in South Australia found he 'thoroughly loved Kapooka. I rang Mum,

[said] jeez, I get bacon and eggs for breakfast every morning and don't cook it or clean after.'

The controlled nutrition has another levelling effect. The increased physical activity more commonly burns away excess fat, but in the tailor shop Bub Noack is sometimes required to upsize. 'Weight and shape adjusts to their new physique. We had girls lose ten kilos and one who put on seven kilos. It was the first time she had three meals a day.'

Finding a moment to interview the recruits is another challenge. In the mess over lunch I snatch conversation with a small group hunched over plates piled high: stroganoff, vegetables, salad, bread rolls and large beakers of coloured cordial. Eighteen-year-old Rebecca Jones from Bunbury in Western Australia is flushed and buoyant; having entered via the try before you buy gap year program, she has decided to sign on. After eight and a half weeks Rebecca has lost her fear of the Section Commanders, having learned they are 'good souls, father figures, human. You can even crack a joke.'

Nicholas Cope is ten years older and from Manchester in the United Kingdom. After six years in 'Oz' he decided to join up—recruits must have either Australian citizenship or permanent residency status. Nicholas says: 'Australia has given me lots of chances and I want to give something back.'

Hurried mouthfuls and they move on. Brendan Schmidt, eighteen, from Beerwah in Queensland, says a key moment was six weeks in when he realised he was not recognised and needed to 'graduate from the grey zone'.

The instructors are even busier, their day generally starting an hour earlier and finishing an hour later. The job where you see more of other people's sons and daughters than your own has long been resented and avoided. 'Fucking babysitting', they complain when transferred to a training post. Only in recent years have allowances improved to make it more appealing. Instructors will also understandably grumble about imparting skills applied to deployments where, through generous allowances, the students swiftly earn more than their teachers.

But it is also a privilege. Sergeant George Griffin, in his second year of his second instructor's posting to Kapooka, says, 'The people here are a reflection of the *esprit de corps*. It is an honour to do this.'

In one of their cramped offices, three instructors are persuaded to talk shop. Sergeant David Adams, the most experienced, joined in 1994. Bombardier Brad Cowan signed on in 1998, and Lieutenant Annie Francis in 2003. 'Our approach is forever changing, like fashion.'

They acknowledge the newer intakes are less robust but that the approach is to regard them as not yet competent. 'They come from a background where you can't smack a kid on the bum. This generation has no experience of failing anything . . . The blokes take it hard. We can't tell them they are not up to standard. Their world falls apart when we do . . . You look in their eyes and at first the light bulb is only working at five watts. There is no comprehension . . . and you will see the smirk of someone who thinks they know everything but they are not in control . . . Over time they come to recognise a mate's weakness is his weakness. The older guys with families know better when it is time to share. The body language betrays the struggle.'

'They need to keep a straight face. Stand with shoulders in and head half down.' Imposed discipline is applied for the first weeks, when self-discipline usually begins to kick in, and the instructors begin to notice the lost puppy look fade and focus sharpen in the eyes of the jubies.

Sometimes the loners without well developed social skills can be seen standing distant or heading for the regimental aid post in hope of being excused. The instructors say they generally come around. They also say they don't yell any more, but you still hear plenty of raised voices. The approach to breaking down recruits and rebuilding them might have changed, but the idea is much the same. If they don't conform, there is not much point. And if they don't get the message from their instructor, they soon get it from the group. The 'fuck you, stick that' attitude has a narrow lifespan.

Some instructors, though, still despair at the greater freedom and second chances never conferred in their day. When Tony Gilchrist returned as an orderly sergeant, he endured a sleepless night chasing up three recruits who had gone into town on the drink. 'All they got was restraint of privileges, and I got into trouble for the way I spoke to them. In my day they would have been out.'

Ryan Ingold, a clear-eyed, no nonsense soldier, is another of many to have equal suspicion of the touchy–feely approach. Ingold, who joined in 2000, says 'It's a fine line. You need to be able to go to it, but not over it.' And while no one speaks up for the old bastardisation rituals, neither are they completely rejected. The older soldiers still refer to it as 'sorting out the weeds'.

Like the recruits, instructors muster satisfaction after the first weeks when their sections and platoons begin to move in step. 'You see it in the march. Square gate. Left arm and left foot struggling. We have to teach them to walk. They over-think.' Like reporters pointlessly perambulating towards a camera, apprentice soldiers need practice in order to lose the stilted marionette march.

At the end of the first month, in mind and body, the individual and the group begin to acquire fluency, ever so gradually developing muscle memory. And then there is the wonderful moment of the epiphany, when the Rubicon is crossed, often achieved without ceremony, perhaps in the dead of night or crouched after a pack march drawing deep breaths in the shade.

The high-wire confidence course is designed for that very purpose. Rebecca Jones was encouraged when she saw 'an Alpha male petrified'. Sergeant Adam West has seen it, too. 'At physical training a bloke carries fifty kilograms and the girls think I can't do that, but then they see them struggling on the high wire. It is another big moment when they realise they have their mate's safety in their hands.'

The recognition that you are capable of not just doing it, but doing it with competence, is received like a lottery win. 'I don't know how to explain it,' Rebecca tells me, 'but it's really cool.' Adam West says: 'When they turned [the corner], they took off in leaps and bounds. It does click.'

Watching the recruits shiver in winter rain, Bub Noack sometimes wants to take them home. But she also sees the self-assurance that succeeds discomfort. After seven weeks recruits return to be fitted for their dress 'polyesters'. 'By the time they get their polys they are switched on. They come back walking better, with confidence.'

An eagerness to fit in encourages what for many will be a career-long search for an ideal role model, and the instructors come easily to mind. Young crushes develop, not so much the romantic kind as more of an 'I am going to be like him' swelling within the soul. So as well as day one, soldiers remember their first squad—'31 platoon Delta Company'—and their instructor. 'I had a really great Section Commander, Corporal LeCornu. I'll never forget his name,' says Nichol Anderson.

Inevitable bonding occurs as mother hen instructors attend to recruits who don't know how to apply for a bank account, had never washed up or put out a bin. Rachel Ingram, looking after a platoon of soldiers aged between seventeen and fifty from all walks of life—the poor, the well off—found 'you need to be a point of family contact. You can't handle them properly if you don't know that Pop just died.'

The recruits in turn identify with their Section Commanders, sometimes conspicuously so. After the first two or three weeks George Griffin could 'tell by the mannerisms of the recruits' which commander they had. Bub Noack would hear them talking in the line: 'I am going to do that, I am going to go there.'

The 'Gucci' jobs (another borrowed British expression) come in and out of fashion. Post-2000, combat engineering became the flavour of the decade. Lieutenant Damian Bignall, not long returned from Afghanistan when he became an instructor, found recruits soaked up any practical lesson. And having come back from operations, 'You care about what you teach them. The details become that much more important and relevant. On operations you don't want to go back over old ground because you left a pouch open and dropped something.' Recruits touch the pouches on their uniform as he talks to ensure they are fastened.

Simone Wilkie found instructors were 'careful about the too keen, the brown nosers, the smart arses. The best is the team player. You can't hide personality traits. They will be found out.' The favourite recruits, according to George Griffin, are the ones with lots of ticker. 'The bloke you like is the one who makes the greatest effort.' They tell of one recruit who was a pain to teach but fought to comprehend all the way. 'Got injured but would not drop out. Ended up with a cannula in the arm, dropped twenty kilograms, but got there. An inspiration to others as well as us.'

When Rachel Ingram thinks of a young boy with a bad stutter she still smiles. 'When the last person comes back into the room they are supposed to say LAST MAN. He would not say it. He was a bent-over boy, a grey man, used to bend over like a mouse and sit close to the walls. We worked on him and it wasn't easy. After a couple of weeks I decided I would not treat him differently and soon we could not shut him up. It blew us away.'

After the first month the drop-out rate falls away. Despite constant fifteen hour days there is time for a pizza and even a beer and a weekend movie. *Alien v Predator* is showing. Some phone time is now allowed, and formerly confiscated mobiles are heard more often chirping through the barracks.

At the midway mark they pull on their civilian suits and hop back in the bus for a trip to the Australian War Memorial in Canberra. While in the broad Army there is general suspicion of the Anzac industry's amplification of the digger, at this indoctrination phase legend is a useful conscript. Young faces peer at the galleries as an old soldier takes them on a tour. 'So the mateship, never forget it, that's the word they learned on Gallipoli.' The faces in the old photographs staring back from the Dardenelles and the Western Front, though battle worn, are about the same age.

Like all generations of young soldiers the newcomers will do much for the sake of a piece of coloured ribbon. Upon arrival they wear a red tab, which means few privileges and no consumption of alcohol. By week three, if they have stayed the distance they graduate to a blue tab and start to receive free time. By week seven there is a gold tab and additional privileges. By this stage they move and march with fluency and rhythm.

Drill is still imposed despite a fading regard for its value. When the modern recruits, who are allowed more questioning of the point of all aspects of training, ask about drill they are told it is not about marching, but discipline. They are told the parade ground is like a battlefield; that the soldier who marches well fights well. They are told what their great grandfathers were told: 'Arms-drill as it should be done . . . is beautiful, especially when the company feels itself a single being, and each movement is not a synchronized movement of every man together, but the single movement of one large creature', wrote World War I veteran Robert Graves.[4]

After the close order marching, washing of civvies and oral hygiene the recruits will move on to more of what they expected: camouflage and concealment, how to assemble and operate a radio, and how to strip and fire a weapon.

Some free time in Wagga Wagga is allowed. At the McDonald's where only weeks earlier they would have been swiftly lost to the crowd, though now in civvies they are readily identified by staff. They are polite. They are well groomed. They always put back their tray. When they leave, instinctively they walk in step despite trying to break out of it.

Former Chief of Army Peter Leahy is one of many senior officers to speak of the magic of Kapooka, saying it has intrigued Australia's US allies. Brigadier Gus McLachlan, who had a stint there as a Platoon Commander, calls it 'mysterious and marvellous'. He says the Americans came to observe and then shamelessly copied what they came to call 'the crucible', a 13 kilometre pack march (including obstacle course and bayonette attack) known as 'the challenge' conducted at the end of recruit training. Blue Mawson says what the Americans most wanted to blueprint was the way Australians taught their junior leaders.

Major General John Caligari, a former training command chief of staff, is in agreement with Peter Leahy when he identifies the march-out as his favourite day. 'The best thing I have ever done is reviewing officer at Kapooka. Stand there in the crowd as the young soldiers, now with a shining Rising Sun badge on their hat, march onto the parade ground and you hear the parents trying to identify their kids. "Look, there he is, no, it can't be." When the march breaks up the young men and women find their parents, often calling them "sir".' Caligari says mothers and fathers have wanted to hug him.

Rachel Ingram will never forget the mother of the former stutterer watching open mouthed as he talked to his mates. 'She walked up to us in tears. The experience unlocked him.'

Kapooka did the same for Major General John Cantwell, who became commander of Australian Forces in the Middle East in 2010. At school he had neither excelled in sport nor study but he took off during recruit training, topping the course. Ironically, the subduing of self and embrace of the collective can be like a transfusion to individuals. Becoming a friend of someone who would not have formerly occupied your world can enlighten as well as equalise. Mateship has propinquity; useful characteristics are borrowed and shared. As Tony Gilchrist puts it, 'Some are good at sit-ups, some are good at push-ups.'

While the majority of names at march-out are white Anglo-Saxon such as Taylor, Campbell and Jones, Commanding Officer Max McIntyre is noticing a gradual change. 'We are beginning to see Asian, African, Indonesian soldiers.' But Indigenous recruits are still rare and women are still resistant to signing on to an overwhelmingly male environment. He has also noticed the high proportion of recruits who come from broken homes; Simone Wilkie puts the figure at 30 per cent. Retired Lieutenant Colonel Tom Rogers came to see the entrance of Kapooka 'like the Statue of Liberty. Bring me your poor and hungry.'

Private Simon, who started his Army training aged fifteen and would be fighting in Afghanistan while still a teenager, joined after his parents divorced. 'I needed direction.' The young soldier, fit and smart, completed his Higher School Certificate after he graduated from Kapooka in 2005. The opportunity to fight in Afghanistan was very much in his mind when he joined. For actions five years on he would receive Australia's second highest bravery award, the Star of Gallantry.

While many jubies come from poorer circumstances, they are not from the fringe. Unlike other armed services, Australia has few recruits joining for the money or the dental plan or to avoid incarceration. Australia's all volunteer defence force continues to recruit from the mainstream. The Special Forces Direct Recruitment Scheme specifically seeks the brightest and fittest.

Tapping the mainstream is most evident in something else you can't help but notice: how many recruits come from families with an existing link to the Army. Both Dan's parents were soldiers. John Caligari, the son of a soldier, has two sons of his own in the Army. And on it goes.

The first eleven weeks are an important beginning, but a beginning only. What the new recruits have mostly learned is how to be in the Army. The finer points of soldiering, be it firing a rifle or driving a truck, will come later.

The jubies learn something else that is a marvel to all who watch closely. As Blue Mawson and Rachel Ingram comment, while they will go through their careers generally seeing government property as fair game, theft from one another is virtually non-existent. 'Pinching is worse than murder,' says one. From here on soldiers will think little of leaving wallets and cash unlocked. Kapooka, it seems, builds not only soldiers; it builds self-respect, and (if you can forgive the nicking of Commonwealth property) fresh notions of integrity.

CHAPTER 3
BIAS FOR ACTION

Mick Moon is immaculate in his Brigadier's uniform. Large and muscular, you could imagine him in something different, say World Championship wrestler togs. Or maybe not.

Mick has a story that reveals something of the interior self. He tells me of his decision to join the Army in 1981. Although he had received an offer of acceptance to officer training, he instead took a job with a finance company. Soon he found himself at work at 8.30 in the morning in Springvale, Victoria, repossessing a grandmother's XA Ford. As he drove away, he saw her in tears in the rear-view mirror. When he dropped off the car, Mick tossed in his job, finding the uniform of the Australian Army a better fit.

When we speak he is the Commandant of the Royal Military College (RMC). His office is directly opposite the front entrance. Anyone driving between Canberra city and the airport will pass it. The RMC, better known as Duntroon, is Australia's West Point or Sandhurst, the home and heart of officer training.

However, unlike the American and British military colleges, if you decide to take a left into Duntroon no guard will stop you at the boom gate. Indeed, there is no boom gate, guard, machine-gun post, broken glass or barbed wire. At Australia's premier military academy the local bus passes through on its way to elsewhere. Civilians can wander in, have a look around and even play a round of golf.

The manicured grounds house not only the college, but also Australia's top brass. Follow Staff Cadet Avenue and you enter the 'Milky Way', as it is called, because of all those stars. Again, there are no sentries outside the Chief of the Defence Force's front door. The side gate of one of the grand old homes adjoining the golf course ended up being left unlocked so errant golfers could recover their balls. The panic room in the Chief of Army's residence was used to store wine. And, with his troops deployed in the Middle East after the Twin Towers attacks of 2001, Lieutenant General Peter Leahy would ride his mountain bike alone from his residence to military headquarters in neighbouring Russell.

In 2011, with the Afghanistan mission in its tenth year, Duntroon would celebrate its centenary, the RMC having been established ten years after Federation. The Anzac reputation, born soon after, can shroud a founding principle of containment of Australia's military. The grounds, historic buildings and absence of security reflect a peacekeeper rather than war fighter ethos. Duntroon looks more scholarly than military. Its motto, *Doctrina Vim Promevet*, translates as 'Learning Promotes Strength'.

Not that by any reckoning is it a place for the faint hearted. Major Jason Groat, who led a company through a bloody and brutal deployment in Afghanistan in 2010, would tell me, 'Anyone who says they enjoyed RMC is lying.' His Commanding Officer at the time, Lieutenant Colonel Jason Blain, when on a first return visit to his old room noticed his window framed a pleasing view, said: 'At the time I never saw it. When I was in the room I was either sweeping, polishing or sleeping.' Lieutenant Ashley Judd, who went on to command troops in Afghanistan soon after surviving Duntroon, thinks of it as 'the meat grinder. I look back on it fondly but don't remember thinking anything fond of it while I was there.'

Paul Graham, seventeen years of age when he joined in 1997, would be awarded a Distinguished Service Medal for action in Afghanistan in 2008. Back then, as a newcomer, 'instead of having fun like mates at uni I was polishing boots and getting yelled at by blokes two years older'. But in time Paul 'found his groove', and when returning to Perth on leave came to realise 'it was the last time I felt at home with civilian mates'.

What is tough about Duntroon is not the physical demands or the classroom. It is not the specifics of spit and polish, peer group scrutiny, lack of freedom and free time. It is more the way it all gangs up.

It is also not the bastardisation. As at Kapooka, hazing rituals involving abuse and humiliation have been outlawed following recurring scandals. In 1969 an inquiry was undertaken and a purge initiated. In 1983 it happened all over again. The beast of bastardry has prowled the Brindabella hills for many a year, and for many a year the rituals were not only excused, but encouraged. The beast was an honoured watchdog enforcing discipline and upholding tradition.

Looking into the film archive of Duntroon, I find footage from 1926 showing cadets being given a jolly good rollicking.[1] Initiation ceremonies at the time saw them crammed into closets, where they would be locked for hours. For the sake of the grace and comfort of senior cadets, the juniors would be forced to warm water pipes with their bare bums. (The broom closet tale is now enshrined as legend. 'Staff Cadet Casey' in skeletal form, encased in glass, is a permanent guest at the RMC mess hall. Tradition requires the last cadet to leave to seek the skeleton's permission. The true stories of cadets jammed into a black hole have morphed into an entertaining fantasy of Staff Cadet Casey being locked up before the Christmas holidays and not discovered until January.)

Almost a century on, it feels like the rituals have probably managed to be disassembled without removing the regulation. It is only the older intakes who admit to observing and experiencing hazing. The newer intakes, such as Lieutenant Jake Kleinman, who joined in 2006, highlight the strict, prison-like rules. 'There is no hazing. There is strict discipline but it is not out of control. There are a few traditions, but nothing over the top. My sister was at a college at Sydney University and nothing worse happens here.'

Most cadets contend the scandals of hazing and harassment are more evident at universities and organisations such as the Australian Institute of Sport, but as Jake Kleinman puts it: 'Because public money is involved it is an issue. People look at the Army and they expect more, as a reflection of their society's values.' While most cadets rue scrutiny that can seem unfair, they also generally accept it is due.

There are two paths to graduation. One is a direct entry eighteen month course. The second follows university training on the other side of the hill at the Australian Defence Force Academy (ADFA). Psychologist Colonel Peter Murphy believes 'you need systems in place that are robust and alert. RMC has done better. ADFA continues to have problems. They [the students] are younger and more are there for the degree.'

Opened in 1986, ADFA, the bland brick outlying campus of the University of New South Wales, is even more undergraduate than military when compared to RMC. Tri-service classes stick to university routines; Midshipmen and Officer Cadets are seen marching past the lecture theatres carrying briefcases, and weekends are for themselves. Because of the younger student body, ADFA carries more *in loco parentis* (parental responsibility). And like many a school boarding house, discipline has been delegated down.

When scandals surface they seem more often to do so on this side of the hill. The April 2011 Skype affair, as it became known, spread from allegations that a female Officer Cadet was unknowingly recorded having sex, with images broadcast to fellow students via the internet. Eighteen-year-old 'Kate' took her story to the media, after which Sex Discrimination Commissioner Elizabeth Broderick investigated.

Thirteen years earlier, when a cadet broke ranks, Bronwen Grey, an executive from Defence personnel, oversaw the inquiry. One 'dully'—first year cadet—from that time told me senior students would make it clear 'you did not cross the road' to complain to staff. According to the-then Army cadet and to rumour of the day, one offence too many, in this case penises flopped on the shoulders of females, was the catalyst for a thorough investigation that would wrest disciplinary control from senior cadets to staff.

You would have thought the lesson learned. But late into the 1990s at ADFA—or Legoland, as the brick block campus was known—ritual punishment and humiliation was commonplace. 'Fluffy bunnies' saw mouths stuffed with marshmallows until the victim spewed. 'Running man' offered two options: after being taken a distance from the college, junior cadets were required to run back wearing either running shoes or underpants. 'Naked was the best option, as otherwise your feet would be shredded.' 'Woofering' described using a vacuum cleaner to inhale a penis.

Entry to both ADFA and the RMC requires candidates to front a selection panel consisting of an officer at least the rank of Lieutenant Colonel, an Army personnel representative and a board psychologist. Acording to Commandant Mick Moon, the board is a 'funny beast'. There are two intakes per year, with selection panels conducted months in advance, and as with Kapooka you get the sense the black art of determining soldierly qualities has been honed over time. Another officer who has sat on the panel explained that it would see up to ten applicants at a time. The panel tended to look for 'the guys in the middle who could communicate, think and work together'.

The applicants arrive the night before the selection process begins. Ten to 15 per cent are serving soldiers, while civilians from a range of backgrounds and aged between seventeen to fifty-three make up the rest. They work together, outdoors and indoors, throughout the day and are asked a range of questions such as: 'Have you done anything you are ashamed of?' Answers such as, 'I once caught an undersize fish and did not throw it back!' are not unusual.

Each candidate is given three minutes to talk on a subject of their choosing. According to one officer, an applicant started talking about Adolf Hitler being misunderstood, another about aliens who occupied this planet before humans. The officer then saw other candidates trying to stop them from giving these kinds of answers.

And as at Kapooka, the applicants don't all look like Olympians. One female doing a physical training test explained she could not run, as she had never done so before. Basic drill can break down into mayhem and confusion, with some candidates struggling to differentiate left from right.

The day ends with individual interviews. Cadet Paul Nolan, who immigrated to Australia after serving in the Irish Army, found 'you have to sell yourself. People who see it as a job don't go far. Nor should they. It is a vocation.'

Mick Moon says that despite increased demand as Australia seeks to grow its armed forces, the selection criteria have not been adjusted down. The figure of 50–60 per cent of candidates being accepted has remained 'historically, surprisingly stable'. Another officer tells me the panel looks more for the 'eight out of ten': the stable, intelligent team player. This is not an environment where loners, such as Julian Knight, are approved of or thrive. Knight is the RMC's most notorious mistake, selected to Duntroon in January 1987. Six months later, after an assault on a colleague, his appointment was terminated. Then on 9 August 1987, in Hoddle Street, Melbourne, Knight went on a shooting spree, killing seven people. He was sentenced to 460 years in prison.

The new approach seems to work. 'There is obviously a good screening process. You never see anyone who can't suffer crap,' says Tobias Raimondo from Launceston, who completed the full four years—three years at ADFA, gaining an MA major in History and English, before going on to the RMC.

Once accepted, the preference is to pass and not fail people. And like at Kapooka, the process is more of survival of the willing rather than of the fittest. Cadets will strive to be neither 'grey man' nor 'heat seeker'. But, unlike Kapooka, drop-out rates are higher.

*

The eighteen month direct entry course to RMC is divided into three classes, beginning at third and ending at first. Third class is more like Kapooka, where recruits confront the basics: 'Running around, navigation, first aid, weapons.' Much of this occurs in bushland at Camp Blake, in Majura on the fringe of Canberra. Lieutenant Jamie Smith noticed 'the ones who were diggers beforehand didn't like the crap, the hoops they were being put through'.

For soldiers who have joined from the ranks it is a pain to be back in kindergarten. Former private soldier Edward Keating found being from the other ranks helped, but he did not like 'in the first six months being treated like a child, told to hold weapons with both hands, six months after returning from Iraq'. According to Brigadier Mark Bornholt, the sections with ex soldiers 'do better'.

Recruits are exposed again to the 'splits', the two minute gear change from physical training outfit to full whites and all the rest of the 'crazy room' rules. There are the classic room inspections, with probing eyes and fingers searching for dust under the bed or any skerrick of organisational detritus. Leisure time shrinks. Phones are denied and drinking in the lines or residential quarters is banned. Mick Moon believes that recruits need to be taken away from their comfort zone and iPods.

The instructors tend to be the Army's best, drawn from the ranks of experience, some fresh from the battlefield. 'Gone are the days when cadets run themselves.' Moon says they have to meld fast or they have difficulties: 'RMC becomes a meritocracy, a collective, very fast.'

The ADFA stream experiences a similar six week basic military training in the early stage of their studies. Again, this shakes out most of those who are seen to have 'got on the wrong bus'. The ones who drop out first do so less because of the physical demands as through recognition that the highly ordered and controlled existence, and the narrowing space that crushes time with partners and mates, is not for them.

'He hasn't got it' is a common explanation for someone's choice to leave. As a second-class cadet, Chris Appleton, the son of a Brigadier, sees it as being more than an issue of the right stuff. 'I have had a few surprises. Some friends who appeared suited have left. They were fit and smart but they had to also enjoy it. You may be suited but not enjoy it.'

The physical training can leave a visible scar on the person and the place. Cadets trooping from class to class on crutches are a common sight. The pressure to avoid back classing means constant fear of injuries. And the term 'linger' is difficult to kill. (Squeezer is another term used for a cadet who 'squeezes' out of having to work.) Being assigned to Neville Howse, a rehabilitation platoon, bears a stigma, despite many cadet injuries occurring through no fault of their own.[2] Cadet Edward Keating felt that if he did get put back he would not be able to stick it. He also thought the term 'linger' was 'mostly affectionate'.

You notice in the Army that despite the one uniform there are lots of internal variations. And despite a unifying *esprit de corps*, there is also a baffling and sometimes brutal degree of rivalry.

At RMC a first profound divide is between those who have directly entered and those who arrive via ADFA. The ADFA lot call the RMCs 'Bakers'. No one is quite sure why, a presumption being that someone with that name in the past had demonstrated a flair for ignorance, or that the cadet is 'half-baked'. When a 'Baker' says something less than clever in class, the ADFA cadets can be seen and heard drumming their rings on the desks. The RMCs in turn call ADFA cadets 'FAC'—ostensibly 'former ADFA cadet', but just as likely 'fucking ADFA cunt'. The ADFA lot will forever bear the stain of being a bit 'too Canberra'.

After the two streams come together in second class the differences are not so noticeable. The RMC stream does tend to say that once they all flow into the broader Army the ADFA bonds and networks hold tighter, even extending to other services. But they also say strong friendships frequently overwhelm old boundaries. Career networking can have an important start here, with successful cadets and mentors providing 'top cover' for trusted mates.

Australia is supposed to be classless, and while the armed services are full of many shining examples of egalitarianism, if you choose to study class in Australia there is probably no better place to start than Duntroon. Formed from recommendations by the famous British Field Marshal Lord Kitchener, there is still 'a trace of the last days of the Raj', certainly in the officers' mess, according to Lieutenant Colonel Malcolm McGregor. Retired Lieutenant Colonel Tom Rogers, arriving in 1983, thought there must have been a car show on because of all the British sports cars on display.

Brigadier Gus McLachlan, who joined a year earlier, did so after 'Mum brought a Duntroon brochure home. There was a picture of a young man with an MG, a surfboard and a girl in a bikini. It looked a bit shallow but I gave it a go.' Once there, he found: 'If you turned up in a panel van someone would have whispered in your ear. One kid from a private school had a straw boater and a rowing oar on his wall. You had to learn to behave in the officers' mess. Part of our formal learning was etiquette.'

While the sports cars are now harder to find, class is still visible in the parking bays. Lieutenant Colonel Bruce Murray tells me:

'There is still a bit of demarcation. The young soldier has the panel van, ute or HSV. If an officer gets into one, he can be referred to as having ORTs—"Other rank tendencies".'

The attitude to tattoos, or 'tough stickers', is much the same. You will see officers sporting them, but not often. Conversely, in the ranks they are conspicuous, except among the Army Reserves.

Lieutenant Jake Kleinman, the son of an associate professor of surgery from Newcastle, New South Wales, saw bloodline as still being a factor as recently as 2006. 'As far as institutions go it is one of the oldest. It's a snob institution, one of the last elitist places in Australia.'

Unsurprisingly, team building at Duntroon and the coaching of competitive sport finds many parallels. If officer cadets have a weakness with ropes training, their technique and strength training is worked on; frailties are ironed out in the same way a footballer is taught to improve his left-hand pass.

Rugby, a popular private school sport in the eastern states, tends to be the favoured game. If you are good at rugby you will be more likely noticed. And if you incur an injury playing rugby, you will be more likely forgiven than if doing so, say, on a ski slope. 'RMC, rugby makes careers,' says one former cadet. What they also say is that once on the field there is no rank. Within the prescribed limits of the rules and the referee's application, all and sundry are allowed to bash the stuffing out of one another.

Former stockbroker and captain of Sydney's prestigious King's School, Lieutenant Richie Varvel was fighting in Afghanistan not long after his 2006 graduation from Duntroon. Having overcome rugby injuries, he thought his private school conditioning helped in a way that was more practical than privileged. 'They are not out to hurt you if you do the hard slog and communal living. It depends on your background and walk of life. I had been in boarding school and saw others without a similar background struggling.'

Dublin-born cadet Paul Nolan brought a broader perspective. 'In Australia you don't have to come from a privileged background, which was the case in England and Ireland to a degree. There was more of a back door to a Queen's Commission if you happened to be the son of a general.'

Australian soldiers on frequent secondment to the ranks of allied forces often comment on differences. In the United Kingdom they notice that officers come more from the educated class. In the United States they see the officers coming more from the north, while the soldiers tend to be from the south.

Just as boundaries blur following the merging of the RMC and the ADFA, so are class lines leavened. Australians don't mind a bit of tradition, formality and regalia, but only up to a point. What works inside RMC is what works outside. Class divisions are not so rigid as to limit talent. The powerful middle of Warrant Officers, instructors and general experience exerts itself. Gus McLachlan found the senior non-commissioned officers were the ones to listen to. And here there was 'no snobbery. They would walk on cut glass for you.'

Mick Moon credits the same driving force. 'Training objectives and military skills are more important than where you come from. There is not a lot of time to focus on those issues. In small teams, strengths and weakness quickly come to the fore that have little to do with background and how much money you have.'

If there is a new elite it is in the 'gym generation, where you see no sign of obesity', says Malcolm McGregor. At Duntroon, while unquestionably a socialisation process occurs, if anyone is declassified it won't be because they are not the right kind of 'chap'. But it might be because the organisation has failed to physically shape them. McGregor sees most entrants as being drawn from Australia's 'great middle'.

It is in the RMC's middle or second class where diverse talent begins to blend into a more cohesive whole. The son of a dry cleaner and brother of a fellow Brigadier, the former commandant of RMC Mark Bornholt speaks up for both sport and academia: 'People who have played contact team sport know what it is like to lose . . . tertiary trained people think better.'

Second class sees a range of field exercises, including a parachute jump. This occurs close to the biggest and most feared physical challenge, 'Shaggy Ridge', which, according to Bornholt, the ADFA intake will have 'talked about for two years'. The exercise, in bushland near Berry in southern New South Wales, starts on a Friday and is over by Wednesday. Cadets confront set objectives, enduring without food or sleep. The experience is not about passing or failing, according to Bornholt: 'They learn simple orders work and are fatigued to such an extent they also learn to bond.' For Mick Moon it is a rite of passage. 'We have it at the front end of second class. The older hands mix with ADFA. It is tough but they all survive and learn to work together.'

Lieutenant Jamie Smith would find Afghanistan in 2009 tougher than Shaggy Ridge in 2006, and therefore appreciated the preconditioning. He is one of many large soldiers to find that his size is not always an advantage. 'At the time it was a struggle. The smaller guys and the females did well. I was reduced to eating grasshoppers and whatever.'

Former soldier Paul Nolan found the parachute jump over water at Jervis Bay unnerving. 'No one backed away and it sure as hell wasn't going to be me. But I had the time of my life once I was out the door.' Shaggy Ridge was 'not as hard as it is made out to be but it was interesting to see what I could take'. Anthony Purdy took a few lessons from the trial. 'When soldiers tell you they are tired you now know what tired is like . . . It teaches you to be sure the soldiers are looked after. It was a great feeling when we finished.'

Second class also sees the most drop-outs—20 per cent, after a rate of 13 per cent in the preceding term. Early starts, late nights. It piles up: tutorials, map exercises, running over hills and digging holes. Chris Appleton says his mates saved him: 'They dig the pit next to you and get you through.'

'Outsiders don't get it because it is not a normal situation,' explains 28-year-old Lisa Schulz, who had transferred from the Army Nursing Corps. 'And you have to get it. Those that don't they get rid of. We call it the merry-go-round. If you get punishment after punishment, you never catch up.' Ashley Judd recalls: 'No day's so difficult you can't cope, but still [there are] plenty of difficult days. The constancy of having so many eyes on you twenty-four hours a day means if you make mistakes it really affects you personally. Shit, I have to find a way to make it up. You can't hide anything at RMC.'

Unlike at Kapooka, where mates are important at the time but more likely to drift out of touch later, the longer and more intense Duntroon inculcation does forge enduring friendships. 'The best mates you have apart from during service overseas are the ones who shared RMC,' says Judd.

So how much is mateship a key to getting through? How crucial an element of survival is it? And how, if at all, is it turned against those who have a harder time fitting in? Loners tend not to survive because the engine of the corps of cadets is fuelled by the internal combustion of co-operation, with sole operators a mistrusted contaminant.

Those with experience of RMC applaud the same synergy of effort that is seen at Kapooka. The physically strong in the field will help the mentally strong in the classroom, and vice versa. While the group no longer use bastardisation rituals to exclude the misfits and force conformity on stragglers, the force field of the group packs the explosive power of a joint direct attack munition. The collective can and will continue to exclude the individual.

Most cadets told me the group would not deliberately engineer the failure of a non-team player, but nor would it be likely to go out of its way to help. Mateship is most important because of the ever-faithful 'good bloke' test. Major Justin Elwin remembers Duntroon 'was hard but there is a difference between hard and horrible. If you are not suitable, the group subconsciously turns it back on you. People can turn their back and not be available.' Equally, the group will help 'the good bloke' get through. According to Anthony Purdy, 'The learning tool is the volume of people around you.'

While RMC is clearly a meritocracy, there will be occasions when personality trumps results. Edward Keating, likeable and talkative, told me of an older cadet who was 'useless in the field but a great bloke'. So, 'He gets helped. If you always try and you are a good dude, no one has problems.' Conversely, 'Another guy, a former digger, was awesome in the field. He was very good at his job but a dickhead, so no one had anything to do with him.'

It is a toss-up as to whether the four-letter word most often heard at Kapooka, RMC and every Australian base across the world is 'brew' or 'jack'. Brew means a hot drink, probably made with a teabag or instant coffee. It is a fundamental currency of mateship. Having a brew ready for someone who is coming in from the dripping rain is an obligation that reaches through all ranks. Going 'jack' means letting down a mate or the team. A 'jack man' is someone who invents an excuse to have another carry his pack or sleeps through a picket. The term is thought to derive from the British expression 'I'm all right, jack, pull up the ladder', meaning you look after yourself and don't bother about the others.

'It is worse to be called jack by your mates than be chewed out by the CO,' says Ashley Judd. 'The jack man gets cold shouldered,' explains Jake Kleinman. 'He is less likely to help out, interact and socialise. If you are not jack everyone helps. The group looks after itself. The jack man makes it harder on himself. They most probably would not do it for you.'

Paul Nolan did not see deliberate exclusion by the group. 'There are some arseholes, that's life. But you don't hear people say why not let that person hang? People want each other to pass.' It is more that they are allowed to stray into a kind of campus no man's land. So it happens more subtly, in the way of the herd abandoning the runt in the dead of night.

With all the pragmatism of a former nurse, Lisa Schulz sums up the lot of the jack man. 'They don't have an easy time of it. They don't have many friends. They are not considered highly. Out in the field you see it. Some don't really care. But they are in the minority, and generally don't make it through.'

Organisational psychologist Lieutenant Colonel David Schmidtchen recognises that an institutional urgency to form the group comes at a cost: 'We are harder on someone who genuinely thinks differently. The Brits better tolerate eccentricity. We do unintentionally grind out differences.'

*

One difference that can't be ground out despite some persistent and misguided effort is gender. The historically male Army remains, if anything, silverback gorilla Alpha male. When the first female cadets began training at Duntroon in 1986, women made up 8 per cent of the cadet population.[3] December 2011 saw the female graduation figure climb to 13 per cent and in June 2012 fall to 6 per cent.

Brigadier Simone Wilkie acknowledges ongoing trouble in a boy's club environment: 'There is a problem attracting women. There are negative issues, abuse of power and bullying. Respect and trust are not always due.'

Undergo eighteen months as a woman at the Royal Military College and you can begin to see why. Lisa Schulz, ever sensible, accepts an unfair reality. 'Being female comes into it. You are expected to carry the same weight and do the same. But we are smaller and slower. We can't dig as strongly. It is bad to feel you are the weakest link.'

Colour Sergeant Schulz, the only woman in her section and one of three in a platoon of thirty, performed well. She worked harder at physical training to better prepare herself for the field. With an eye on a role in Intelligence, her capacity to think and reason and show some generosity became an understood asset.

Among the many gripes the men have about women, being weaker is not prominent. They might not be able to dig as hard, but if they work as hard they are generally respected and supported. What does figure, however, are issues of natural authority and organisational bias.

Just as was once said of women newsreaders, there can be reservations about the force of amplitude and authority in the female voice. And there is the 'lumpy jumper assist': perceptions of affirmative action advantages to women, operating above and below the radar, are widespread. The grumbling about favouritism is also directed at foreign cadets from Singapore and the like who are sometimes seen to be given an easier ride.

The softer, civilising restraint on bad boy behaviour is probably not so well recognised. 'You do get a bit of blokey stuff. Sometimes, if they go too far, you put them in their place. I can see how some would be offended, but I brush it off. My closest friends here are the guys. The girls do as well.' And as Lisa Schulz points out, 'It is our world as well as theirs.'

In the last term, or first class, the drop-out rate falls away. There is more room for socialising; the girls and boys get together. There are plenty of mess functions, and the bar is open after work. As is the case in the broader Army, while up front the energy goes into the group, once it is formed there is more encouragement for independent thinking. Indeed, if you are to flourish, it soon becomes an essential asset.

The world ahead, with far more murderous complexity than will ever be covered in a military textbook, awaits. Mick Moon says this is the time of the gearshift. After developing the basics of leadership, cadets 'move to thinking of complex operational requirements, asymmetric threats, where they move out of the theoretical to actual preparation'. When this happens, he says, 'we see a lift in cadets'. By now it is expected that they will have absorbed the RMC mantra of a bias for action.

By the time they graduate to stand on the edge of the parade ground and toss their hats in the air the young officers will, like the other ranks passing out of Kapooka, stand taller. You can see it in their bearing. You can hear it in their conversation.

They have confidence, measure and maturity a step above their civilian counterparts.

Whatever age they graduate at will be their military age. A thirty-five year old qualifying in 2010 will forever be the same military age of a twenty-five year old from the same year. And they will all be institutionalised. When in town having a drink at Mooseheads, although out of uniform they are easily recognised as soldiers or, as they put it themselves, 'AJs'—'army jerks'.

Some of what they have learned could be done without. Civilians, who see them as different, figure in an alienation process that started long ago, well back in training. The toll for this indoctrination is ironic considering the strong citizen soldier ethos that distinguishes Australian military service.

In Canberra the term 'Cordie' for a Duntroon cadet is now not so often heard, having faded like the corduroy fashion generally associated with the expression. At Sandhurst, denim has long been considered the fabric of the devil, not to be worn even out of barracks. The RMC, following suit, is also inclined to consider jeans *déclassé.*

So in their neatly creased chinos you see the cadets standing apart, arms crossed, 'scoping chicks', as if on a mission. The stance, the fashionless haircut and G-Shock watch, the 'fist on a wrist', are all give-aways. 'Would you root her? Did you root her?' the boys grill one another. The girls can find meeting civilian partners particularly difficult. While being so intensely imbued in the art of soldiering and leadership, social skills falter. The worst among them they self-describe as 'social claymores'. Civilian brothers and sisters in universities and the broader workforce become more adept at basic mingling. Hanging out is more the province of the aimless. It does not work with soldiering, where everything, even indolence, has a purpose.

Cadet Edward Keating, a doctor's son from Rockhampton doing what 'I always wanted to do' at the RMC, admits to feeling 'like I have missed out. I see my siblings in Brisbane with their lives progressing, getting married and meeting girls.'

The militarisation process can also do worse, engendering what some admit is a 'hatred of civilians'. 'Fucking hippies, commo wankers,' the AJs murmur. For outsiders there is an arsenal of derogatory terms, 'CJ' or 'civvie jerk' being the mildest. According to Bruce Moore's *A Lexicon of Cadet Language*, others include 'civvie arseholes, civvie fuckwits, civvie poofters, civvie slugs and so on. Civvie even becomes, as well as an abbreviation of civilian, an adjective meaning useless.'[4]

On the credit side cadets learn behaviour that would not be lost on many a CJ, conduct much the same as that seen at Kapooka. Colonel Andrew Condon, who would later become CEO of Legacy, explained that for all the conditioning and civvie bashing, the cadets are taught to retain faith in people. 'The value sets stay with you—integrity, loyalty and a sense of service. At Duntroon we would muck up, but it stopped at dishonour.'

Captain John Crockett, whose decent and patient approach to mentoring Afghan soldiers would impress me in 2010, explained it this way: 'The worst is to have your integrity questioned, for academic misconduct, plagiarism, copying TEWTs [Tactical Exercise Without Troops] etc. We are expected to lead soldiers on operations. If we don't have it we could get them killed.' Gus McLachlan remembers being expected to learn 'officer qualities. There was a strong emphasis on integrity. You were allowed to beat the system, as long as you owned up to it immediately.'

The graduands, as they are called, the fledgling lieutenants, will be paid around $55,000 a year, about $20,000 more than they received as senior cadets. While at the RMC they can drop out at any time; once commissioned, they are expected to stay for at least three more years (nine years for the ADFA stream). The return of service obligation means service for every year the government underwrites the cost of training, plus one.

Closely watched, and even more closely marked, there is a keen eye for those expected to go far. The senior cadet, the Battalion Sergeant Major, might one day become Chief of Army. The Sword of Honour or Queen's Medal recipient may go on to head the Special Air Service Regiment or win a Victoria Cross. Equally, graduands might be back in civvie street within the decade.

At Duntroon, the strength of the corps is at its core. Very successful cadets sometimes, but not always, become outstanding soldiers. The opposite is also true, as was Peter Cosgrove's experience. One of Australia's most popular and successful soldiers, the former Chief of Defence tells of his Duntroon days being conspicuous for a 'bloated punishment record and emaciated academic marks'.[5]

Once the former cadets graduate mid year or on the second Tuesday in December, their order of merit status will help determine whether postings match preferences. While this matters, from top to bottom all wear the one uniform. With this in mind, John Crockett poses the question: 'What do you call the guys who came first or last in the Queen's Medal count?'

'Sir.'

CHAPTER 4
GOING GREEN

Looking back, Lieutenant General Peter Leahy would say the Army had its own momentum. 'As boss, it felt more like it was leading me.' Leahy had been absorbed into the living whole of the Australian Army after his start as a staff cadet at the Royal Military College (RMC). In the story of Ken Gillespie, his successor as Chief of Army, there is proof of its democratic reach. In contrast, Gillespie began as a private soldier, apprenticed to the ranks of the sappers (or engineers).

When recruits and cadets leave Kapooka or Duntroon it is often said they go green, outwardly acquiring the uniform and inwardly the military state of mind. They now belonged to a community roughly the size of an AFL crowd at Sydney Cricket Ground, much larger in the popular imagination than in reality. As of 2010, the Australian Regular Army (ARA) numbered just over 30,000. At the time, research suggested only about 4 per cent of Australians found the idea of going Army-issue green attractive.

Sleeping in the mud and risking your life has never been a strong selling point but, for all that, there remains an appeal. For the private soldier all manner of responsibilities suddenly disappear. If they live on base they no longer have to buy groceries or even cook. Beyond the nights under the stars, which many find part of the allure, they can expect a roof over their heads, health care on tap, and a regular, respectable income. Warrant Officer Nichol Anderson, who would make it many times to the Middle East, asks: 'Where else can you live in Australia for $100 a fortnight and have all your meals cooked for you?'

One mother of a Special Forces soldier, puzzled by her son's career choice, pointed out to me a passage in D.H. Lawrence's *Lady Chatterley's Lover*: 'The Army leaves me time to think, and saves me from having to face the battle of life.'

For the officers, when it comes to responsibilities, in some respects the opposite is true. They assume a realm of obligations that are rarely fully anticipated. Captain Rob Flynn had to not only take charge of soldiers, he had to take care of them. 'We have to fix soldiers' problems: marriages, parenting, budget advice. A significant advantage for the ordinary soldier is the absence of responsibility.'

Officers often say that 80 per cent of their time is given over to being dicked around by 2 per cent of the diggers. If you are not a career soldier, copping a charge can be more a problem for the nearest non-commissioned officer (NCO) and officer if the indiscretion also casts a stain on their record. Perhaps that is why so many leaders, the Warrant Officers in particular, have less than spotless CVs—one reason they become adept at knowing their soldiers is because they have done it all themselves. They are so good at it, this middle sentinel of senior NCOs could qualify as the organisation's most effective early warning system.

It is often said that about one-third of Australian officer come through the ranks, which, if so, is unusually high by international standards.[1] Major General John Cantwell, once a callow private, saw the advantage of the other rank (OR) experience. 'Soldiers expect competence, for you to look after them, to find them somewhere to sleep, something to eat, to put them forward for a course. That responsibility further devolves to responsibility for wives, partners, kids and the noisy dog. If you are the gobby Captain; if you are arrogant and talk down to them, you will lose them in a second.' As one Warrant Officer observed: 'We have junior officers, 23 to 24 with no life skills, dealing with 27- to 28-year-old soldiers, giving financial advice when half of them live from pay to pay.'

In the 7th Battalion, Lieutenant Ashley Judd, not long out of Duntroon, was both acculturating and earning regard as a platoon leader. 'You rock up with pips and they are not going to give it to you. You have to fight for respect. Probably not all understand the responsibilities of an officer; they don't see you doing a lot of your job. You communicate more directly with the Section Commanders. If you ask the diggers about their commanders, the biggest thing they will say is he was good at looking after us, and standing up for us. Slowly they let you into the platoon. You might think you own the platoon, but they are in it longer. For all that they don't want to run it. They want to be led.'

Having done it all—from Kapooka recruit to Kapooka instructor to RMC cadet—Anthony Purdy 'never stopped being amazed at the sight of a junior officer talking to a rough, burly Sergeant. Soldiers will see through you. You can't bullshit them.' As Peter Leahy suggests, the callow private is able, if not visibly so, to exercise a degree of organic control. Plenty of young officers will admit the diggers can break them, or at the least make them earn respect an inch at a time.

Poorly performing officers will readily find trouble if they do not look after their soldiers. Once he reached his battalion, Lieutenant Paul Graham found: 'Soldiers don't care whether you get in the shit for something. Your welfare and career prospects are not their concern.'

Junior officers, sometimes even the best among them, can find to their cost that giving the diggers a break might be equally disrespected. You let them go into town and buy beer and someone overdoes it, and it is the officer who is in trouble. So it is an odd dynamic. The ranks will press for an advantage, but just as easily think less of the officer if they gain it. The Infantry, it seems, has many ways of testing the enemy's perimeter.

There can't be too many armies in the world where a young officer craves to be called something other than 'sir'. In Australia the word can swiftly become pejorative, uttered with unmistakeable disdain. An officer running into one of his soldiers in the supermarket will not be called by his first name; that would be too familiar. But there is a reason why many officers would prefer to be acknowledged as 'boss', a more reliable indicator of respect. And even better is to be given a nickname, depending of course on what it happens to be! There is an army of them—many ingenious, many more profane. 'Blister': pops up after hard work. 'Circles': an officer who gets lost trying to navigate. 'FONC': friend of no cunt. 'FINCLE': fucking idiot no cunt likes. Peter Leahy says grimly, 'Some officers prefer not to know.'

Major General John Caligari tells me: 'After a transport stuff-up when the vehicles for the Townsville High Range were not ready the next day there was a chorus: "Have you ordered the trucks yet, skipper?"' If a mistake has been made the soldiers will chide an officer to get it right 'in a good natured way.'

The higher tax levied on officers can apply to physical as well as mental endeavour. While Lieutenants and Captains have the power to order privates and Lance Corporals to dig holes and fill sandbags, there is an unspoken convention that unless they appear fit enough to do it themselves, authority will weaken. According to Anthony Purdy and many others, there is a 'culture of being fitter than the soldiers. The expectation comes not from the staff, but from ourselves.'

Doing initial employment training (IET) is the next step after graduation from Kapooka. Soldiers speak of two armies: first and second. The second means entering a support role in Logistics, Transport, Medical or Ordinance. The first is more at the sharp end—in Artillery, Armoured or Infantry.

As a young Lieutenant, Jake Kleinman made a popular choice. 'I don't sit in an office. I don't always produce something at the end of the day. But I shoot weapons and blow things up and run around in the bush. It is what I always wanted to do.' Sergeant Adam West from Kleinman's 7th Battalion says the same: 'Infantry is what I wanted to do—booms and bangs and playing with weapons.'

Australia's School of Infantry at Singleton in country New South Wales, 200 kilometres north-west of Sydney, is not known for its charm. In winter temperatures sink below zero, turning the ground white with frost. In summer humidity bakes the dull scrub-land. Soldiers drenched in sweat from hauling lead-like packs over hill after hill yearn for a trace of breeze. Even the kangaroos and dingos wilt.

'Tas' McGinley loved 'Singo'. After turning up at Kapooka as a seventeen year old in 1990, the Tasmanian would forever after be known as nothing else. Frighteningly taciturn, unerringly considerate, Tas would go on to become Company Sergeant Major in the 6th Battalion, Royal Australian Regiment (Motorised) and be seen as a soldiers' soldier. 'Kapooka taught you discipline and teamwork, but Singo made you a soldier. It gets smashed in.'

In time the smashing would call for limits. At the height of summer 2003, just weeks into his IET, Private Jeremy Williams had taken enough. According to a later inquiry, following altercations with other trainees and some heavy drinking in town, Williams returned to base 'tearful and distressed'.[2] Close to midnight on the first weekend in February, the twenty year old found a rope and a tree and took his life.

In the preceding weeks, after sustaining an injury on a pack march and being back squadded to a rehabilitation platoon, Williams feared discharge. Not being able to keep up at Kapooka or Duntroon is hard enough, but at the School of Infantry there was open denigration of the 'window lickers', who had struggled with a spell of hard training and been relegated to the role of spectator. The justification at the time for aggressive abuse was less to punish and humiliate as to discourage submission.

The soldier who, as former infantryman Travis Robinson put it, 'is always copping out with an injury' will always be resented. 'I mean, it could be a ridgy didge injury, but if someone is always sick or at the RAP [regimental aid post] trying to get a chit to get out of duty, you're always going to carry his stuff out field so that's going to create some anger in the team.'[3]

The suicide of Private Williams forced changes at Singleton. No longer were staff and fellow trainees given licence to bully those struggling to keep up. After the changes were implemented,

I watched a retraining platoon being retested for basic fitness. The finish time for a 2.4 kilometre run had been adjusted up from 10 to 11 minutes. Most crossed the line in time, but success and exhaustion could neither erase nor explain the look of misery on the soldiers' faces. When so much effort goes into building a sense of belonging, perceptions of not keeping up or not fitting in are hard to bear.

Tas McGinley would return to Singleton as an instructor to confront the Gen X junior soldiers in an evolving era of equity, diversity and imposed tolerance. 'I used to think the newer generations were soft. At Singleton you would find them: never mowed lawns or played sport. Into XBox. Now I don't think that at all. You get to find the ticker. You suck out the weakness like a snakebite. One drill and they suddenly get it. I like watching them turn into infantry soldiers.'

Another instructor at Singleton, Sergeant Todd Noble, says: 'We don't punish, we allow people to be disappointed in themselves. But there will be people who don't keep up on a run, and some guys who have to be made to do it.'

The process involves 'getting in their headspace and getting the civilian things out of them', explains Tas McGinley. But, importantly, he also says total institutionalisation is avoided. 'I am not a robot. I am green, but not military programmed.'

Bram Connolly, bound for 1RAR and later Special Forces, 'relished' IETs, appreciating the fine balance of both fitting in and flourishing. 'We were given our freedom back in some ways. I always looked back on the experience and realised that it was the hard but fair approach that instilled within me the trait of self-discipline.'

For Corporal Dan, bound for the Commandos, there was no concern about fitting in. He made plenty of friends at Singo, among them Private Luke Worsley. Luke and Dan both went on to the 1st Battalion, where they did well enough to apply for Special Forces.

The Commando Selection and Training Course made the three months at Singleton look like a farm stay. Four hours of personality testing. Ten days of exercises, including a 30 kilometre pack march. No sleep and food for three days, feet a mess. The worst of it was being dumped at sea at night some way offshore, Dan's first time in the ocean. He recalls his heart almost leaping fully from the water when he was nudged by something with a large fin—a pod of dolphins, as it turned out. But soon he started to think: where there are dolphins, there are sharks. It was not until first light that he reached the shore.

By this stage of the selection course, many starters had pulled out. And of 120 who began the training, only 30 finished, Dan and Luke among them. They were accepted into the 4RAR (CDO) at Holsworthy, sometimes known as 'Hellsworthy'. 'A totally different world,' reflects Dan, who at the comparatively young age of 21 qualified to wear the Sherwood green beret.

Another Commando, who joined the 1st Commando Regiment (Reserve), Private Andrew did a direct entry course that combined Kapooka and Singleton training. Nineteen years of age and 69 kilograms in weight, the university student from a privileged background got quite a surprise when he stayed the course and became an elite soldier. 'I saw people who were cage fighters and prison warders fail.' What made the difference? 'The key is not being a dickhead. The dickhead factor excludes a lot. My best trait was I could get on.'

Having figured out working in the film industry would mean being unemployed for most of the year, Troy Simmonds tossed in a work experience position at the South Australian Film Corporation and studies for a law degree with a clear objective in mind. He loved his Singo IETs—'all sorts of exciting shooting, field craft and obstacle courses'—before joining Bram Connolly at 1RAR. Troy had his mind set on Australia's elite Special Air Service Regiment. 'I finally did selection in late 1995 and had an accident, badly dislocating my shoulder. I was taken off the course and was devastated but vowed to try again. In 1996 I had a shoulder reconstruction and trained like crazy. I got on the November selection course and was one of nineteen selected out of one hundred and forty starters. Very exciting times.'

Talk to anyone in Infantry and you could come away believing they are the Army. Aaron Cimbaljevic, or Cimba, had different ideas. Having joined as a digger, he did his IET in Cavalry and as an officer chose Armoured. 'Carrying a pack was not for me. God invented the diesel engine for a reason.' Cimba's reckoning was that modern wars would be more likely fought from behind a steering wheel or joystick. Later in Afghanistan and to his peril, Captain Cimbaljevic would find himself carrying a pack and putting one foot in front of the other along with the other grunts.

Kyle Faram, who joined in 2000, wanted a trade and hoped to train as a carpenter, but he was refused and was instead directed to the School of Artillery. After eight weeks at Puckapunyal, in chilly Victoria, he was transferred to 107 Field Battery in steaming Townsville. 'I was arrested on the first weekend for underage drinking.' Faram, or Faz, would find his feet, qualifying for 4RAR

(CDO) and later the crucial joint terminal attack controller role. Like Aaron Cimbaljevic, Sergeant Faram would also feel more than the heat of battle in a range of tours of Afghanistan.

More evidence of the permeability of rank and position is found in the story of Jason Groat. Tas McGinley's company commander in Afghanistan began life in the Army as a truck driver. By the time this thoughtful and ingenous soldier came to lead men in combat he had crossed from private soldier to Major, and from the Royal Artillery Corps to Infantry.

Lisa Schulz, graduating from Duntroon in 2009, did not buy into this soldier first, soldier second school of thought. Australian women are banned from the ranks of Infantry but are hardly exempt from the risk of casualty. On the modern battlefield they drive the vehicles that strike the roadside bombs. They occupy bases targeted for rocket attack. They command engineering companies and fly helicopters. The rigorous Duntroon experience adjusted some of Lisa Schulz's attitudes to eligibility for a combat role. 'It made me look at it and recognise I probably shouldn't be in it.' But Schulz is still, as she puts it, 'a soldier first'.

Likewise Corporal Rachel Ingram. When the former Kapooka instructor was deployed to Afghanistan as a 'phot', or photographer, there was something of a nervous flurry back in Canberra. Female soldiers are weapons trained and Rachel, like all the men patrolling with her, would be armed. A country girl from a family with Gallipoli veterans on both sides, and having grown up wedded to her pony, Ingram had wanted to join the Light Horse.

For her IET she was sent to 5th Aviation in Townsville, where she was assigned to the catering corps. 'It was devastating, but there was then no choice about a trade unless you were a musician.' Rachel would go on to Signals, following a circuitous route that saw her achieve a personal goal of being the first Australian woman on patrol in combat. In Afghanistan she would lose 14.5 kilos in three months. 'My weapon came first, ahead of my camera. We are one section, one platoon. The only person who will get you through is you. We all finish together, only ever as fast as the slowest man,' she had told me before she deployed. When she returned she would proudly say, 'They never waited for me, no problem.'

When marching out of Kapooka in 1991, Nichol Anderson was 'the only girl from her room still in'. At that stage she saw the Army as a stepping stone to the police force, so had an immediate eye on enlisting in the Military Police (MP). At the time women had first to gain experience in another field such as transport, catering or ordinance. Private Anderson got transport, and with no driver's licence had her early training behind the wheel of a massive Unimog.

Once there she found it strangely comfortable, developing enough situational awareness to recognise that the life of an MP had drawbacks. 'They called the women MPs bush pigs. All they did was bang in star pickets.' With a career similarly constricted, the young private suffered further the blunt and unbridled chauvinism of the time. But she also found she 'loved the Army discipline and social life'.

One other source of satisfaction for the young driver was noticing that when sent to haul soldiers back from exercises outside Townsville on the high range, they would fight to get in the back of her truck. Hungry, tired soldiers develop an advanced order of rat cunning, and they had worked out that the female drivers took the rough roads with greater care. A smoother ride back meant they could get some sleep in the truck and be fresh for a top night in town.

Private Anderson would rise to Warrant Officer Class One, the ceiling rank for ORs. She would become a 'mover', helping organise the transportation of entire task forces, steering an even larger green machine around the globe. There would be plenty more occasions when the range of skills she learned and demonstrated found broad appreciation.

It is sometimes said of Australians deployed abroad and working alongside foreign allies that among them will be someone who has trained as a diesel mechanic and can get you going again; or a carpenter who can affect bush repairs; an electrician who at a pinch can wire up an alarm system; and so on. A small army without the option to call in specialist tyre changers, bore diggers and the like needs to be agile and resourceful. Anthony Gilchrist saw this for himself in Iraq. When he left Kapooka he wanted Infantry, but got Ordinance. 'I was told I scored too well in aptitude.'

Soldiering has always needed a lot more than soldiers carrying guns; it also needs clerks, cooks, storemen, linguists, computer technicians and more. Lieutenant Colonel Bruce Murray from the Army's career management section explained 'there are nineteen critical trades and it can take six years to train specialists in some technical fields'.

Gilchrist, who had a knack for reading manuals, applied to become an ammunition technician. The move to the Royal Australian Army Ordnance Corps (RAAOC) at Albury–Wodonga on the New South Wales–Victorian border was the first of fifteen in the next twenty years. As many soldiers attest, in those days the standard of Defence housing was so poor you took your carpets with you.

Tony developed skills in handling munitions and explosives, which were soon in increasing demand at a time when the homemade bomb was becoming the other side's force multiplier. Although progressing only to Year 11 at high school, Army career management soon found it needed Gilchrist, who was fast tracked as a special services officer to the rank of Captain.

The transformation was never as smooth as either side might have wished. 'I kept being told I had OR tendencies. I did not seem to have the levels of diplomacy and tact they wanted.' But he did have a great deal else to offer, notably his living, breathing self, which in the ranks of the Explosive Ordnance Disposal Engineers can disappear in a blinding flash.

If anyone in the peculiar precinct of counter-insurgency warfare can find the front line, it is the engineers. Michael Lyddiard wanted to be one after he saw a poster showing a soldier with a mine detector crossing a creek. Lyddiard, from Ipswich in Queensland, joined the Army in 1995 at the age of seventeen. His father, a 21-year Army veteran, tried to discourage him. With some feeling, Lyddiard tells me: 'He knew more than I knew.'

Beyond the obvious *Hurt Locker* dangers associated with mucking about with high explosives, a more general deterrent is the indentured service—which can stretch beyond four years. As infantryman Josh Dowsing explained, 'If you do a trade you have to pay back the time you spent learning.'

For others the craft is what makes it appealing. Lance Corporal Rod Johnston did a carpentry apprenticeship in Perth. 'I love building things and I liked the idea of the military with a trade.' Corporal Michael Montgomery, from Logan in Queensland, told me, 'The skills help you later in life.' And on the job, out on patrol, 'You inject yourself into the community, which is better than sitting and staring with your back to the wall, as in the Infantry.'

Sapper Daniel Swinburne transferred after seven years in the Infantry. 'When I was in the grunts I realised I would have little to show for it. So I went to RAEME at Albury and then to Sydney, where I spent eighteen months contracted to a civilian builder putting up townhouses. I liked carpentry and I wanted to help people.'

At the sharp end of this corps are the combat engineers like Michael Lyddiard. Behind those out in front with the mine detectors and the sniffer dogs are all the others who put down rifles to pick up tools to build patrol bases, gun towers, accommodation blocks, schools and bus shelters, who fix failing generators and get the water pumps going again.

Daniel Swinburne makes another point often referred to when there is talk of Army engineers: 'We have our own character.' While obviously clannish, sappers have an easier attitude to outsiders like myself. Maybe it is the trade base holding up a bridge to civilian society that makes engagement easier. Maybe it is the required interaction with ordinary people. Or maybe the constructive nature of their work rubs off on the collective personality.

When I meet Sapper Rowan Robinson of the 3rd Combat Engineering Regiment he is full of good cheer. Easy going, fit, suntanned, 'Robbo' is the Aussie digger from central casting. My descriptive notes are brief: 'laconic, laid back, no false modesty, not afraid of hard work, an engineer'.

Robbo had joined at the age of eighteen, an older brother already in 1RAR. 'After a time I spoke to my brother, who told me you don't get a lot out of the Infantry that can be translated to a career, so I transferred to the Engineers.'

When we speak, Robbo has returned from his first trip to Afghanistan. Then aged twenty, in two years of service the young sapper had trained for jungle warfare in Malaysia and urban warfare in Singapore, and experienced counter-insurgency warfare in 'The Ghan'. I would later have cause to pore over my notes of our conversation. Clearly the young soldier loved his life in the Army. Unaffected and unselfconscious, he told me: 'I would definitely go back. I feel like I am achieving something.'

Outsiders often don't understand why anyone would want to help people they don't know, who live on the other side of the world. Furthermore, they don't always connect with a sense of duty to their own country. Insiders view this gap as being so wide they hardly bother to try to close it. In the hundreds of interviews undertaken for this book, I heard soldiers expressing these sentiments many times, that they wanted to do something for their country and they wanted to help people. If you don't have those feelings you are unlikely to understand them.

As we part, energetic, effervescent Robbo, with boundless life and optimism, tells me he has put in for Special Forces selection.

CHAPTER 5
MISSION DRIFT

My first trip to Afghanistan in 2007 brought me to a conflict remarkable then for having dragged on longer than World War I. For all that the story, like the barren wastes of Uruzgan province, was a mostly empty canvas. This is partly because of remoteness, partly because secretive Special Forces units conducted most of the operations up to then, and partly because of inherent internal complexity that continues to challenge an outsider's comprehension.

Landlocked Afghanistan occupies two-thirds of the area of New South Wales. The centrally located Uruzgan province, about the size of the Australian Capital Territory, has a population that is slightly smaller than all of Canberra's—97 per cent live a rural life, much the same as that experienced by centuries of forebears. The literacy rate for the male population is about 5 per cent and for females less than 1 per cent. Strategically positioned at the centre of the Pashtun tribal belt, the river valleys intersect all points of the compass. From steep and rocky observation posts, locals have observed many a passing army.

Apart from the few Toyota HiLuxes and jingle trucks on the unpaved roads, Tarin Kowt, the provincial capital of the Uruzgan province, looked little different then to the way it appeared in 1901. To the west of Tarin Kowt is Deh Rawood, where you can visit the remains of a fort traced to the time of Alexander the Great. It is also the home of the Taliban's spiritual leader, Mullah Mohammed Omar. A Pashtun, Mullah Omar is from the world's largest tribal society, one of around twenty million people awkwardly positioned on both sides of the Pakistan–Afghanistan border.

The tribal map of Uruzgan, like much of Afghanistan, is a patchwork. The two main groups are Durrani Pashtuns, who dominate Uruzgan's east, and Hotaki Gilzai Pashtuns such as Mullah Omar, who are concentrated more to the west of the province. The Hazara are a tribal minority who are still found in small enclaves, as are the Kuchis, who have seemingly forever moved their herds across this disputed earth.

The population, although almost exclusively Islamic, is mostly Sunni Muslim. The Shia Muslim Hazara, with their distinctively different Mongol features, once in the majority, have for centuries resisted displacement. The impact of ethnic and religious persecution reaches far as well as deep. Many of the boat people turning up in Australia from Afghanistan proclaiming a well-founded fear of persecution are Hazara.

The picture I am trying to paint here is hardly one of harmony. Historically, along the narrow river valleys the reach of government has been weak to non-existent. And when outsiders arrive, despite the *Pashtunwali* obligation to be hospitable, there can be fierce resentment and an allied code compelling retribution if wrong is perceived to have been done.

A history of outsiders abducting females, press ganging males and imposing taxes has generated distrust in the very notion of governance. Rule of law is something Afghans have had to work out for themselves, so each small community is its own fortress. And when they fight it is not only because the enemy is from a predatory tribe, but because they are defending a patch of fertile ground or a watercourse that helps feed a family.

Over the centuries invaders have come and gone, the most recent being the Russians—who pulled out in 1989. After a decade of futile bloodshed they left behind the burned out hulks of tanks, helicopters and as many as thirty million land mines, one for every still living Afghan.

Mujahadin warlords who helped oust the Soviets with the aid of allies such as Osama Bin Laden and the United States held power briefly until the likes of Mullah Omar intervened. Mullah Omar's Taliban were at first popular for standing up to cruel and oppressive banditry, but the Talibs, or 'religious scholars', had no idea how to run a country. The village elders dragged Afghanistan backward from the clutch of modernity, applying medieval rule that sanctioned the abuse of women and children and drew world condemnation.

When Osama bin Laden's Al Qaeda launched attacks on the United States from his Taliban sanctuary in September 2001, retaliation was swift and effective. Less than a month later Tomahawk missiles rained down on every compound and cave target cells could identify. Despite the airborne holocaust, the population did not back their new oppressors. After five years, Afghans were well and truly sick of the Talibs.

Tarin Kowt was one of many areas where locals turned against the Talibs. In November 2001 they stormed the residence of the provincial governor, who they had come to consider 'a very bad man', killing him and stringing up his body in the main street.[1] Days later Tarin Kowt fell in a telling episode, its liberation emblematic of a new ruling alliance.

Hamid Karzai, an ethnic Pashtun from the Popalzai tribe, born just to the south of Kandahar, had fought with the Mujahadin. His resistance of the Taliban saw him now again joined with the Americans, and within months of the World Trade Center attacks an extraordinary mission evolved. Linked with eleven members of Operational Detachment Alpha (ODA) 574, US Army Green Berets, Karzai persuaded the Americans of the massive strategic benefit of vanquishing the Taliban from its heartland.

ODA 574, the first team to infiltrate southern Afghanistan to help co-ordinate the resistance, made it to Tarin Kowt on 16 November 2001. With Karzai's help, the Green Berets rallied a small band of local fighters to oppose an estimated 500 Taliban heading north from Kandahar.

Once in position Karzai's military adviser, 30-year-old Green Beret Captain Jason Amerine, called in American airpower. US Navy F18 fighters spotted the first convoy. 'Smoke 'em,' instructed Amerine.[2] Caught in the open, the Taliban convoy was destroyed.

This pivotal action demonstrated that Taliban rule was unpopular, even in this heartland, and in contrast reflected the might of a superpower that could hurl thunderbolts from the sky. Further, it brought weak and strong together, forging an unequal yet influential alliance. The action helped elevate Karzai; educated, multilingual and able, he had cache enough to lead a tribe. Leading a nation of tribes might prove another matter.

*

By the end of 2001 the Taliban retained small toeholds in the mountains and the southern provinces, but across the broad Afghanistan battlefield they were resoundingly defeated. The Americans gained a stronger toehold, setting up their main southern base in Afghanistan's second largest city of Kandahar, where the Taliban had staged its last stand.

America's Operation Enduring Freedom became Australia's Operation Slipper. Prime Minister John Howard, who had been in the United States at the time of the September 11 attacks, had made it clear that if asked for military assistance, Australia would oblige. A month later, in keeping with ANZUS treaty obligations, Australia announced details of a military contribution.

In November the Australian Special Operations Task Group (SOTG), led by Lieutenant Colonel Peter 'Gus' Gilmour, arrived in Afghanistan. By 2002, in this first phase of Operation Slipper, SOTG worked from both the Kandahar air base and from Bagram in the north.

1 Squadron of the Australian Special Air Service Regiment (SASR) enjoyed greater freedom of movement than would later be the case, as small teams in long-range patrol vehicles embarked on intelligence, surveillance and reconnaissance missions. The 'chicken stranglers', as they are sometimes known, are trained to live off the land and in some respects disappear into the landscape, watching and collecting intelligence and usually avoiding confrontation.

This was a kind of phoney war period when vehicles could be taken far and mostly free of improvised explosive device (IED) attack. 'In the old days there were fifty-day patrols, when we were resupplied by helicopter. They were the best of times, the poor old "terp" [interpreter] in the back, bouncing around,' says a trooper.

The SASR found its way along rocky tracks that took patrols where the tracks wanted to go. Sometimes they crossed into Pakistan, sometimes into a former world. They entered villages where electricity had not yet reached. One trooper remembers an ancient villager speaking of 'Britannia', family history somehow connecting the Australians to the Anglo-Afghan wars of the nineteenth century. Sometimes villagers would confuse the SASR with the Russians, not knowing they had left thirteen years earlier.

With a laugh, the trooper recalls rolling into a village and, above the caterwaul of livestock and greetings of *'Assalaam alaikum . . . Inglesi'*, hearing a distinct Aussie accent. Thinking there was an opportunity to gather useful intelligence the patrol eagerly conversed with the man, who had not long returned from a stint in Melbourne. They were out of luck—the AFL fan only wanted to talk footy. 'He asked about Tony Lockett. He did not want to talk about anything but Lockett.'

Trooper Troy Simmonds has similar recollections of encountering locals carrying Martini Henry and flintlock rifles, which some of the Australians were able to purchase and souvenir. 'We also bought some amazing handmade carpets.'

The mission was still a long way from adventure tourism. On 17 January 2002, Corporal Tristan Salvadori was badly wounded by a land mine outside Kandahar. On 16 February, a Land Rover carrying five Australians struck an anti-tank mine in the neighbouring Helmand province; Sergeant Andrew Russell later died of his wounds.

Beyond supporting the US alliance, Australia was also engaged in the primary mission of destroying Al Qaeda sanctuaries and remnants of Taliban protection. Small SASR teams set up observation posts near snow-capped peaks of the Hindu Kush, where the air is so thin you can barely walk, let alone run.

The troopers watched in silence, with a particular eye for a tall, bearded man in robes accompanied by bodyguards. On the roof of a kind of Talibanistan, not far from the famed Khyber Pass, altitude sickness caused symptoms similar to those of a throbbing hangover, as eyes strained and backsides froze.

Troy Simmonds recalls US soldiers from the famed Delta Force being surprised at the fitness of the Australian SASR. The Australians, with warmer jackets and better conditioning to the thin air, helped carry the Americans' gear as they 'humped their arses up the mountain'.

Operation Anaconda began early in March 2002. With their comrades positioned in their eyries, two members of the SASR joined a large force of Americans from the 10th Mountain Division and Afghan soldiers. The plan was for a hammer and anvil type operation to crush one of the remaining Al Qaeda outposts.

As is often the case, meticulously planned operations can stumble over a tripwire, triggering chaos in an instant. On the coverless slopes of the Shah I Kot Valley, this group of soldiers soon found the enemy to be better equipped and appearing in greater numbers than anticipated. For eighteen hours, exposed, surrounded by wounded and under constant fire, Martin 'Jock' Wallace, a signalman from 3 Squadron SASR, held on to his radio as well as his nerve. His actions of attending to the wounded, fighting off the enemy and helping call in air support earned Wallace a Medal for Gallantry.

Two months later, a different team from a different squadron of the SASR fought another battle that spoke of a different order of chaos. A six-man patrol, Redback Kilo Three, set out on a surveillance and reconnaissance mission in the province of Khost, in the north-east. According to a later investigation by *Time* magazine, the team stumbled into a range war. They sought cover from the gun emplacements they encountered, but were spotted. When a gun battle developed near the village of Bhalkhel the Australians withdrew towards another village, Sabari, attracting more gunfire.

In serious trouble, Redback Kilo Three called in air strikes to help them manoeuvre to safety. They managed to get away unscathed but not so the locals, who claimed eight of their own had been killed. They also claimed they were not Al Qaeda or Taliban. The Sabari villagers were 'guarding their homes as they did every night, from their rivals in Bhalkhel, with whom they had been feuding for months over rights to the area's forests'.[3]

At this stage, with a decade of war barely begun, the battleline contours that score these ridges were not understood. The tribal mapping had not been done, and locals were used to defending their own ground. It is not hard to understand how they would view the arrival of strangers with weapons as unfriendly. The episode demonstrated something else as well: Australia had some work to do shaping its own code of conduct in an environment where Western notions of rule of law and principles of armed conflict had little traction.

The learning curve would be every bit as steep as the daunting Hindu Kush. After the firestorm, with Redback Kilo Three back at Bagram, the recriminations began. One soldier had taken and left behind a prohibited camera, as well as souvenired a dead man's turban and rifle. An inquiry determined the patrol had fought to defend their lives and operated within prescribed rules of engagement. The soldier who carried away trophies of war was disciplined.[4]

Collecting souvenirs from the battlefield might not seem much of a deal in Australia, where German medals and Japanese swords can still be found in Granddad's shed. But that was then. The new era of the strategic private is also the era of the 24-hour news cycle. Camera phones can collect images that are then swiftly distributed to all points of the globe. The narrative that explains and contextualises the episode will not so easily carry.

For many soldiers, particularly those operating in secret, the news cycle is another threat. Special Forces in particular are known for a dread of ink over blood. There is clear wisdom in the application of strict discipline that encourages decent conduct and constrains the prospect of scandal. Just to be sure, Australia's elite SASR would also eschew the use of helmet cameras.

This would mean that in subsequent years Australians saw and heard barely anything of the work of this regiment in perhaps the busiest decade of its existence, which suited the culture of an organisation programmed to avoid the spotlight. It also suited military commanders, who saw media attention as generally unprofitable. The policy of neither needing nor seeking recognition also generated a vacuum too readily occupied by rumour and suspicion.

In November 2002 2 Squadron, the last of the Sabre squadrons to then deploy, rotated out of Afghanistan, drawing this phase of Operation Slipper to a close. Prime Minister John Howard later acknowledged an underestimation of the resilience of the Taliban, but at the time the decision seemed correct. 'The military advice we had was that we ought to withdraw. It was always intended that we would have highly trained effective forces there for a short period of time. That happened.'[5]

Australia's contribution in the next phase would be in the form of a desk officer in Kabul and another engaged in mine clearance work. Attention was turning to Iraq.

*

The conflict in Afghanistan, sometimes described as the 'good war', gave way to the 'bad war' when in 2003 Australian soldiers joined another US-led Coalition to eliminate weapons of mass destruction from another rogue state, Iraq. While none were found, in pursuit of them the Australian SASR and 4RAR Commandos enhanced their reputation.

To their chagrin, many of the rest of the troops deployed were quarantined from the worst of the fighting by Prime Minister Howard. Corporal Ryan Ingold, who marched out of Kapooka in 2000, was by then trained to the hilt. His expertise as a 2RAR infantryman was unsurpassed, having led a section to victory in a 'DOG', the Australian Army's Duke of Gloucester Cup, a five-day competition that tests the training and endurance skills of each Infantry battalion. Now he was stuck in a 'sand trap'. 'We had a lot of skills but did hardly anything. I take my hat off to the US National Guard. Their soldiers were getting blown up by the day. They were not as well trained, but they had to do what we could not do.' Australia upheld its ANZUS commitment by undertaking protective security work, largely in the quieter Al Muthanna and Dhi Qar provinces.

In contrast, Tony Gilchrist, a Kapooka graduate from 1987 working bomb disposal in Baghdad, was 'too bloody close'. The first sight to greet him when he arrived at the airport in 2005 was of ramp ceremonies to send home the flag-draped coffins of dead soldiers. While United States losses alone would climb above 4000 lives, there will never be an accurate figure for how many Iraqi lives were lost but it is thought to be over 100,000 at a bare minimum. Gilchrist saw too much of it. Working with American and British bomb disposal teams, he went out on 157 jobs in 160 days, learning like the rest of them to tuck his feet back while travelling in a vehicle in the hope they would less likely be torn from his body if an IED was tripped.

'I saw some horrific injuries. We pulled bodies out of cars, collecting bits, the biggest part fitting in one hand: one head, one leg, one shoe. You felt like shit but you could not show it to the others. One time five blokes in the lead vehicle were killed. By the second month enthusiasm waned and excuses for not going out began to emerge. Every day we expected not to come home. Every day I would leave photos and a letter to my wife on the desk.'

It remains a remarkable fact that in the six years of Operation Catalyst in Iraq, no Australian military personnel were killed in action.

Even before the Iraq venture was started it was clear the objectives in Afghanistan had not been met. In October 2002, bombs detonated in and outside the Sari nightclub in Bali killing 202 people, among them 88 Australians. This and further attacks on Western targets throughout Indonesia were linked to Jemaah Islamiyah, which in turn had connections to Osama bin Laden and Al Qaeda.

Ironically, following the swift victories of 2001 and 2002, the Iraq distraction had taken pressure off terrorist sanctuaries in Afghanistan and Pakistan that now more clearly represented a direct threat to Australia. While the Taliban had been ousted from government and Al Qaeda seriously weakened, their leaderships had recovered and regrouped in Pakistan. And Osama bin Laden was still at large.

David Kilcullen believes that in counter-insurgency operations 'the initiative is everything'. A former Australian Army Infantry officer, he began his study of guerrilla warfare in West Java in the 1990s. Later, as a Lieutenant Colonel with a PhD in Political

Anthropology and advising Australia, Britain and the United States on strategies for Iraq and Afghanistan, he counselled: 'If the enemy is reacting to you, you control the environment. Provided you mobilize the population you will win. If you are reacting to the enemy, even if you are killing or capturing him in large numbers, then he is controlling the environment and you will eventually lose . . . Focus on the population, further your game plan, and fight the enemy only when he gets in your way. This gains and keeps the initiative.'[6]

When the Australians returned to Afghanistan in August 2005 a better defined plan had been developed, but there was more learning needed than was yet to be comprehended. It might have seemed simple enough—take on lesser-armed Islamic fundamentalists in a primitive landscape. Special Forces could pick up where it left off, resuming counter-leadership missions and this time finishing off the bad guys.

However, little in Afghanistan is simple. The Australians would face a fanatical enemy, a poorly educated and mistrustful population and a weak and corrupt goverment presiding over a flimsy economy heavily underwritten by a massive illegal drugs trade. Afghanistan's criminal class would merge indistinguishably with the insurgency, like the border region to the east, forming an invisible narco-state.

Afghanistan is commonly referred to as a graveyard. The perceived wisdom is that invaders who don't end up under a pile of rocks instead retire to lick their wounds. The experiences of the Russians in the 1980s and the British a century earlier are invoked, as are comparisons with wars in Iraq and Vietnam.

Soldiers I have interviewed, with actual battle experience to draw upon, are frequently irritated by the comparisons. While most are happy to do what soldiers are trained for and go there to fight, none see themselves as invaders. They will turn up in Afghanistan, but no one wants to stay. One experienced Australian Special Forces soldier told me: 'There are as many differences as similarities to Iraq and Vietnam. The biggest difference is that Afghanistan is far more complicated.'

The experience of Australians being cushioned within a softer corner of the conflict, as in Iraq, would not be repeated when Special Forces units made their way back to Afghanistan to set up the base they still occupy in Uruzgan. While Uruzgan did not have the population density to be as fierce as provinces such as Kandahar and Helmand (where the British, Canadians and Americans were deployed in larger numbers), it was fierce enough.

Often referred to as the badlands or the Wild West, the deep river valleys of Uruzgan are like corridors providing an insurgency passage from Pakistan. The steep mountains offer sanctuary and overwatch all that goes on below. Beyond the thin green strips of farmland alongside the rivers the place appears desolate, like a planet in *Star Wars*.

In September 2005, when Australian C130 transport aircraft touched down, it was a bit like arriving at Dodge City. The Americans had been there for a year, setting up Forward Operating Base (FOB) Ripley beside a 1830 metre runway they had bulldozed on a not quite flat stretch of dirt outside Tarin Kowt. They had established other bases in Uruzgan: FOB Anaconda to the north in Khas Uruzgan, and FOB Cobra to the north-west at Char Chineh. FOB Tycz near Deh Rawood had been going since 2002.

The Australian base, Camp Russell, at the elevated end of the air strip, was at first a small cluster of tents pitched within a sea of grey-coloured, talcum powder-like dust. The Special Forces contingent was about 200 strong, forged from SASR and 4RAR (CDO). Water was scarce here, 1341 metres above sea level; there were only a few showers. Camp stretchers were unfolded and plastic wrap torn from MREs (meals ready to eat) for a four month rotation.

The Australians' role was to head out on surveillance and reconnaissance missions. One member of Rotation I recalls these missions as 'soft and slow', like much of 2002. 'It was totally different. They just watched us. There were a few IEDs and some contacts in the Khod Valley. We climbed up to find a few abandoned and rusting 107 mm recoilless rifles. It was like we were inside the onion, and yet to peel it back, layer by layer.'

Rotation II reached further, taking greater firepower such as mortars into Helmand province, travelling longer distances, experiencing fewer ambushes and little to no threat of IED attacks.

By the time Rotation III arrived in May 2006, the Australians were well into it. Summer saw the first of what became routine fighting seasons. In the green zone foliage had thickened, providing cover. With the mountain passes no longer blocked by metres of snow, weapons caches were topped up and fighters assembled.

It is often said that when the fighting is thickest you see the same figures rising to the occasion and this was true of lofty Lance Corporal Ben Roberts-Smith, who had joined the SASR from 4RAR (CDO) back in 2003. On 31 April his small sniper team climbed for ten hours through the night to the top of the Chora Pass to establish an observation post. The eyes on the valley below provided vital intelligence, supporting what became for the Australians their most intense action since the Vietnam War.

In the Chora Valley the predominant Gilzai population was more supportive of the Anti-Coalition Militia (ACM), as the

Taliban were then known, after watching the foreigners 40 kilometres north in Tarin Kowt cosying up to their main tribal rivals, the Durrani Popalzai. By the end of May, the ACM had grouped to overrun the police station at Chora. Afghan National Army forces, as well as Americans, Canadians, Dutch and Australians, were also moving into position to engage in fighting that would stretch over the following months.

On 2 June, Ben Roberts-Smith was forced to fight for his life when his observation post came under attack from two flanks. He split and manoeuvred from his team, catching sixteen approaching enemy in the open. Roberts-Smith took them on with his sniper rifle, attracting accurate return fire but holding the enemy off for the forty minutes it took for air support to arrive.

A United States AC130 Spectre gunship lumbered up the valley. With its 105 mm howitzer, 40 mm cannon and Gatling guns blazing, the hills ahead became swirls of dust flecked with coloured mist. With ammunition exhausted, the gunship turned for home. So too would the Australians, their patrol vehicles riddled with gun shot.

By 3 June the Taliban were repelled, but the fighting was far from finished. On 6 June there was close-quarter fighting high on a mountain when the Taliban attempted to overrun an observation post. Commandos provided fire support with mortars and they were in turn engaged by rocket-propelled grenades (RPGs) from three fronts. Watching from the high ground, they could see Afghan women and children being forced to resupply ammunition. Sergeant Matthew Locke charged the enemy, throwing hand grenades and firing his M4, killing Taliban who had closed to within 5 metres of the observation post. He would be awarded a Medal for Gallantry.

On 7 July, during Operation Nile, Sergeant Ray was part of a quick reaction force of Commandos to rescue Canadian Special

Forces soldiers who were in pursuit of a Taliban leader. The Canadians from Joint Task Force 2 had been surrounded and, having one killed and two wounded, risked being wiped out. The Australian Commandos led by Captain Justin rushed to support them by securing a helicopter landing zone. At the front of the convoy it must have looked a bit like a scene from *Black Hawk Down* as rocket and small arms fire from the ridges rained down on the mounted patrol as it raced through the night.

New Zealand-born Sergeant Ray and his platoon secured the site, providing accurate covering fire for an hour. In superior numbers, the Taliban closed to within 50 metres but were repelled before and during the perilous helicopter extraction. Even so, the robed and bearded fighters still saw advantage on their side, setting up a range of ambush points along the return route.

Special Forces soldiers are trained to take the initiative when under attack, to overcome a natural urge to duck, hide or withdraw and instead directly retaliate. This is known as the hinge effect, when you seize the moment and try to swing advantage your way, and it is exactly what the Commando platoon did as it surged towards the ambush sites, in one instance Sergeant Ray destroying a machine-gun post from 30 metres. Another Commando who was there described it as 'an incredible kinetic night. We were taking fire from all 360 degrees. It was amazing none of us were killed.'

Platoon Sergeant Ray would later receive a Star of Gallantry, Australia's second highest bravery award. Introduced to the Australian Honours system in 1991, it was the first Star of Gallantry ever awarded. Sergeant Ray explained his success and survival to 'being a better shot'. Captain Justin would be awarded the Medal for Gallantry.

*

On 17 July 2006 Australian Special Forces teamed with the American 10th Mountain Division for Operation Perth, as they had done in March 2002. Corporal Brett Wood's Commando patrol joined the American Infantry on a clearance mission, again in the Chora Valley. Just after noon, in the wilting 50° Centigrade heat, they came under heavy RPG and small arms fire.

One American soldier, Sergeant Robert Chemento, was killed. The wounded included six Australians, among them Brett Wood, who had been struck in the foot by RPG fragments. With the Australian fighting strength down to one third, Corporal Wood did not report his injury.

Again the initiative had to be seized. Wood's Platoon Commander called on him to take his section forward and attack compounds sparkling with AK47 and PKM machine-gun fire. He did so, allowing the wounded to be evacuated. However, the attacks persisted, forcing Brett Wood to ignore the pain and blood and break into the enemy positions, the Commando and his team killing six.

The now limping Wood told his commander of his wound and was sent to the casualty clearance station. He was soon back receiving treatment at the Camp Russell regimental aid post. Brett did tell his partner Elvi that he had been injured, but said it was because a box had fallen on his foot while unloading a truck.

Elvi, like most wives and partners, mums and dads back in Australia, heard nothing of these exploits. Slight, pretty and elfin like, Elvi Neeme had met Brett Wood two years earlier at an Emergency Services party and fallen in love. 'I did not know soldiers and soon realised how naive I had been. At that stage Brett had been in Iraq. I wondered why he did it and came to learn how much he loved it. In civilian life, you wear blinkers;

you have little idea. Dad, knowing I craved stability, asked: are you sure?'

At this stage home contact occurred via a borrowed satellite phone. There was nothing like the banks of telephones that would later be set up to make international connections as simple as a local call, and gratis to boot. The opportunity for direct contact had obvious strengths, but weaknesses also.

Beyond the requirement to observe operational security, soldiers are not eager to pass on details of the everyday dangers they face. Equally, at home, partners see the value of erecting another shield to deflect knowledge of domestic difficulties that can't be sorted from a world away.

The Australian casualty list in Afghanistan would ultimately grow into the hundreds. Over the twelve month period from 2005 to 2006, eleven soldiers suffered wounds, one Commando having his jaw blown away. A similar number of bravery awards were also conferred. Brett Wood and Ben Roberts-Smith both received Medals for Gallantry.

Brett's proud partner Elvi was in tears when the award was conferred. She was also a touch taken aback by the reaction from his comrades. 'His friends paid out on him so much. It was so brutal I asked whether he should ask them to tone it down. So much flak from them. Non stop. Isn't it a bit much? He told me this is how it is. "They are embarrassing me because of the honour".'

A year later 4RAR (CDO) received a Meritorious Unit Citation for 'extraordinary gallantry'. The task group had been able to 'successfully neutralise the enemy on a number of occasions in previously impenetrable sanctuary areas'.[7]

Another award would eventually find its way to a member of the same Task Force known as 'H'. In an environment where protected identity is as common an accessory as dark sunglasses, the Australian Warrant Officer comes with a ready-made pseudonym; within the international Special Forces community he is simply 'H'. 'Do you know H?' the Americans will ask an Australian on exchange to one of the posse of US Special Forces units.

In that tight, exclusive world H is known as much for direct speech as direct action, which may be how he ended up with the Americans in 2006. Not that I can pretend to know all the details—within this tight-lipped community, checking and cross checking is more than usually difficult.

There is unit rivalry at all levels of the Australian Defence Forces, which in the heightened climate of Special Forces can be even more intense. The sand-coloured berets of the SASR don't always blend easily with the green-capped Commandos. The story goes, as a Platoon Sergeant with Delta Company 4RAR, H fell out with a Commanding Officer, and there was said to be some trouble during Rotations I and II. After an altercation H was moved, fortuitously as it turned out.

In the main, Australian Special Forces units were deliberately separated from US operations because although considered to have optimum capability and able to qualify as Tier One, the Australians did not have the same operational flexibility. In short, US Special Forces such as the famous Navy Seal teams could range into Pakistan, something the Australian government would not allow.

H, broad shouldered and amiable, ended up in Bagram, where he soon made friends with the Americans and in doing so gained entrance to a community that excluded most of its countrymen, let alone outsiders. Special missions units (SMUs) are recruited from the broader United States Armed Forces, the best known of which are Delta Force from the US Army and the United States Naval Special Warfare Development Group (DEVGRU). The by invitation only DEVGRU is better known as Seal Team Six.

H achieved a rare feat for a non-US national, to be accepted into DEVGRU. The Americans, with a high degree of pride in their warrior spirit, were said to be surprised to find H right up there alongside them as they swooped into battle.

What impressed H about the Americans is what impresses most Australians who join joint forces: that is, the entire Australian Defence Force is roughly equal in numbers to the American Special Operations community. SMUs have their own dedicated assets, their own intelligence platform, aviation support and more.

SMUs pursue high-value targets. H soon found himself very busy on three to four 'kill capture' missions a week, the ones that did not range into Pakistan. For vehicle operations the SMUs preferred civilian wheels such as Toyota HiLuxes, which by night presented a conveniently familiar silhouette. The low profile was also maintained in other ways, with small teams of only three to four heading out.

For larger operations the Americans mostly took to the air. On board the modified MH47s—more heavily gunned, powered and armoured Chinook rotary wing variants—they would usually set off in the dead hours beyond midnight. While the kill capture missions have been criticised for botched targeting, H believed the intelligence relied upon was almost always accurate. The SMU would drop on top of a target and be gone within an hour or two, the target more often captured alive than dead.

However, one mission into Kandahar in which H was involved did not go to plan. Two MH47s dropped onto a target and came under attack. Heavy machine-gun fire raked the aircraft and rockets began to streak through the night. The Americans had more support above, but could not bomb or strafe because the Special Forces teams were too close to the enemy targets. The MH47 with H on board took off in order to draw fire away from the other. They were successful to a fault—about 2 kilometres distant, an RPG found its mark.

The large chopper began to groan and sway; the Australian thought he was going to die. Turbines screamed and hydraulics squealed. The pilots fought mightily, but gravity won. The heavy twin rotary Chinook hit the ground hard, but did not burn. And H did not wait. Unhooking his harness, and with a senior Ranger, he pulled survivors, many of whom were injured, from the wreck and then set up defences. Considering comparable crashes, remarkably there were no serious injuries.

Against orders, the other MH47 'winchestered', or remained on target, to provide fire support until it ran out of ammunition. An AC130 Spectre gunship also tracked overhead, sticking around until the approach of daylight. When a rescue helicopter arrived and all were clear, the AC130 turned its 105 mm cannon on the downed MH47, leaving it to burn.[8]

The American soldiers on board that MH47 returned with a special regard for their Australian ally. H later took part in further missions, one with a US Rangers regimental reconnaissance detachment (RRD), the US Army's answer to the Seals, that also positioned him at the centre of the action and the top of the world.

Midway through 2006 the American Central Intelligence Agency identified that one of its most wanted men, Badruddin Haqqani, a leader of the Al Qaeda-linked Haqqani network, was on the move between Pakistan and Afghanistan, aided by complicit Pakistani intelligence operatives. H and the RRD were dropped above the snowline and trekked into position at 3657 metres to intercept Haqqani and his bodyguards as they traversed the Hindu Kush.

The small team was at the very edge of its capability; the air was so thin the helicopter could take only six men. It was hard to breathe, let alone move, and cover was non-existent. They were supposed to be on the ground for only an hour or two, but would stay for 24. And there was no hiding; they were forced to place themselves in a position where they could in turn be observed.

Within line of sight were between 100 and 125 enemy clustered around cave entrances, Haqqani believed to be among them. The RRD team came under fire. The joint terminal attack controller called in air strikes, a B1 bomber speeding from the Indian Ocean base of Diego Garcia. A mass of ordinance crashed into the caves. Seven 2000-pound bombs shook the very mountains on one run, and seven more on another.

Estimates of enemy killed in action in Afghanistan are rough at best. The battle is not to gain ground so ground is rarely examined, especially as there is rarely the time or opportunity. The number of insurgents killed was put at 100 plus, but it was not the victory sought—killing large numbers of enemy is acknowledged as a weak metric of success. The target sought, Badruddin Haqqani, lived to raise another army and plot further attacks until killed by a drone strike in 2012.

A few years on, H would be able to place alongside his Australian medals a US Bronze Star for valour. While the global war on terrorism is often derided as a myth, it did not seem so then to H and the Americans, up there above the snowline.

CHAPTER 6
ANOTHER 20 YEARS AT LEAST

The war was made personal for US soldiers by the September 11 attacks, a holy war even to the disquiet of some of their allies—who watched them praying on their way to battle. For the Australians, too, despite the lack of defined battle lines, it was real enough. Following the first Bali bombing in 2002, there were more terrorist strikes in Indonesia, another targeting Westerners including Australians, again in Bali in 2005.

The notion that this Talibanistan was a haven for global terrorists had credibility for those Australians who saw the enemy up close at this time. Special Forces soldiers were struck by the strength, training and motivation of tall, strong and fierce Jihadist-like combatants; H was one of many who in hand to hand combat had fought for his life. 'They were the business,' the soldiers tell me.

Five years into the conflict it was becoming clearer that defeating even the best the enemy could assemble was not enough. Australia was eager to move to a new phase of reconstruction and development. In military speak it meant moving from kinetic to non-kinetic operations; in soldier speak it was time for the touchy feely stuff.

In 2004 Hamid Karzai, who had helped liberate Tarin Kowt three years earlier, became president of the Islamic Republic of Afghanistan, reinstating the first government since 1979. In the preceding year a new International Security Assistance Force (ISAF) had taken over command from the US-led coalition, Operation Enduring Freedom. ISAF would try to manage a balanced objective of maintaining security while assisting the rebuilding of the country and the functioning of government.

In this nascent stage, ISAF was made up of 37 nations. One of the eleven non-NATO countries in the Coalition, Australia joined principally with the Dutch, as it was too small to do much on its own. In 2006, 1600 Dutch deployed to help form Task Force Uruzgan. Forward Operating Base Ripley, or Davis as it was also known, became Camp Holland, the Dutch leading the mission.

Soon after the Dutch arrived, Australian Special Forces pulled out for the second time. The Special Forces commitment to Iraq had been upgraded and, with further operations running in East Timor and the Solomon Islands, capability was stretched. The Australian government believed, or perhaps hoped, that in Afghanistan the time had come to switch emphasis from killing the Taliban to winning the population, and that Dutch allies would supplement force protection.

The Special Forces contingents withdrawing in September 2006 to make way for a Reconstruction Task Force (RTF) did not agree, expecting their replacements would be exposed and vulnerable. 'It's not right to pull out . . . there are lots of baddies out there and you need a strong reaction force.'[1]

Australia had already sent a forward scout. In March Army Engineer Captain Michael Scott arrived to spend seven months working with American and Dutch Provincial Reconstruction Teams (PRTs). There were 25 scattered across Afghanistan, with various nations taking individual approaches to the provision of health care, education and general infrastructure.

Scott was candid and perceptive in his appraisal of the task ahead—corruption and governance would be a serious challenge. Uruzgan governor Mullah Abdul Hakim Munib was on the United Nations sanctions list, which meant ISAF dealings with him were restricted. Government officials were largely illiterate, with a skilled workforce being hard to find and harder to attract. Security remained a serious concern. If outside contractors were brought in they could be attacked and their projects destroyed.

Scott saw that the United States PRT approach of providing gifts in the form of school books, medical supplies and buildings was not working. The worst example was the provincial administration building in Tarin Kowt; completed at a cost of nearly US$250,000, it was opened by the US Ambassador in January 2006. In September, after local officials reported cracks forming in a wall of the building, it was found upon inspection that as the result of a lack of supervision by a qualified engineer the roof was unfinished and building defects in structural members had been hidden by cement rendering. 'Originally roads were built without bridges, schools without teachers and farm machinery was provided without a maintenance plan.'[2]

It is sometimes said the Americans do war better than they do peace. The problem was not only a lack of co-ordination between different entities, but contradictory conflict. The PRTs would organise to dig a well to provide fresh water to locals, only to see them blown up by US soldiers wanting to deny them to the Taliban.

One American PRT official, Chris Mason, told me: 'The bottom line is the PRTs are window dressing. There is an average of one PRT in the southern insurgency zone for every 1.2 million Pashtuns, most of whom are living in mud huts with no electricity, access to safe water, medical care or anything we would call a school . . . At the strategic level of the war, the handful of PRTs and their few dedicated civil affairs specialists have had no significant impact on the lives of sixteen million people in desperate poverty.'[3]

Michael Scott was impressed, however, by the different approach taken by the Dutch PRT in first undertaking a conflict analysis to get an understanding of where along these river valleys tensions, enmity and rivalry stirred. This understanding would prove important: giving a generator to one farmer could alienate a neighbour; digging a well to liberate women from a 3 kilometre walk could cause annoyance, depriving them of their one opportunity to get out and about; provision of electricity to one tribal enclave could win its approval, but help make an enemy of a rival community.

When the first Australian RTF arrived in August 2006, what it confronted was a job far more about construction than reconstruction. RTF1, under the command of Lieutenant Colonel Mick Ryan, found a corner of Camp Holland and accommodation for under 300 engineers and a solitary platoon of Australian Infantry. Further protection was supposed to be provided by the Dutch battle group.

According to Colonel Stuart Yeaman, who would command a later task force: 'The decision to deploy a full reconstruction team to aid a new Dutch deployment was seen within the Australian military as something of a novelty. Engineers had never been deployed this way.' Yeaman described Tarin Kowt as 'still a lawless, barren mud-brick town and the Australians' role in trying to bring peace and stability started there'.

When Australian engineer Captain Clare O'Neill arrived at Tarin Kowt, her experience was very different to her later work as an aide to Governor General Quentin Bryce. Looking immaculate was somewhat beside the point in Afghanistan. 'I will always remember my first patrol. The town was like something from a western movie. There was no economic activity. The streets were deserted. There were bullet holes everywhere and bloodstains in the street.'

Looking down from Camp Holland at night it was mostly black as pitch, with only a few lights from the houses of those who could afford a generator and fuel. If the night was otherwise illuminated it would be through the streak of tracer and rockets and via the intermittent glow of flares.

Providing protection to the reconstruction teams, Corporal Andrew Booth from 7RAR was struck by the different reception they would receive from one hill to the next. 'People would invite us to sit on a mat and ask about having a patrol base built. A kilometre away another group or tribe weren't interested.'

From the same battalion, Private Josh Dowsing had his nineteenth birthday in Afghanistan while still learning his job. He remembers long, hot days standing guard over engineers installing water tanks and laying concrete slabs. RTF1 did not move far from Tarin Kowt and tellingly, at that stage, there was 'no drama'.

Many of the soldiers would complete an entire rotation without sighting a local woman. The ones who did saw only a fleeting glimpse as figures in full *burqa*s hurried out of sight. Clare O'Neill gained a different perspective; her burly bodyguard waited outside when she became the only Australian soldier allowed into the women's wing of the Tarin Kowt hospital. It was 'quite a sight. The roof had collapsed. The birthing room was a mouldy mess.'

The operational restrictions on RTF1 meant it would have limited effect, moving as it did only far enough to get out tools and put something up before turning back in order to reach base by nightfall. Overnight the Taliban could destroy what had been put up. Further apparent was recognition that the Dutch forces were not providing adequate protection. Thirty-two-year-old Major Justin Elwin, commanding an Infantry company, felt the frustration of 'fighting and building at the same time', but also a sense of accomplishment in 'paving the way'.

RTF1 endured the below zero winter, returning to Australia in April 2007. In the same month, Australia announced it would again deploy the Special Operations Task Group. The fierce fighting of 2006 had bloodied but hardly beaten the Taliban. As would be seen year after year, the insurgents had a way of leaking like snowmelt back into the valleys.

There were still plenty of pockets of Uruzgan such as at Gizab that were no go for the ISAF. The Taliban continued to intimidate through the distribution of 'night letters', threatening all who dared interact with the government or infidels. The Taliban also continued to tax the locals and operate as a shadow government. Adjustments were made by trial and error to the balancing of kinetic and non-kinetic goals—of killing enemies and of making friends.

A contingent of 300 Special Forces soldiers, made up of SASR, Commandos and at this stage a smaller combat engineer element, were back in Camp Russell in May bristling with weaponry. At about the same time, 393 personnel from RTF2 settled across the Hesco barriers, bearing weapons and gifts in the form of a US$4 million budget for planned construction projects.

My first visit, with a crew from *Four Corners* to report on problems and progress to date, soon followed. The closest I would get to Special Forces was on the plane, in the cafe and from a distance as they tested their weapons on the range.

My 'embed', as it is uncomfortably described, would be with RTF2. I say uncomfortable, because it can sound like winning access equals losing control. The stigma that attaches is not always deserved—journalists negotiate for access all the time, and editorial control is not part of the deal. That is not to say being transported, fed and having your life protected by a bunch of soldiers does not present a threat to objectivity and judgement. This risk was one I much preferred to take than the alternative of free ranging the hills of Uruzgan, offering myself for execution or kidnap.

On 21 May 2007, we flew out of Sydney on a charter flight to an undeclared 'location in the Middle East', which turned out to be Kuwait, where we boarded buses to take us to a massive American staging facility near the Iraq border.

When an army moves it is something to behold. Beyond the personnel, heavy vehicles and weaponry, there is a small city of prefabricated warehouses and workshops, refrigeration plants and water purifiers, even kennels for the dogs. Australian Warrant Officer Nichol Anderson explained that her job as a 'mover' was like a military version of being a travel agent: calling names from a clipboard, giving directions to accommodation, barking warnings about carrying prohibited ammunition and not being there for the next 'bag drag'. One difference was the call, 'Anyone who wants to piss better do it now.' Another is an insistence on leaving on time. While other nations give leeway if someone forgets a bag, the Australians stick to strict procedure.

Warrant Officer Anderson could average eighteen hour days that were both strenuous and unforgiving. 'It is always our fault if transport is not there or the plane breaks down.' And with all the pre-surgery like checking and counter checking, how could anything go wrong?

A year earlier, in April 2006, Private Jake Kovko had been fatally wounded, a military inquiry later finding he had been accidentally shot by his own weapon. An error somewhere in Kuwait meant the wrong body was repatriated to Australia. To that date, Australia had had little practice of returning flag-draped coffins. One clear outcome of this compounded tragedy was an upgrading of weapons discipline, evident every time a bunch of soldiers arrived back at base. An unauthorised discharge is a grave sin. Using a buddy system, soldiers paired off to do safety checks, inspecting and test firing weapons into sand-filled drums to ensure barrels were clear.

It was probably true in Hannibal's time, that whenever huge armies move, the lumbering caravan is initially a danger to itself. A look at the casualty list for all the allied forces in the Middle East showed that the Kovko incident was not unique. What is obvious at this massive United States staging area is soldiers sporting reflective sashes over their physical training gear as they pounded the dust on fitness runs. A surprisingly high percentage of casualties, as many as one in four among the Americans, were non-combat related.

The American mess facilities are jaw dropping in more ways than one. Front of house, a civilian contractor counts the numbers to sit down. Here as elsewhere in the history of human conflict, someone in some place far away is doing very well.

Beyond the cheeseburgers and enchiladas and 50 flavours of ice cream, there are salad bars and glistening trays of fruit. Soldiers can also have a Maccas, KFC or Pizza Hut fix, with queues forming directly outside the government-sponsored smorgasbord. Fast food and fitness are two of the many contradictions encountered in the world of soldiering. And like back at Kapooka, no one says very much. The mess halls are human refuelling stations—it can take decades for soldiers to break a habit of sitting down to eat rather than talk. The Australians say the Americans are even worse, becoming irritated if their intensive mastication and digestion are interrupted.

At the staging camps, that is what soldiers mostly do: eat, mark time, exercise and undergo final pre-deployment training. A short bus ride from the base is another large facility, where as much time as can be spared is devoted to teaching split-second reaction. When manning a checkpoint or staring over the machine gun from the back of a Bushmaster, that is all the time a soldier might have. How do you know whether the vehicle rushing towards you harbours a suicide bomber intent on obliterating you, or a heavily pregnant woman racing to the hospital?

It is at the range that I met Warrant Officer Tas McGinley for the first time. Warrant Officers can be scary, and in the scary stakes Tas places somewhere between Norman Bates and a great white shark. When Australian soldiers are questioned about what most pisses them off, the media usually makes the list. A 2006 survey of Warrant Officers querying what they most hated about Army life listed 'adverse media' ahead of 'incompetent superiors', 'dishonesty' and 'pay'.[4]

I would get to know Tas better three years later; at this time talking to me did not seem like his best experience of the day. I asked him to explain how a soldier can be trained to see inside the mind of an approaching stranger. 'Obviously the soldier has got to have his wits about him. You obviously won't be comfortable, but doing more and more of the training gets the drills down pat. When and if the moment occurs they will more likely do the right thing.'

The training must have had its benefits. A few weeks earlier, on 3 May, Private McNab from 1RAR and attached to RTF2 was manning a crossing point at the Wanow Bridge outside Tarin Kowt when he saw something in the approach of a sixteen-year-old Pakistani male that caused him to train his MAG 58 machine gun in that direction. (The Taliban had used a local six year old to mark platoon headquarters.) Suicide bombers, often school age and recruited in distant Madrasahs, are promised the reward of a martyr's funeral—affording entry to paradise—and then sent in search of the oppressors. The terror tactic is difficult to counter. On this occasion the soldier's movement appeared to trigger a premature detonation, which killed the attacker. Private McNab, about 10 metres distant, was slightly wounded by shrapnel strikes to his left arm and shoulder. [5]

On 25 May, as the Australian C130 banked steeply towards the dirt strip at Camp Holland and banged to earth, sending skyward a billow of dust, it was well worth hammering home recognition that the distinctive blue body armour of the non-combatant advanced no superior protection. In asymmetric warfare, the civilian aid worker or journalist can be a higher value target, attracting more publicity for the cause and applying more pressure on foreign governments to pack up and go.

Our welcome was mixed. The Australian Defence Force's reputation for hosting media would improve, but never to a point that matched partner forces. The disparity was such that many

Australian journalists came to prefer embedding with the far less controlling Americans.

Investigative reporters can't so easily walk away from obstacles, and are given more time to overcome them. This had meant trying to understand why the Australian Defence Forces sought to over-manage us. Part of the problem, obviously, was fear of unfavourable reporting, but there is more. Unlike the Americans, who can often seem like contestants in a talent quest, the diggers do not perform on cue.

When we walk into a recreation room and declare we would like to gather footage, the soldiers all flee. A consequence of the intense group bonding is the individual's aversion to attention. To enforce this, Australian soldiers have what they call a 'carton rule': anyone appearing in a newspaper or on television is obliged to buy a carton of beer for his mates. The custom may well have a worthy genesis, reflecting a suspicion of 'big noting' and 'bunging it on'. But it does not help when trying to tell their story, a story they universally conceded was not getting through to the broad public and their own families back home.

Film crews can go a little crazy when they are restrained on the edge of the action. Commanding Officers worry junior soldiers will misbehave; junior soldiers resent the intrusion, particularly in their free time. There is the further burden of herding chooks, which can be the way it seems for soldiers forced in an already difficult circumstance to provide additional safeguards for ill-disciplined media. In the military, chain of command is everything; the best way, sometimes the only way, forward is by starting at the top. The Commanding Officer of RTF2, Lieutenant Colonel Harry Jarvie, took a deep breath and said, 'Make it happen.'

Our first patrol began at 0400. Soldiers keep appalling hours, the idea being to move in as unpredictable a manner as possible. We head into town. I am folded awkwardly into the front passenger seat of the Bushmaster. My driver is nineteen-year-old Queenslander, Trooper Brendan Davis. When I later call my wife, she tells me her hairdresser's friend has a son in Afghanistan named Brendan. On the other side of the world, Australia is still a village; they are one and the same.

At dawn we are assembled in the bullet-riddled governor's compound on our way to a project reconnoitred a year earlier by Captain Clare O'Neill. The engineers are renovating the Tarin Kowt hospital. Nothing in this place happens easily; the engineers can't work without massive force protection. Corporal Igor Moravcik, or 'Czech', searches locals entering the hospital. This is his third Afghanistan tour, having come twice earlier with the Russian Army.

The team of engineers have learned to lower standards and adopt the Afghan way. They can't permanently supervise the work, on this occasion returning to discover local contractors have plumbed the bathroom where the kitchen should be.

The local medical workers have it tougher. Thirteen-year-old Ben Rahmulla is being treated by Dr Ajab Noor for a bullet wound in the knee after being caught in crossfire. Dr Noor works his own no-man's land. If he treats the Taliban he makes an enemy of the government, and if he treats members of the government he risks execution by the Taliban. One of his staff tells me twelve medical workers have died in the preceding year.

It is mid summer and the days are long and exhausting. I am like a toasted cheese sandwich jammed between the ceramic plates of body armour. My 58 years do not make me an ideal candidate for this work. I drift off, mouth falling open. With my helmet permanently askew, I've been dubbed 'Dad's Army'. The amused soldiers take photographs before heading back to work.

Eighteen hours after we set out we are back. The next job calls for an even earlier start, and at 0230 we again clamber into the Bushmaster, treading carefully around the electronic cabling and inexpertly strapping harnesses over the bulk of our outer shells.

We are out in the desert when dawn breaks and I enter another age. A Kuchi shepherd moves his flock past the strung out convoy, paying no attention to this century's intruder. The sappers up ahead are searching a gully, where there is a choke point. It will take about an hour with dogs and mine labs to ensure no improvised explosive devices (IEDs) were planted the night before; when we return the routine will be repeated.

Australia's comparatively low casualty rate is attributed to luck, patience and discipline. On this tour RTF2 would have three soldiers hit by Taliban bullets, none penetrating protective equipment. Sometimes the soldiers don't even know until after tearing the Velcro free from their body armour and hearing a 7.62 round clatter to the floor that they'd been hit. In the neighbouring Special Forces camp four Commandos are counted as being saved by their body armour, bullets striking chest plates rather than their chests. Some Australians tell me of discomfort working with British soldiers, who retrace the same route after being hit by IEDs because they don't want to be cowered by the enemy. They are also bothered by the way some of the American units barrel through villages with no time to pause wearing death masks and playing heavy metal.

This time we make our way to the village of Talani, where a school is being built at a cost of $110,000. Many of these new schools, particularly the ones built for girls, have been burned to the ground. Local employees talk of intimidation, but they are surprisingly defiant. In order to win some confidence and overcome suspicion, a *Backyard Blitz* approach had been adopted by the sappers. The point of these quick impact projects is to deliver results rather than the empty promises that were experienced in the past.

Plumber turned Warrant Officer Brendan Johnson, one of three plumbing supervisors in the Army, cheerfully totes a rifle as well as a wrench. I ask him why he is here risking his life instead of making a fortune in a civilian occupation back home. 'I could do that, but [in Australia] you can't carry a weapon around at the same time you are fixing drains,' he says. Captain Liam Hansen explains that soldiers are no different to others in deriving satisfaction from 'doing the righty'. 'To be able to help people who have nothing is quite satisfying and ultimately a humbling experience.'

It is fair to also say, the diggers do like it outside the wire. Given a choice, the appetite for excitement tinged with risk seems to trump any desire for the comparative comfort and monotony of base life. Soldiers who stay behind in the Forward Operating Bases are known as 'Fobbits'.

The Tarin Kowt base, a sprawling military, industrial complex, has a touch of 'blokesworld' about it, albeit without the alcohol. The ultra low-alcohol 'near beer' in the fridges is rarely touched and no one seems to complain. On Anzac Day and other special occasions a few beers might be allowed. Across the Hesco at Special Force's Camp Russell exceptions are sometimes made following intense missions.

Soldiers do develop heightened degrees of cunning, so it would be naive to presume no one bends the rules. Supplies on an industrial scale flow in daily, and the same restrictions don't apply to the civilian contractors, who are there in numbers. 'Where there is a will there is a way,' some of the soldiers tell me. The same is true regarding rules forbidding fraternisation, but the bans, as well as scarce practical opportunity, do not stop them trying.

The Dutch have plenty of fit, healthy and attractive female soldiers, and at Camp Holland they draw more attention than they would catching a suntan at Bondi Beach. But the relationship is not one of mutual attraction. In a queue at the Windmill Café, an Australian soldier who can speak a little Dutch hears one of the girls caution another not to make eye contact with the Aussies. The story does the rounds that male Dutch soldiers have warned the females about Australians abusing their women. It is either a clever ploy, a misunderstanding of Australian dress codes, or a bit of both. Australian diggers in their down time often wear singlets known as 'wife beaters'.

The diggers would sometimes interpret NLD, for The Netherlands, as 'no one likes the Dutch', which is not quite true; regard is varied. When calling for combat support the Dutch are criticised for lacking aggression, but what is censured is also praised—the Dutch are known for determined avoidance of civilian casualties.

In the Dutch-run mess, the story is much the same. The Australians can't quite cop the herrings, but they plunder the smoked salmon. Each national force tends to keep to their respective tables; neither openly warring nor enthusiastically bonding, the Task Force Uruzgan allies assume a posture of armed neutrality.

While the Dutch apply greater emphasis to the non-kinetic work, they have at this stage in 2007 incurred more combat casualties than the Australians. And it is not as if the Australians are blind to other ways of fighting. Indeed, next to PRT House is an Australian initiative that has become an exemplar visited by royalty, politicians and generals.

A trade training school built from an idea formed from Major Michael Scott's reconnaissance mission has proved a useful weapon ranged on the long war. Teaching young Afghans basic carpentry, plumbing and small engine maintenance skills helps distance them from recruitment by the Taliban, generates local income, provides the youngsters with a minor skills base and advances goodwill.

When we visit, the mood on the floor of the workshop is buoyant. The pride in the faces of kids who could hold in their hands the product of their labour is also apparent in soldier–tradesmen instructors who have encouraged them to pick up a saw rather than the sword. The students are paid $3.50 a day, about three times the average local income. In Afghanistan, boys enter the workforce, such as it is, when still children; the trainees are mostly in their early teens. If and when they graduate after a month of training, they receive a certificate and a tool kit worth around $500.

Warrant Officer Shane 'Johno' Johnsson is realistic about progress. 'If they are here for the money the tool kit usually ends up in the markets at the bazaar, but if they're serious there are opportunities in town. The majority are motivated when they come here and want to learn. You do get the few here for the money. They are generally lazy so they stand out, and you eliminate them so you can concentrate on the ones here to learn.'

When we go into town, kids whose arms reach for goodies such as pencils, papers and sweets commonly swamp us. The soldiers warn us to keep a distance. If battle suddenly erupts, the kids will be in the line of fire. This does happen—on 15 June a suicide bomb-laden vehicle strikes a Dutch armoured car travelling through the Tarin Kowt main street. Dutch PRT soldier Timo Smeehuijzen is killed, along with five local children who had been running alongside.

Not long after, on 24 June, a civilian truck driver is shot dead when he moves too close to RTF soldiers in an Australian Bushmaster. The vehicles display a large red sign, and graduated warnings via loudspeaker and signalling are given, but in similar incidents across Afghanistan civilians continue to be killed and wounded. Any gain via the creation of a job or construction of a mosque can be lost in one burst of fire. Winning hearts and minds from behind the sights of a machine gun has its challenges.

Notions of innocence face regular challenge. The blamelessness of civilians, particularly children, is obvious, but it is also a weapon. Children are exploited. Not only are they strapped into suicide vests, they are caught carrying IEDs, are used to recover weapons on the battlefield, and are sent forward to scout the foreigners' positions.

Australian bomb disposal specialist Tony Quirk helps dispel some innocence of my own. Quirk has seen more of Afghanistan than many Afghans; the 2007 tour is his fifth. There is a picture on the wall of the Explosive Ordinance Disposal (EOD) hut of Warrant Officer Quirk in full Afghan robes. He had first come in the early 1990s as part of a United Nations mine clearance team.

The EOD teams are beginning to receive intelligence from locals about the placement of bombs, and are frequently called out on render safe procedures. The IEDs might be placed to attack the foreigners and government forces, but they might also be aimed at tribal rivals or a nuisance neighbour contriving to divert water. Children are common victims of these blasts.

When we leave the EOD hut we walk past Camp Russell, home to the Special Operations Task Group (SOTG). A base within a base, it is off limits or by invitation only to other military personnel.

Journalism and secrecy are natural enemies. In such an unstable environment the conduct of soldiers, special or otherwise, calls for scrutiny. For me the persistent excuse that operational security counted more than transparency had become less convincing by the year.

The Special Forces soldiers are only occasionally seen around the main base. Sometimes it can look like they overstate the understatement. With their advanced weaponry, looser clothing and longer hair, they stand out like Jedi knights on a lunar landscape. When a random conversation does occur they are friendly and unpretentious, but also unrevealing.

At this stage it seemed to me that a suicide bomber would find getting in to Camp Russell easier than a journalist. It would take a while to learn more of the Special Forces' story, and to understand one reason they were rarely seen is because they were rarely there. Rotation IV spent by far the majority of its three-and-a-half months in Afghanistan outside the wire.

In mid 2007 the fighting season returns, seeing another attempt by opposing militia forces to overwhelm the Chora district. Rotation IV of the SOTG has something to live up to following the intense battles in the same area one year earlier.

In mid June Alpha Company of 4RAR (CDO) moves out in strength. In command in the field is a distinctly uncommon soldier. Major Ian, looking more whippet halfback than lumbering forward, arrived in Afghanistan on Anzac Day 2007. In 1995, his graduation year at the Royal Military College, Duntroon, he had shone, winning the Sword of Honour. Later, as a student at the United States Marine Corps School of Advanced Warfighting, he would top his course. Major Ian is the kind of leader the men liked: smart, composed and brave.

The SASR would operate more discreetly, small patrols moving with stealth, watching, gathering intelligence and fighting when called upon. One Commando from Rotation IV credited them with providing 'excellent situational awareness'. The Commandos, with company strength punch, would go looking for a fight. The formal objective was disruption of the insurgency threat to other ISAF elements around Tarin Kowt.

They move north into areas not so far trespassed by ISAF. The American Patrol Base Anaconda is positioned at Khas Uruzgan, in the north of the province, but acts more as a bullet magnet. The Americans would move out on combat reconnaissance patrols, attract fire, call in air strikes and return. The Dutch also were not moving actively beyond their patrol bases.

The Kush Khadir valley, south of Anaconda and north of Chora, was a known Taliban sanctuary where the foreigners had not so far strayed. In 2007, Alpha Company 4RAR (CDO) would strike out on long-range patrols into the Mirabad and Baluchi valleys and up into Kush Khadir. In the badlands between the northern village of Gizab and Chora to the south, a feature known as the Octagon became a centre of action. They rolled into battle on special reconnaissance vehicles, which took a hammering. Around four soldiers occupied each modified Perentie Land Rover, moving in small separate 'packages' through the night and at around 0400 settling into a 'hide'. Further small teams would foot patrol into overwatch positions. In the *dascht*—the desert—you don't stay unnoticed for long.

Some of the work was non-kinetic; Alpha Company had taken along a male nurse with paediatric skills. 'A great force multiplier. He delivered so many babies,' according to one soldier. The company also pioneered some important diplomatic work, moving into Hazara enclaves in formerly restricted Gizab, encouraging local resistance to the Taliban.

The Commandos lived rough. They went without washing for weeks on end, and put up with less serious injuries. The teams stayed out for 40 days straight, being resupplied by Chinooks or parachute drops from C130s. This would also prove precarious; if the parachutes missed the ridge they could drop 500 metres into the valley below, instigating a recovery chase between the Australians and nimble-footed Pashtuns. Among the items resupplied were entire gearboxes, which were replaced in the field.

Tempted towards the belief they had the numbers to overwhelm the intruders, the Taliban was drawn into battle. But once one patrol was engaged, Major Ian was able to swiftly summons others from different points of the compass.

TIC is a general military acronym for troops in contact. The multiple TICs for this rotation came in the form of blazing battles rather than random pot shots, a total of 49 direct engagements. As soldiers say, when it 'turns to shit' you tend to see the same figures stepping up.

'Todd in contact' became a new descriptor for one of the Alpha Company section leaders. Aged 31, Todd Langley would find his way to the centre of action not because he was reckless but because, instinctively, he knew what to do. His mates say 'it was more a function of him doing his job so well. He did not need to be asked.' In one early TIC, Sergeant Langley came face to face with a previously unobserved spotter, who swung his AK47 and fired. Two rounds cut through the Commando's shirt under his armpit before Langley returned fire from within 10 metres with greater effect. 'Todd in contact' would receive a Commendation for Distinguished Service (CDS) for this and a series of further actions, his second CDS.[6]

Fighting was fierce. Another Commando similarly moving forward towards concealed enemy bunkers was shot three times in the legs from 10 metres distance. He kept going until his legs stopped working. Yet another Commando was shot through the thigh, the bullet exiting through his buttock, and still one more sustained injuries to his lower leg. Casualty evacuation was called for and the fighting went on.

One of the mortar crew earned a Medal for Gallantry. Corporal 'Skeet' ran 150 metres through accurate machine-gun fire to recover a mortar tube that had been blasted from its base plate. Cradling and stoking the mortar on his own, he dropped round after round with devastating effect. Another gallantry award, a Distinguished Service Medal, went to platoon leader Captain Lewis, who time and again led attacks on the Kush Khadir bunkers. According to his mates the Captain's actions made a crucial difference, providing 'a lynch pin for success'.

While soldiers are trained to respond instantly to chaos their officers are forced to go further, in the midst of mayhem attaining order. Major Ian's role was to defeat not only the enemy, but also his opposing commander's plan. On one occasion, in a contact that stretched for twelve hours and in the midst of the noise and tumult, he stood giving orders—to then see an enemy appear in front of him pointing an RPG7 and firing. There was a flash and a puff of smoke. The rocket soared between Major Ian and a signaller standing alongside. It detonated behind with a massive crash and spume of dust and debris. The 32-year-old Major was seen resuming command, bleeding from one ear. 'As cool as cat shit,' commented one watching soldier.

The Taliban fought hard through three major long-range missions, backing themselves, using asymmetrical and conventional methods. Alpha Company opposed trained fighters operating within friendly territory and to a battlefield plan. Special Forces encountered prepositioned firing points and the dreaded Dushka, a 12.7 mm machine gun, the enemy's version of the .50 calibre Browning.

Major Ian was awarded a Distinguished Service Cross for 2007 operations into 'harsh terrain deep within hostile territory'.

The SOTG had surprised the Taliban by not returning to Tarin Kowt for nightfall. The insurgents developed a new estimation of these men who turned up in their 'tanks'. On the radio they were heard referring to them as 'green-eyed bearded devils' who 'did not do the coward thing' (by withdrawing and calling in air support).

Rotation IV was still in Uruzgan when we headed home via Kabul. According to my diary, we are 'bumped from tomorrow's flight by 20 coffins'. A CH47 had been shot down, killing all on board. In a separate incident an Afghan National Police checkpoint was overrun, contributing sixteen further corpses.

As you often hear, in Afghanistan there is no front line: the killing happens everywhere. The stretch of road between the airport and Kabul's green zone, where ISAF is headquartered, is one of Afghanistan's most dangerous, the targets being so large and plentiful.

In Kabul the atmosphere is more tense than bleak. I do my best to get a handle on progress or otherwise, doing the rounds of government, business and the military. At the green zone enclave, 37 NATO and non-NATO nations are represented, each with their small camps and their own rules. The French and Spanish serve profiteroles and paella and are allowed a drink. The Australians and Americans serve lamingtons and frankfurts and are dry.

All nations, Australia included, have come here on their own terms. Caveats apply to how much risk they are prepared to take and what function they choose to perform. Understandably, exposing their soldiers to the high-risk combat zones in the south and east is not a popular choice.

The ISAF Commanding Officer, American General Dan McNeill, admits the uneven commitment fetters a cohesive and uniform strategy. 'Each of these governments wants their resources applied in a different way, so my days are not uneventful.'[7] The government causing the most problem is the one nearest at hand. President Hamid Karzai, in power now for three years, is considered even more than Iraq as the key distractor resulting in the mission drift.

While many of Afghanistan's 34 provinces are comparatively trouble free, others are like splintered shards of a still broken mosaic. Karzai had brokered power in the time-honoured way, accommodating provincial warlords. He was widely known as the Mayor of Kabul, the term reflecting his minimal influence and reach. Plumb jobs went to the undeserving, or to the best worst choice.

General McNeill came to a pragmatic recognition successors would inherit, of chronic paucity of choice. Fighting that had stretched beyond the average citizen's life span meant a lost generation of skills. 'If it's football, whether it's American or Australian Rules . . . somebody gets hurt and the coach wants a change and he turns to the bench. President Karzai wants to make a change, he turns to the bench and there is not a lot of depth.'[8] At ground level ordinary Afghanis could see the government doing no better, indeed, doing what rulers had always done.

The Afghan National Police (ANP) force was a serious problem. Coalition soldiers would hear police on the radio collaborating with the Taliban, advising of the movement of foreigners. When the ANP was asked to man a remote checkpoint, it found it safer and easier to collude. Tribal connections to the insurgency were frequently more robust than responsibility to central government. And the police were badly paid, if at all. Superiors would routinely plunder the salary budget. Ingrained corruption reached deep to the lowly officer at the checkpoint, who stole at will from an exhausted, exasperated citizenry.

Like most with a realistic view of what nation building entailed, the commander of Task Force Uruzgan in 2007, Colonel Hans van Griensven, saw the international community needing to stay 'for another twenty years at least'.[9]

The warmer months of 2006 and 2007 had shown the fighters assembling to oppose the foreigners along the ridges and valleys beyond Tarin Kowt as capable and brave. What had also been demonstrated was that they could be beaten. At this stage, militarily, the contest seemed far from hopeless. And considering the alternative of a cruel, oppressive and visionless Taliban rule, the objective of creating a superior alternative still seemed achievable.

In 2007 the mission was costing Australia $400 million a year. Five years on it would grow to $1.6 billion, the Australian taxpayer spending $1 million for every soldier deployed.[10]

Australians would in time show themselves to be less concerned about the financial cost as they were about the blood tax. Between September 2005 and my visit in June 2007, no Australians had been killed in action. Some had been seriously wounded, their lives forever reduced, but little to nothing was known of this—Defence and government were wary of sharing the load.

There was little public debate about a prospective twenty year commitment; it would take time for a dangerous equation to be assessed and understood. The most effective means of maintaining security was by sending into harm's way well-trained soldiers with rifles. Fighting the war by dropping guided bombs from 20,000 feet served to advance a further dangerous equation: every civilian killed drove more into the ranks of the Taliban.

The cost-benefit calculation that had sent me to Afghanistan in the first place became another puzzle. In subsequent years I would see the Australian soldiers' view of what they were achieving track in the opposite direction to public reckoning back at home.

CHAPTER 7
OPERATION HOME FRONT

When American soldiers are interviewed at the battlefront, and for the sake of the hometown audience asked where they hail from, they will identify the place they grew up: 'Little Rock, Arkansas', 'Sioux Falls, South Dakota' and so on. Ask the same question of a digger and he will say 'Darwin' or 'Townsville', or maybe 'Enoggera' or 'Holsworthy'. To the Australians, home seems more unit, barracks or garrison town.

Corporal Leon Gray, with no partner in Australia because he 'is never in one place more than two months', further explains. 'There is no compromise. The Army has to be that way. I say I am from 7RAR, and 7RAR is my home and family.'

Ask the question of a soldier's wife and according to Susan Blain, veteran of multiple moves and farewells, 'Your family is where the Army sends you.'

In the career of many a soldier, the battle that counts most is the one fought at home, reconciling demands of workplace and family. Of course, this tension is common to all working families, but when the Army is the employer it is like having a second spouse. Marriages can falter as a young wife, struggling with a teething infant, stands helpless as her partner heads off to another seemingly pointless training course, having returned from one only days earlier.

A Section Commander will feel similar tension, obliged to look after the welfare of his soldiers as much as he does his own children. Junior leaders see virtue in not getting familiar with the partners of their soldiers, as knowing them personally might influence the demands they impose in the field. They don't want to be going soft on one at the expense of others.

When soldiers toss it in, a central reason is family. It gets to a point where they can't ask a primary age kid to change schools for the fifth time, or they can't see how their partner, just promoted to account manager, can find the same job at Puckapunyal.

It is hard for soldiers, let alone their partners, to get used to the idea that institutions have no heart. While the soldier often feels deeply for the organisation, the organisation can't feel back. The Army asks for total dedication and loyalty, but no sensible soldier expects a like response.

Basic career arithmetic can have a soldier leaving at the very time they represent maximum value to this big and heartless green machine. That same Section Commander, in his late twenties after ten years of training, is also at an optimum age for parenthood.

When on patrol in Afghanistan and while catching my breath under a tree at the edge of a wheat field, I overhear the company commander and one of his section leaders talking career on the other side of the trunk. Having earlier asked about prospective interviewees, I knew the Commanding Officer Major Jason Groat had high regard for the Corporal, Adam Heemskirk. Struck by what Adam said, I wrote it down (and later asked permission for it to be used): 'I think I'll get out. I want to be a better father. I remember how angry I was with my wife when she asked me to request time off to help her. And I thought later, what a shit husband and father I had become.'[1]

On the day he leaves the Army to start a new career as a personal trainer, Sergeant Jamie Osbourne tells me: 'There is no life in the job. I needed to hold the family together.' Jamie does not look overjoyed; it is just that the time has come.

Soldiering is more than a job. It is a vocation. Going along with the shit deal soldiers can get means understanding that, so it stands to reason surviving partners also need to develop a kind of 'vocational awareness'. When Lieutenant Ashley Judd joined, 'no one in my family expected me to do this'. His girlfriend of seven years got a shock. 'She was a bit like, why?' Partners find that, although not formally enlisting, they sign on too. 'It comes with a compulsory lifestyle. If a partner is not into it, it probably won't last.'

The inherited encumbrances are not all obvious. A partner endures deference to the heartless machine, and what must on occasions be nagging jealousies. They compete for attention and affection with milling, ragged, profane, stinky hoards of others, the mates who come and go, turning up to stay with a box of beer and no pyjamas. Despite this, they can be exceptionally forgiving.

Kate, the fianceé of a Special Forces soldier, intelligent and inquiring, met Steve when working in a clothing store. 'He was always coming in. The others did not want to serve him because he had that curt AJ [Army jerk] way about him. They are not always comfortable talking to women, they are not the romantic types. He came back again and again, spending all his money, so he had to live on Weet-Bix for a week. When he gets together with his mates you see that bond. A whole room full of Alphas, a secret society.'

Captain Lynn Harding, who runs the Geckos Family Centre at Townsville's Lavarack Barracks, sympathises. 'Time stands still for the family while the soldier takes on force preparation, as well as deployment and catch-up training upon return. The family operates in a vacuum. If they have a child in hospital when the husband is overseas they can be at wit's end: no sleep, can't mow lawns and find child care.'

'Civilian wives can have trouble understanding that the majority of decisions affecting them aren't made by them,' explains Senior Warrant Officer Nichol Anderson, who spends a lot of time wrangling spousal difficulties. 'One mum has four boys and a husband often away. It is very hard if they don't understand the requirement for discipline or why the husband has to be at work at 0400 for a stupid reason. I ring them to explain and have a chat. I know they are not fully conversant. Some don't get it. They can't cope and blame the ADF, even though they were married before he joined. And some don't want to get it.'

Guilt surfaces a hemisphere away. In Afghanistan, Major Josh Jardine talks of a son playing up in Darwin. The boys often do, 'a manifestation of you not being there'. Jardine appreciates having a wife who is not in the Army. 'It gives me balance and perspective. She has it tougher. I leave her to cope for nine months plus with kids and a full-time job.'

What is obvious is that so many partners turn out to be teachers or nurses, occupations that call for personal sacrifice as well as having some useful mobility. At a barbeque in Brisbane, before deploying overseas for a fourth time, Private David Deitz is mucking about, rolling in the grass with his three- and seven-year-old children. Looking on is wife Kathy, a nurse who 'works a lot of abnormal hours as well'. 'We put life at home on hold. They don't,' he says in tribute.

One obvious solution to the problem of finding an amenable partner is to marry within or, as the wags put it, 'go for the in-house discount'. Nichol is married to someone guaranteed to 'get it', another soldier.

Nichol met her future husband, Jeremy, when she was posted to Darwin in 1995; they would both become Warrant Officers. Attuned to an industrial-strength organisation, she confesses to managing home life as they would a military mission. That is what soldiers do—they manage. The battle plan is to not let the marriage get in the way of the job, nor the job the marriage. 'We do all operational and exercise movements,' she explains, rattling off her recent deployments: 'Baghdad, Kuwait, Al Minhad, Kandahar, Kabul' for up to six months at a time.

In 2003, Nichol became a mother to Joshua. 'Everybody thought I was making up my husband because he had done three rotations.' They never deploy at the same time, and when she is away Nichol builds a little shrine on her desk comprised of letters and paintings and photographs. 'I could ring every day but don't. I try twice a week. Sunday is a good day to call. He plays football so has something to say, which means the calls last for ten minutes instead of two.'

Exquisite planning extends to financial management. Deployed personnel can do very well; hardship and hostile environment allowances plus taxation exclusion means that along with the Afghan rugs and pashminas they bring back an extra $70,000 or thereabouts. Nichol and Jeremy have bought and paid for one house in Townsville, almost own another in Sydney and are planning on acquiring a third. Sit down with some of the Army's busiest and best remunerated soldiers from the Special Air Service Regiment (SASR) and the subject is as likely the real estate market in Perth as the ratlines in Waziristan.

When I meet up with Jo Aboud for the second time, she is living at Duntroon in 'one of the oldest houses in Canberra'. The first time we met she was at a housing estate on the outskirts of Darwin. Jo also has a list of postings: 'Wagga Wagga, Puckapunyal, Canberra, Brisbane, Townsville, Melbourne, Queenscliff, El Paso Texas, Darwin and back in Canberra.'

Married to Regimental Sergeant Major Rob Aboud, Jo is a science and maths teacher. 'You have to find jobs that have school hours.' At this stage they have four children aged between four and eleven. 'The oldest in Year 6 has been to five schools.' A lack of standardised education is high on the list of problems identified when the Australian Defence Force considers a vexing and high separation rate. If the Defence Force career stretches to a child's final years of high school, the call to throw out the anchor grows even more strident.

Missing a child's finals match or graduation becomes routine. Lena Elwin, wife of Major Justin Elwin, who led the RTF1 Infantry protection company in Afghanistan in 2006, laughs when she tells me she forgives him for missing 'our tenth wedding anniversary, Christmas and birthdays'.

A shadow army of wives and partners offers some compensation, generating bonds similar to those forming on the other side of separation. Jo Aboud says she met her best friend Kim at the airport when farewelling their Iraq-bound husbands. 'When her water broke I went with her.'

Susan Blain's inscribed 'Wonderwoman' coffee mugs bear a cartoon figure of the superhero and the names 'Blain, Hay, Stewart', her friends cum support network. There is an element of profit in the arrangement when circumstance and adversity forces skills and responsibilities that otherwise might not be acquired. She tells me how she learned to use a chainsaw after a branch crashed onto the kitchen roof during a storm.

'Separation is something we have become used to,' Colonel Jason Blain is quick to explain, 'but that does not mean we like it. The morphing to Wonderwoman can infer we like it, but we don't. We learn rather to deal with it.'

Jo Aboud is not laughing when she talks of a related and obvious consequence: 'I have had an easier time of it, but it is not an easy life. The number of separations and divorces I have seen shocks me. So much so I am now hesitant to ask, how is Joyce?'

As at Kapooka and the Royal Military College, Duntroon, stress and pressure can strengthen relationships but it can also break them. The Defence census of 2007 records 'about a 3%' divorce rate, and 2 per cent of members reported they were separated.[2] The national average for divorce in that year was 2.3 per cent.[3]

The anecdotal evidence suggests that the problem might be greater still, taking into account a high number of de facto relationships. After every deployment I heard stories of relationships that did not last the distance. At Enoggera, settled with a group just back from Afghanistan, one soldier talks about the new four-wheel drive he just purchased, which seemed in part compensation for the empty house that greeted him upon return.

Finding a partner prepared to survive the absences is only one of the problems—finding a partner to begin with is hard enough. Not too many romantic opportunities emerge while out bush on training exercises, let alone searching *qualas* and patrolling the *dascht* in Uruzgan.

Romantic opportunity for gay soldiers is also fraught. While homosexuality is formally accepted fraternisation is not, and homophobia is hard to outlaw. The males in particular tell me it is possible to be open but unwise to be obvious, so it is better to quarantine relationships. One SASR trooper tells of an occasion when a fellow trooper waited until a farewell function to announce he was gay. Many soldiers endure a career without letting on.

While the topic of divorce tends to bring on the silence, weddings provoke the opposite reaction: diggers love them. In Afghanistan I could not help noticing how many were being organised and eagerly anticipated, with friends of dissimilar backgrounds planning to travel across the country for a mate's wedding. A Captain tells me: 'I have two on when I get back, one at Magnetic Island, the other in the Hunter Valley.' They laugh about shotgun weddings—'McDonald's drive-throughs'—but there is also serious intent.

Weddings are the aisle way to future partners. The sisters (and brothers) of mates tend to be optimum candidates, already acculturated as they are to a degree. There is a particular Army stamp on the ritual, not only in weddings often being celebrated at the regimental chapel and in dress uniform, but in customs that have evolved. At a wedding I attend, military pragmatism is obvious. The first order of business after we sit down is the MC's announcement identifying the single guests.

A related subject that adds anger to the silence is what is known inside and outside the Army as 'grass cutting'. In the civilian world partners will move on to relationships with partner's friends. In the Defence community it happens too, sometimes with greater tension.

Perhaps I should not have been surprised at how often the partner swaps appeared to occur. But I was astonished, probably because you assume when mateship is elevated to the ranks of the sacred that no greater power could intercede. Plainly, this is not so. Soldiers will joke about sleeping with a hated corporal's missus.

There is a story, no doubt apocryphal, about a wife signalling a lover by way of the laundry window. If she sat the Omo box on the ledge it declared 'old man out'; Fab alternatively warned 'fucking arsehole's back'.

A joke publication, 'Australian Army Man Standing Orders and Directives Volume 1, MANSODS 1-1-1, 2010', itemises a soldier's alpha code. Examples are: 'A man's best friend is his dog, not his girlfriend or wife'. And, 'Only have sex with an ugly chick if you can't be bothered wanking'. Item 36 declares, 'Having a relationship with a mate's wife while he is overseas is to be punished by DEATH . . . you know who you are'.

I have heard enough to recognise Item 36 is at least half serious. Friends can be forgiven for stealing each other's girlfriends, but doing it when a mate is deployed takes longer. 'I will hurt him if he knew' is one soldier's response to the proposition that the wife who walked out found a new partner while he was abroad.

There is no escaping the ugly face of barracks room life. You see it in other similar hyper male strongholds: football teams, surf clubs and so on. YouTube images of soldiers dressed up in Ku Klux Klan outfits or anti gay ranting on Facebook might not be representative, but neither is it unusual.

Single soldiers often still live in barracks on base in their own room, or 'wank-box' as it is sometimes described. There is a requirement to live on base for the first twelve months, after which they can choose to move if accommodation is available.

While the old days of getting on the booze at lunchtime and sleeping it off in an Armoured Personnel Carrier through the afternoon are gone, booze-ups and the maintenance of 'piss fitness' are still features of Army life. To better manage it, sports bars are provided at the bigger bases but don't tend to draw the crowds. While the boys do cluster together, they also tire of each other's stories. And for fresh opportunities they have to go off base. In Darwin the single men remain reliable clients at favoured pubs and strip clubs. And despite police paying close attention to the roads around Robertson Barracks, soldiers with too many schooners on board continue to attempt to run the gauntlet.

When a 'singly' does find a partner, pressure to maintain routines such as drinking with mates persist. They become known for the 'AJ Fadeaway', that is, disappearing in the middle of a round, and are declared 'Jack', or more specifically 'Jack Marriedy'.

Chatting to a soldier about to take leave, I ask where he is heading. 'Las Vegas.' What is the attraction? 'The whores.' I suspect relationship breakdown is not only a consequence of the many challenges born of separation and neglect; Army life can undernourish the concept of equal relationships. In an organisation that is 90 per cent male, the cultural weakness most apparent is plain and simple misogyny.

After 2000, as mission tempo increased, Australia committed $11 billion to grow and sustain the Army. Some of the budget was sensibly turned over to improving living conditions and family life. The old days have passed where cabbage patches of clustered and shabby Defence houses declared a secondary social status. Riam Kent, an 'Army brat' married to a soldier who was another 'Army brat', says, 'We have it a lot better than our forebears. Mitch's mum lived in a condemned house.'

In the old days, Defence families expected the carpets to be stripped by the earlier tenants. The serial movers learned carpet squares were best because they were more adaptable. Today's generation of soldiers are more likely to roll up smart Afghan rugs, having already checked out the floor plan for their new house on the internet. Defence Housing now disperses personnel through the community, in homes less likely to induce in-laws' sympathy, pity or disdain.

The garrison towns, Darwin and Townsville, exemplify on a grander scale a changed community relationship. When John Caligari lived in Townsville in the 1980s, 'It was not a place of choice. We had to order people to come here.' As a young lieutenant, Caligari 'was always visiting hospitals because there were so many fights, often in competition for women'. He remembers recovering one soldier whose forehead bore the crude initials 'AJ', carved by a broken beer bottle.

He did, however, manage to capture a local girl, Narelle, a nurse, who had been advised by friends 'to never marry an AJ'. When John and Narelle returned a quarter century later with John in the top job, occupying Jazzine House at Townsville's best address, it must have been interesting when old friends came to visit. The Caligaris say wives now want to be posted back to Townsville.

Standing on the hill overlooking Lavarack Barracks, with Townsville stretching beyond, the bigger picture is revealed. The single men's barracks, circa 1960s, have been replaced by the latest cyclone-proof, tropical-strength accommodation. Alongside are green and manicured sporting fields, largely empty; the Army is busy with larger contests. The hum of air conditioning carries indistinguishably to the suburbs, where the Army-only ghettos are a memory.

The locals are no longer so likely to sneer at the AJs, and the *Townsville Bulletin* and the ABC less inclined to highlight indiscretions because of the uniform. The Defence community, now 10 per cent of the population, has moved from the fringe—with spending power that shows. The Holden and Ford dealers do well when the diggers return. The same is true of Darwin. Like many returning from their first deployment, Josh Dowsing 'did the typical young person thing, wasted it on piss, heaps, going to strippers, buying new clothes'.

When seconded to other armies, opportunities for comparisons emerge. In the United States, Australians notice the higher regard the public has for service personnel. One Special Forces soldier tells me of people standing in respect when servicemen board an aircraft. Strangers whisper 'thank you for your service' when they pass. He says once when in a coffee queue at Starbucks he found the customer ahead had already paid.

On exchanges to England families are surprised by the poorer living standards. They speak well of British professionalism and, as in the United States, admire the greater capability. Without exception they also make mention of class. Australian officers have an easier relationship with other ranks, and Australian other ranks tend to assume greater responsibility than in the United Kingdom and the United States. Equally, Australians are criticised for being too close, too frank and not so demonstratively patriotic.

Psychologist Colonel Peter Murphy explains: 'In the past in the UK they were shocked to see our officers talking to soldiers. Australia's approach to leadership is different. The role of their NCO is to keep the officer away from the troops. They often talk of the Queen, the Queen's shilling, the Queen's commission. In Canada also.'

When the Blain family was relocated to Canada, they saw something similar. '[In Australia] we no longer have military precincts and married quarter patches. They do, and it is rank conscious. This is Captain's Street, this is Major's Street. Out of curiosity I asked what is over there in the Major's Street and was told, they get a fireplace with a mantelpiece.'

Rank can transfer to wives in Australia as well, where they too have to act as Mrs Colonel. At Townsville's Geckos Family Centre, Captain Lynn Harding says: 'In the cabbage patches exclusion was a problem. The senior officers' wives wore their husbands' rank.' But Captain Harding explains these boundaries are also crumbling. 'Officers' and soldiers' wives are mixing well. They can have no idea what the other wives' husbands do.'

Susan Blain, who works in a law firm, sees that the changes are not all driven from within: 'There were not as many career women then. The wife gave up her career. There have been times when Jason was not the breadwinner. I was.'

Another difference in Australia is a comparative absence of tension. September 11 drew not only America but also American consciousness into a state of war. The United Kingdom as well has felt the after effects of terrorist attacks, and 'the troubles' in Northern Ireland, although in the past, are still fresh in public memory.

When in the United Kingdom, Riam Kent 'got a sense of their different lot. In Australia my husband never brought a weapon home. The tensions in Northern Ireland made for real and present danger. I was shocked and realised how lucky we are to be on Australian bases, where we are isolated from violent reality.' Although for one Australian Special Forces soldier, 'the troubles' did have some reach. Back in Australia after a stint seconded to Northern Ireland, he had trouble breaking the habit of picking a new route every time he drove home.

Coming back from Afghanistan in 2007, I too dealt with the dissonance of returning from a war zone. At first you can be annoyed by the complacency of Australia. You ask yourself, how can people get so hyped up about a horse race or petrol prices? Then you drive over the hill towards home and the warmth and peace of Australia settles you, as mentally you exit an abnormal state and enter the world as it is supposed to be.

In 25 years at *Four Corners* I brought the world home many times. The soldiers do that, too. The psychological balancing act is perilous; they want their loved ones to know, but only up to a point. The protector, once confronting danger, continues to hold the shield high to further deflect the experience of danger. The ones with experience do worry.

In 2008, when Reservist Greg Sher began packing for Afghanistan to deploy with his company from the 1 Commando Regiment, he chose to spare his parents the worry. His dad, Felix, had some suspicion, but as far as the family knew their much-loved son was going off on an exercise somewhere in Australia.

In the same year at Lavarack Barracks in Townsville I met a soldier just returned. Sergeant Michael Lyddiard walked into the interview room with his wife Katri alongside. It was their wedding anniversary. As he sat down he removed his prosthesis and put it on the table, joking: 'I have given my right arm for the place.'

On 2 November 2007 the combat engineer was on patrol during Operation Spin Ghar, which translates as White Mountain, a good description of the winter landscape at the time. The Australians and Dutch had teamed with the famed 1 Ghurka Rifles to clear the Baluchi and Dorafshan valleys. After crossing the Chora River, infantry soldiers had spotted a partly exposed battery pack in the earth that led to a TC6 mine. Sergeant Lyddiard, on his belly in the dirt, worked for three hours to defuse it. He was doing well, but for the first time encountered an anti-handling device. The mine exploded. Lyddiard lost an eye as well as the arm. Still conscious, he asked his mates: 'How's my hands?' They changed the subject. But for their swift attention he would have become the fifth Australian killed in action.

Back in Australia, unlike many with similar injuries, Sergeant Lyddiard was able to return to work. Dealing with the injury would be a lifelong burden for him and Katri.

Not all of my fretting at this time was irrational. Although the lives of soldiers and others more easily merge in places like Darwin and Townsville, the broader community, unlike the military community, knew too little of all this. Some of the knowing, at least for the sake of healing, cried out for a breaking of ranks.

CHAPTER 8
MOWING THE GRASS

By 2008, the International Security Assistance Force (ISAF) had grown to a coalition of 49 allies. Across Afghanistan, each approached the mission as they saw fit; in Uruzgan, the principal partners were the Dutch, Australians, Americans and, of course, the Government of the Islamic Republic of Afghanistan (GIRoA).

The ISAF coalition could clearly state its objective, which was to assist the provision of security, reconstruction and governance. A cohesive strategy to achieve these goals was less clear, approaches varying from partner to partner.

The enemy up to this point also escaped clear definition. Al Qaeda, Taliban and other anti government forces were collectively described as Anti Coalition Militia, Opposing Militia Forces or, the most enduring catch-all, the insurgency.

In many respects, cohesion on the other side of this porous battle line was no better—the splintered tribes were united most of all by a common enemy. In Uruzgan the Popalzai, the tribe of President Hamid Karzai, had gained both influence and enmity.

Opposition to government was not simply tribal or ideological; a Popalzai defending a poppy crop the foreigners now wanted bulldozed could readily side with the Taliban. Commonly, allegiances were also formed through self-interest and self-protection.

There were still many corners of Uruzgan where Kabul and the foreigners had little reach. In these patches, and even in more controlled areas, a Taliban shadow government levied taxes and meted out rough justice. One reason for planting bombs on certain routes was to channel locals towards shadow government tax collection checkpoints. To the ordinary Uruzgan farmer, alternative routes could be no more appealing.

A shocking image that would define the Taliban's brutal justice made it to the cover of *Time* magazine. In 2009, in punishment for eighteen-year-old Aisha fleeing a brutal marriage, a Taliban commander near Deh Rawood in Uruzgan decreed her ears and nose be severed in order to set an example to other girls.[1]

Not that the provincial government was much better. Juma Gul, the Karzai-anointed police commissioner, was notorious for stealing his officers' wages. Over 1500 Afghan National Police were on the Uruzgan payroll, with no one quite sure how many were actually paid. The cost of ingrained corruption was also demonstrated at government-sanctioned checkpoints, where tolls were exacted on long-suffering locals. According to a report by The Liaison Office, an Afghanistan-based non-government organisation at Chora, one police officer admitted: 'For the past five months I haven't been paid. I've got to demand bribes. I have no other source of income.'[2]

After being questioned and then released from Camp Holland at Tarin Kowt and given money to find their way home, Taliban suspects were routinely pilfered.

*

Two years on from 2006, when Australia had returned to Afghanistan, its mission objectives were largely met: a safe haven for Al Qaeda was now denied, and the alliance with the United States had been maintained. But you only needed to travel 100 metres from a patrol base and hit an improvised explosive device (IED) to know that Uruzgan was far from secure, let alone built and governed. The insurgency, though poorly equipped, divided and unsustained by popular moral support, at least had a plan. Lieutenant Colonel Ian Langford, awarded a Distinguished Service Cross for actions in Afghanistan, wrote: 'The strategy of the enemy is brutally simple—prolong the fight as long as possible and the Alliance will become fatigued.'[3]

By 2008 the Australians had a better grasp of whom they were fighting. The Americans defined three tiers of enemy: Tier One were the hard-core global Jihadists; Tier Two comprised more localised tribal opponents melded with narco-traffickers and related elements who saw government as a threat; and Tier Three was made up of part timers, locally recruited and opportunist, picking up a rifle or laying an IED for payment once the harvest was finished.

Australian Colonel John Frewen described the enemy then as extremist, experienced, resilient, accustomed to hardship, clever and reasonably well resourced. He saw the motivation to fight as being partly due to hard-core beliefs and partly coercion. Support from outside 'comes in many forms. It comes in expertise, funding, provision of weaponry and the like, so that's certainly part of the problem,' he explained.

In Uruzgan, if you applied a magnifying glass to what you could see of the enemy, then a blurred portrait would emerge of some experienced hardline commanders with small and irregular fighting forces to call upon. The insurgency was drawn mostly from

Uruzgan or the neighbouring provinces, with Pakistani and Arab fighters sometimes in the mix. Specialist bomb-making equipment and expertise, as well as tactical directives, crossed the border from a Taliban executive at Quetta in Pakistan.

When the Australians arrived in the province kitted out in their DPCU (Disruptive Pattern Camouflage Uniform), they looked much like combatants from any other ISAF nation (or maybe even galactic storm troopers from another planet). At first the locals saw them as Americans, and sometimes British, but that changed over time. The red painted kangaroos on the armoured vehicles the locals knew as 'tanks' were equally misinterpreted as 'red rats'.

According to the survey by The Liaison Office, locals had least regard for the Americans for being blunt and over-aggressive, for poorly managing aid distribution and for a suspected imperialist agenda. Conversely, the Dutch were highly regarded for their sensitivity and diplomacy; their reputation for more cautious use of force was largely applauded, although sometimes disdained. The Australians were seen as too much like the Americans, but better at reconstruction and development and best among all the foreigners at fulfilling promises.[4]

Australia's Reconstruction Task Force 3 (RTF3) and the Special Operations Task Group's (SOTG) Rotation V endured the winter of 2007–08, the former now largely engaged in building patrol bases in outer-lying areas. Patrol bases Locke and Worsley had been named in honour of the two Special Forces soldiers killed in 2007; Patrol Base Lyddiard in the Chora Valley was a tribute to the Australian Explosive Ordinance Disposal (EOD) specialist torn apart by an IED in November.

Combat engineer Rowan Robinson saw the winter through, at times waking to find his sleeping bag tarpaulin turned rigid. 'I snapped my bivvy bag. It was minus 14.' Robbo's job was also to go searching for IEDs. 'There were seven in our section, and the terps [interpreters]. We had two finds. They used homemade 10 kilogram explosives and a pressure sensitive activator. We would pull back and get the EOD [expert] to deal with it. It's nerve-racking but it's your job.'

In Special Forces there had been an expectation the tempo would reduce with the cold but, as was often the case, it did not. Going on patrol meant getting the clothing balance right: too much and it was overly hot when you moved, and too little meant it was numbingly cold when you stopped. Repeated crossings of watercourses on foot meant water froze on trouser legs, the ice shards breaking off as the troopers moved—mostly at night in deeper pursuit of Taliban sanctuaries.

Lieutenant Richie Varvel provided closer infantry protection for RTF3 Engineers. 'The guys did up to six weeks in Chora living out of a platoon base,' says Varvel. 'We did not stop for any weather. The locals at the time got more used to you. They support whoever provides protection. While we were there they supported us. The next day they would support the Taliban.'

Varvel described a pattern of encounters that would become routine. Attacks often occurred at 'stand to', that is, last light when the enemy had the sun behind them. A patrol would approach a *quala* (or compound) and see women and children departing, a good indicator the shooting would start. And then, 'It all happens quickly. You don't have time to dwell on being shot at. You hear bullets and RPG [rocket-propelled grenade] motors—bullets through pants and packs, bullets passing between us.' The skirmish would extend into the night and then stop.

Through night-vision equipment, the Australians would detect some movement and then in the morning search a particular haystack to recover weapons hastily cached. 'There were no bodies or blood trails. They had fired from the *quala* because it affords protection but the people in the *quala* were not necessarily the enemy. The shooters had more likely come and gone on motorbikes.'

The insurgents did learn to fear the red rat tanks, the Australian Light Armoured Vehicles (ASLAVs) of the cavalry with thermal imagery that could find them hidden in a tree line. The call would go out: 'Enemy 150 metres moving south', and the 25 mm cannon would open up. 'Pink mist—like shooting a watermelon,' says one soldier.

'The LAVs were swift and violent,' explained Sergeant Todd Noble. 'Once they arrived it would be over in milliseconds.' If there was time to inspect the battlefield, he found the insurgents 'were outstanding at clearing up after themselves. You can't find brass. Locals sell it. The dogs lick the blood. We did find several caches, hidden in paddocks and stuck in the roofs of houses. People claim they had no idea it was there. They could be right.'

Dog handler Sapper Andy Sichter had to keep his Labrador Ingrid well away from local hounds, which were like 'grizzly bears'. He remembers patrolling through snow and locals being generally respectful to Australians. 'We did not tiptoe. If they needed help, if their car wouldn't start, we gave them help. There were amazing scenes. I once counted twenty-three people getting out of an Econovan.'

The mountains were still frozen when Special Forces Rotation V returned to Australia in January 2008, and thawing when RTF3 withdrew three months later. The winter, the harshest in decades, had been followed by a poor poppy harvest, making the climate just right for the insurgency to increase its fighting strength by leaning on the hard-pressed locals.

RTF3's departing Commanding Officer, Lieutenant Colonel David Wainwright, had pursued the counter-insurgency doctrine of population protection. The patrol bases were being relocated away from better-secured areas and positioned closer to communities for the sake of local safety. The population-centric inkblot or oil stain strategy is as old as Napoleon: the incoming force settles in a manner designed to hold the people close and become familiar to a point where goodwill begins to soak outward. The idea continued with RTF4, commanded by Lieutenant Colonel Stuart Yeaman, when it arrived in April 2008 with a $9 million redevelopment budget.

The nature of the fighting, the swift and violent on again, off again clashes also had a temporal dimension. The Taliban would say: 'They have the watches, we have the time.' To the locals, the calculation was as obvious as the irregular surges of beefy strangers with their heavy equipment trundling through the villages. Trust and goodwill would last for only as long as they stuck around.

Stuart Yeaman surprised both the locals and the Taliban when at the beginning of the 2008 fighting season he deployed most of the Task Force to the village of Sajawul. In the Baluchi Valley between Chora and Tarin Kowt, Sajawul was a known junction for Taliban fighters moving forward and for injured repatriating to the rear, often to government-funded clinics. 'Confused, the Taliban leadership opted to sit out and wait for the RTF to leave, convinced the usual ISAF pattern in the area would continue, and soon the soldiers would move on.'

The Australians stayed put through the fighting season, answering intermittent rocket attacks with mortars. The insurgents would set up 107 mm rockets (about the size of a golf bag), crudely aimed in the direction of the patrol bases. They would often fire them using a similarly simple timing device, a cigarette slowly burning down to ignite a fuse, enabling the attacker to get well distant before ISAF counter measures picked up the signature and directed return fire.

The insurgent's arsenal was in some respects more primitive than that available in the world wars of last century. Indeed, when weapons caches were uncovered, World War I vintage Lee Enfield .303 rifles were often found. And in isolated pockets insurgents known for their shooting prowess were sometimes called 'old Mujahadeen'.

In contrast, the young Australians arriving in Uruzgan carried into battle not only weaponry, but also education and training of a higher order than had accompanied armies of old. The basics are now far more complicated; beyond the significantly greater firepower at their disposal, modern soldiers are kitted with radios and with night-vision and GPS navigation aids.

Of course, if you are RTF, you also carry electric drills and shovels, bags of cement and portable generators. In the Baluchi Valley, on the rocky northern slopes alongside the Dorafshan River, Patrol Base Qudus (named after a slain Afghan soldier) began to take shape. The base, which owed its existence to the clearance operations in the area one year earlier, was well positioned, acting as a barrier between insurgent groups in the Baluchi and Chora valleys and Deh Rafshan in the north.

Driver Private David Deitz was also a qualified sniper, scout and combat first aider. He remembers 'living in swags in the dirt'. The soldiers dug weapons pits with picks and shovels in 45°C heat. Engineers constructed Hesco walls and machine-gun platforms, while beyond the base the infantry patrolled, both watching and being watched.

By now, insurgents had learned to attack in numbers only if they could see a clear numerical advantage. That might have been the thinking around Anzac Day 2008 when they began to track the movements of a vehicle patrol moving out from Tarin Kowt.

The dirt tracks through the Chineh Kalay Valley to Langar, 25 kilometres south-east of Tarin Kowt, were less travelled by the Coalition and conversely well known to the Taliban. (When ISAF created a security bubble in one valley, it frequently displaced insurgent forces into another.)

Delta Company from 4RAR (CDO) of SOTG, Rotation VI, struck out with the conventional objective of 'ground truthing', gathering intelligence and advancing greater freedom of movement for the RTF. It had four compounds of interest in its sights when it moved off in strength for a planned two day patrol. Thirty-two special reconnaissance vehicle (SRV) Land Rovers and Bushmasters raise plenty of dust.

Bombardier Kyle Faram, with a *shemagh*, a traditional headscarf, over his face had come some distance since he was arrested for underage drinking soon after joining up. Now a father of two, he had passed the Commando selection course and further qualified as a joint terminal attack controller (JTAC), often described as being like an air traffic controller on the ground. His first deployment to Afghanistan had followed eight years of training. Lance Corporal Jason Marks, a friend since 2001 and also a father of two, was on the same patrol.

The Australians were split roughly into three, further sniper and overwatch teams in support, one of them led by Sergeant Ray, who had earned a Star of Gallantry back in 2006. On 27 April,

Faram was in the Platoon Commander's SRV manning a radio that was in touch with Dutch Apaches, held off so they could not be heard; Jason Marks was behind him in one of the other three-man Land Rovers. With the Australian flag billowing from one of the vehicles they moved through the village of Chineh Kalay, with locals smiling and waving.

After completing a daylight clearance, they were punching south. It is fair to say the convoy was not prepared for what lay in waiting. Just before last light, as the Commandos rounded a corner on the return trip, they saw a trail of locals heading away and within an instant the rocky high ground to the south-east lit up like a Christmas tree. An RPG and 107 mm rocket exploded near the lead car. Accurate small arms and RPG fire then smashed into the vehicles, which wheeled into defensive order. The Commandos were trapped in a killing ground. Some of them dismounted, rushing to return fire, the voices over the radio backgrounded by the roar of battle. 'There, top of the hill, where's it coming from?' 'They're close, boss.'

The sparkle of gunfire was also seen coming from compounds in the greenbelt to the north, the Platoon Commander's vehicle, the only one with four on board, attracting concentrated fire. The Commandos returned fire with their 50 calibres and M4s. Kyle Faram's M4 jammed. He jumped from the vehicle to clear it, but because he was still hooked to the radio handset he was held back. He felt a punch in the arm, and as he took cover to clear his gun his arm lost all strength. He looked down and saw a perfect hole spilling blood. More bullets whizzed close by, one passing between his legs. The tyres on the vehicle shielding him were shot away.

Unable to reach his field dressings, Faram began bandaging the wound with electric tape. With splinters of bone leaking from his wound, a mate asked: 'What's the matter, princess, not enough milk?' The Australians are known for straining amusement from the direst circumstance.

Behind him, Jason Marks' vehicle, the third last in the convoy, was also taking hits. One side was riddled, the tyres also shot out, five bullet holes through one headrest. A MAG58 container was hit, scraping Marks' face. He kept fighting as Private Rudi alongside wiped the blood and pronounced him 'fine'. Rudi, the combat first aider, soon wished he was wearing his helmet rather than a baseball cap. He jumped from the SRV, unhooked a 66 mm rocket and aimed it at muzzle flashes coming from the tree line. Then, realising they were also receiving fire from behind, he got off another 66 mm in that direction.

At this point Lance Corporal Jason Marks fell, shot through the back of the head. Seconds later, Private Dan (the 50 calibre gunner in the same SRV), was shot twice, one bullet hitting his elbow. He rolled off the back of the SRV. Rudi dragged Jason's body to what shelter he could find and attended to Dan.

Medics ran the length of the convoy to do what they could. Corporal 'Dipper' was hit in the pelvis and leg while trying to help Rudi move Jason. Rudi then dragged Dipper to cover and tried to patch him up, ripping off the Corporal's pants. It must have been a day for it. Dipper looked up at Rudi and said, 'This does not mean you get to see my cock.'

The attack was well co-ordinated and positioned in depth. The local fighters were practised; an enemy PKM gunner dug into firing pits would lean back into the elbow and bum scrapes to take cover after a burst and then pop up to resume firing. The

Commandos, calculating the pattern of fire, took turns to time return fire perfectly, the bullets finding their mark as the gunner raised his head.

Private Rudi alternated care for the wounded with return fire from a range of weapons. He fired four 66 mm rockets, hoping that one of the strikes took out the sniper with the Dragonov who had killed his mate. Getting a bead on the enemy was difficult. He emptied 8 Minimi magazines, about 600 rounds, in less than five minutes, while pumping 40 mm gold top grenades. He later counted that 23 had been pulled from the vehicle racks. Even pistols were used. Men were lying across wounded mates to afford protection.

'Victor Alpha, we have one possible KIA, the other one to be confirmed. We are moving back to the south to establish a HLZ [helicopter landing zone], over.' Smoke canisters were fired to lay a protective screen.

The wounded Faram, as JTAC, called in air support. 'Victor Charlie, can we get those Apaches in to try and identify those targets, over?' Dutch helicopter gunships arrived, but were slow to pinpoint the enemy. Faram became angry, struggling with the language barrier as the helicopters passed again and again without firing. 'Go, go, go . . .' On the third pass rockets began smashing into the hillside, but still the firing persisted. 'We walked into a fucking face slap . . .'

The battle continued for two hours in waves: heavy, sporadic and heavy again until after the sun went down. Faram, and three other wounded, were hustled to the casualty collection point. His friend Jason Marks was lying in a zipped body bag. A US Blackhawk Medevac chopper arrived at the defended HLZ. Half an hour later, and dosed up on morphine, Dutch nurses were cutting away Faram's uniform and 'wife beater' singlet.

Intelligence later suggested the enemy force of around 30 fighters were locals intent on sending the foreigners a message that they were unwelcome. Sometimes the fighting was like that—a kind of sport—prompting one Commando to suggest the Australians would do well to introduce rugby league as an alternative means of venting aggression.

Private Rudi's mates marvelled at how the tall redhead managed to duck bullets screeching like wasps. For this and previous conduct, Private Rudi would be awarded a Medal for Gallantry. Four men were returned to Australia for surgery. Kyle Faram had bone grafted from his hip and was not able to rejoin his beloved Commandos.

Australia had lost a fifth soldier in Afghanistan. Cassandra, Connor and Ella Marks were now without a husband and father.

In the next days the martyrs' funerals atop the rocky hills and wounded making their way to the hospital, delivered to ISAF a rough portrait of the cost to the other side. But no one did a formal count. As they often tell you, the numbers of enemy dead here is the poorest measure of success.

Gauging redevelopment progress was a touch easier: you build something and there it stands. Through the summer of 2008 the Tarin Kowt Primary School took shape, built by an Afghan labour force supervised by RTF4 engineers. Construction of the Afghan Boys High School had also begun, and further improvements were made to the Tarin Kowt Hospital.

In the middle of the year a new SOTG arrived and another Special Forces soldier was killed. Special Air Service Regiment (SASR) signaller Sean McCarthy from 3 Squadron was on his second tour of Afghanistan. On his first tour nine months earlier he had asked to replace the signaller on the patrol that took Sergeant

Matthew Locke's life. The 24-year-old was acting selflessly, as good soldiers do, in consideration of the other man's workload. McCarthy's strength of character was evident again on the patrol when he broke from cover twice to place a marker panel as a fire support reference. While exposed to enemy fire, and on his own initiative, he climbed a tree to give the panel greater visibility. When it was shot from his hands he climbed the tree again. His actions enabled effective fire support and the medical evacuation of Matthew Locke.

On 8 July 2008 Sean McCarthy was on Rotation VII's first operational patrol. He was standing upright in his long-range patrol vehicle when a 20 kilogram IED detonated beneath his feet. All four occupants were thrown clear, an Afghan interpreter sustaining serious leg injuries.

They call the 60 minutes that follows a life-threatening injury the golden hour; if a life is to be saved intensive care must be received within that timeframe. It is for this reason that all patrols take into count operating distance. High priority is accorded the swift response capacity of the air medical evacuation wing.

The IED strike occurred about 10 minutes flying time away in the Mirabad Valley to the north-east of Tarin Kowt. Two hours after the explosion, McCarthy was confirmed dead upon arrival at the hospital; a later inquirer could not determine whether a faster evacuation would have saved his life. The inquiry officer wrote: 'I have no contemporary medical evidence that could determine whether Signaller McCarthy's condition was beyond resuscitation or surgery'.[5]

The tragedy did force changes in the way the SOTG went about its business. There was increased reluctance to continue using unprotected vehicles, and recognition sharpened of a need to boost the presence of specialist combat engineers, bringing larger elements of the Incident Response Regiment (IRR) into the mix.

In August, the combat engineers of RTF4, including Captain Clare O'Neill, who had deployed with RTF1 two years earlier, finished building their Baluchi Valley patrol bases and headed far further afield. In four days they drove 400 kilometres out of Uruzgan to rebuild bridges blown apart by the Taliban along Highway 1, the main route between Kabul and Kandahar. After surviving one ambush attempt, they returned unscathed to Tarin Kowt two weeks later.

In the following month an action that was in keeping with the pattern of conflict to date but significant on a range of levels occurred. It would be described as Australia's biggest engagement since Vietnam and was the first involving Special Forces that the Australian public was able to learn about, if in sparse detail. It brought into the spotlight a shy, decent, extremely capable and obviously brave soldier, Trooper Mark Gregor Strang Donaldson.

Donaldson had gone through Kapooka six years earlier. After joining 1RAR he became SASR qualified within two years. He had first travelled to Afghanistan in 2005 and now, typically of Special Forces soldiers, was in his late twenties, a husband and father. Another member of 1 Troop 3 Squadron was patrol commander Sergeant Troy Simmonds, now a veteran of Somalia, Afghanistan, East Timor and Iraq. 1 Troop commander Captain 'James' was another outstanding soldier, the top cadet at the Royal Military College (RMC) Duntroon eight years earlier and considered 'the pick of the crop' during SASR selection.

Made up of four six-man patrols, on 26 August 2008 1 Troop flew 80 kilometres to Patrol Base Anaconda in Khas Uruzgan to assist US Operational Detachment Alpha (ODA) Green Berets from the

7th Special Forces group. The SASR was not always enamoured of the way the Americans operated—as 'bait', moving predictably, drawing fire, calling in superior retaliatory forces and retiring. But as always it is a mixed story. The Australians also admired the way the small US ODA teams hung so perilously close to the population as well as the action, fighting with enormous bravery.

The joint patrols went immediately to work. This time the Taliban would be lured into a trap. A five-vehicle Humvee convoy moved to the north-east with an expectation of ambush. On the preceding night a sniper team trekked 7 kilometres on foot to set up overwatch in the same area. And it worked. The two-way radio (ICOM) indicated an active enemy presence, which soon materialised. From the observation post (OP) SASR saw three Taliban from a command element moving into position 500 metres below. They were brought down by accurate sniper fire.

The Taliban had no idea where the fire had come from, and soon a dark blue dual-cab four-wheel drive bristling with weapons moved to recover the bodies. India 3 patrol of 1 Troop fired again as India 2 patrol engaged more enemy. The US ODA, using 40 mm grenades, cut off the retreat. A later battlefield clearance counted eleven dead enemy.

The patrols married up and moved towards the valley of Ana Kalay, a no-go zone. At 2030 on 1 September, and intent on a similar result, Major James led India 1 and India 2 Patrols on an overnight haul across the mountain range to establish more OPs.

On the following day at 0400 India 3 and India 4, with two engineers and the explosives detection dog (EDD) Sarbi, hopped on the back of three US Humvees at Patrol Base Anaconda. In all there were five Humvees; the first and last contained ten Afghan soldiers, while ten ODA were in the other three.

The movement of the convoy again drew Taliban into the sights of patrols India 1 and India 2 to the north, and seven of the enemy were killed. India 3 and India 4 to the east sighted Taliban at about 800 metres. But it was windy and among the men carrying RPGs and rifles were children. SASR did not shoot.

As Captain James and India 1 and India 2 began the long walk back, Troy Simmonds and Mark Donaldson along with the others in India 3 and India 4 confronted a problem: there was no alternative return route other than the one they had come. They needed to get back before dark, as the Afghans among them had not been issued night-vision equipment. And in the meantime they had stirred a hornet's nest.

It was 1500 when they moved off, with the usual 'smack talk' crackling over the ICOM. The well-spaced five-vehicle convoy worked west along the *dascht* between the green zone and the high ridgeline. And this time the tables were turned: the 37 US ODA, Afghan and Australian soldiers became the bait, lurching desperately ahead of the jaws of a well co-ordinated, 4 kilometre long rolling ambush. According to one member of 3 Squadron, Rob Maylor, who later wrote a rare insider's account of SASR, the radio traffic culminated with an instruction from the Taliban commander to 'kill them, kill them all'.[6]

Mortar bombs struck first. Seeking cover behind their vehicles, the Australians and Americans returned fire as best they could with 50 calibre and 7.62 machine guns as well as MK19 40 mm grenades. But the Taliban, well concealed and in greater numbers, had the ascendency. The rough ground held the Humvees to a walking pace, they became bullet traps as they lurched through a locust swarm of fire. One of the Americans behind a 50 calibre machine gun was hit in the left arm. After attending to him, Australian Corporal Jim took over the weapon.

The US JTAC called for fast air support, directing 500-pound bombs which silenced the mortars and reduced the rate of small arms fire. But still the convoy could only crawl forward, many of the soldiers now on foot ducking behind rocks while the enemy looped around to attack again.

One kilometre on the swarm of incoming fire, emanating mostly from the green zone to the south but also the high ground on the other side, graduated. The air splintered with RPG bursts. One American fell dead, shot in the head. As two Australians carried Sergeant Greg Rodriguez away, two more bullets hit him in the back.

Sergeant Troy Simmonds, spotting a Chinook and knowing there would be Apache escorts, ordered Corporal Gibbo, the Australian JTAC, to call them in. But the Dutch rules of engagement restricted firing into the urban green zone, where from 1500 feet distinguishing civilian from enemy was difficult. As Corporal Gibbo moved to a more exposed position to better direct fire at the ridgeline in the *dascht*, he was shot in the chest.

Troy Simmonds had every reason to worry that the Taliban command to 'kill them all' might soon be realised. Miraculously, no vehicles were taken out by multiple RPG attacks as they bounced and weaved towards a choke point. They were surrounded by intensifying incoming fire. ICOM chatter suggested the Taliban might have mined the narrow ground. The lead vehicle, manned by Afghan soldiers, pulled up in a creek line. Hunched behind bulletproof glass, the Afghans effectively stalled the convoy strung out behind.

As bullets and RPG fragments smashed around, more men spun backwards. Another American was hit in the legs; Rob Maylor raced to assist. Trooper Johnny also suffered leg wounds.

An Incident Response Regiment (IRR) Sergeant, Ben, took hits to the hand and leg.

Troy Simmonds was in the second vehicle. 'Rounds were impacting all around me and there was nowhere to go to escape the fire.' Then, 'It felt like a baseball bat had bashed my leg. I turned to the American beside me and said, "I just got shot in the leg". He said, "God damn, so did I".'

They ducked to the rear of the Humvee. Simmonds knew he had to keep moving. Adrenaline and a lot of training kept him upright. Another RPG burst nearby, knocking him off his feet and sending his weapon cart-wheeling. Rob Maylor and the IRR dog handler, Corporal David Simpson, or 'Simdog', were also fragged. After he tried to call his dog in, Simpson sustained more serious wounds from another airburst.

Barking was heard above the roar of battle as the EDD Sarbi scooted. The black Labrador-cross was well trained to search out IEDs, but no amount of training is going to keep a dog still when the air is shattered and the earth erupts.

Trooper Brett was hit by a round grazing his buttocks. Though both were wounded, Brett and Rob Maylor went forward to try to get the lead vehicle moving.

Unable to feel his arm, soaked in blood and trying to co-ordinate escape from the killing ground, Troy Simmonds was then shot again, a bullet passing through his right hip and lodging in his left hip joint. He fought back, aiming at two Taliban sighted fleetingly on the high ground. Then his weapon suddenly smashed in his face. Another round had struck his M4 in the ejection port, putting it out of action.

He moved to the door of the vehicle to explain to the US Captain that his men had gone forward to get the convoy moving.

The movement seemed to attract the attention of the enemy, who poured so much fire at him he had to look for cover. All he could find was under the vehicle, where he saw 'the rounds striking the ground around the Humvee looking like rain on the surface of water'.

Then at last the convoy began to move after Trooper Brett had taken control of the lead vehicle, shunting the Afghan driver to the rear and undertaking a perilous three point turn. Losing blood and strength, Simmonds willed himself to hang on to the undercarriage of the Humvee. However, about 25 metres on, a large rock dislodged him. Stiff from wounds, he was still dodging bullets as he hobbled to climb onto the back of the vehicle. But he found he could not lift his leg and there was no room. Injured soldiers were sprawled across the back and the cabin was crowded. Simmonds struggled to the front and managed to throw himself 'into the space between the bull bar and grill, adopting the foetal position. Rounds were hitting the bull bar and bonnet, so I wrapped the tow chain over my head.'

Behind him Trooper Mark Donaldson was manoeuvring and firing at Taliban, some of whom had closed to within 50 metres. He got off seven rounds from an 84 mm anti armour weapon and some 66 mm rockets. Then another RPG exploded above one of the Humvees, knocking an Afghan interpreter from the vehicle and blinding him.

Sighting the stricken Afghan, Donaldson sprinted 80 metres to hoist him over his shoulder and race back for cover. Mark Donaldson later told Peter Pedersen of the Australian War Memorial that the 'terp' had ' been with us for about five days, so we'd got to know him a bit. But if someone's been knocked you go and get them no matter who they are.'[7]

The Victoria Cross is awarded for conspicuous gallantry, a daring act of valour or self-sacrifice; or extreme devotion to duty. Mark Donaldson's fighting rescue saw him rise to all heights, to be awarded Australia's first VC in Afghanistan. Four further gallantry awards would go to the Australians. Trooper Brett, who got the convoy moving, earned a Medal for Gallantry.

Whatever criticism might have been applied to the way the patrols got into trouble was reversed by their magnificent efforts at getting out. Donaldson's honoured gallantry was pivotal to reversing their fortune. He would say of the action: 'I did my job like all the other blokes and we got out of there.' [8] Mark Donaldson's punishment could be seen as the demands of an eternal publicity circuit. He sees his duties not as a punishment, but additional responsibilities that are part of the job.

A far more serious price was paid as a result of this action, however. According to Rob Maylor, 'nine of the 13 Australian soldiers had been wounded during that contact. Of the 11 SAS guys in the battle, seven were wounded; the other two casualties were engineers from the Incident Response Regiment.'[9] The Americans lost one killed and several wounded. Afghan soldiers were also wounded. According to Troy Simmonds, 'among those who escaped being wounded all had bullet and frag holes in cams and body armour'. Simmonds later found one bullet had passed through the neck cover draping from his cap. A round creased the top of the head of one trooper. Sergeant Bob had a bullet clip his upper wrist and hit his body armour. Mark Donaldson also had bullets pass through his gear.

Telling of the strict controls applying to media and information is the story of the action that was allowed to run, with all the energy of its subject. When the EDD Sarbi turned up in

October 2009, more than a year after her disappearance, she would become far better known than all other members of the patrol, with one possible exception.[10]

Despite the surrender of his protected identity status, Corporal Donaldson would return to fight in Afghanistan, as would the badly wounded patrol commander Troy Simmonds. The road ahead for injured Special Forces soldiers can be particularly rugged; trained to elite standards, they face the prospect of being ruled incapable of continuing to operate at that level. These furious actions, over in minutes or hours, sometimes produced physical and psychological wounds that would ache for all time.

The morale in Special Forces has been generally high, but exceptions were now more apparent. After Sean McCarthy was killed, one powerful soldier with a pregnant partner back at home did not want to go out again. His comrade told me: 'We did not think the worse of him, but he later cut himself off.'

Two weeks after the battle at Khas Uruzgan, 3 Squadron, including some members who had escaped unscathed, was engaged in another bitter encounter. SASR generally operates in smaller units than their Commando comrades; beyond the 'eyes on' intelligence collection work, they hunt Taliban leaders and bomb makers, the high-value targets.

On the night of 17 September 2008, on such a mission, the squadron became involved in a gunfight that killed a key Afghan leader, unfortunately the wrong one. Rozi Khan was a locally grown, democratically elected leader with an admired past who had thrown his weight behind the government and the foreigners. Some of the locals saw his killing by the SASR as evidence that enemies of Khan, including the Barakzai tribal leader, were manipulating ISAF. The SASR saw it as another of the stuff-ups that happen in war.

Khan had rushed to help a friend who believed the Taliban was surrounding him. Khan's forces and Australian troopers fired upon one another, each believing the other was the enemy, and the SASR doesn't tend to miss. Khan's son Daoud Mohammed accepted the death was a mistake, although it was not one with an easy recovery. He also understood that the killing of his father by the Australians would drive many erstwhile supporters into the arms of the enemy.

The death of Rozi Khan became one of the many stories from Afghanistan that gives us pause to consider whether any effort in such a murderously complicated environment could ever be worthwhile. However, SOTG Rotation VII could also lay claim to progress. It had significantly reduced the Taliban command structure in Uruzgan and pulled off a 'jackpot' during one mission, capturing Mullah Bari Ghul, the shadow governor of the province.

Among the array of awards bestowed on this rotation was another Star of Gallantry, to 2 Commando Private Scott for intense fighting near Sorkh Lez in the Mirabad Valley. The nature of the combat again demonstrated that the enemy was still capable, brave and determined. The Khas Uruzgan battle was not the only one in 2008 in which Australian Special Forces soldiers feared they came close to being overwhelmed.

To the other Australian soldiers in the reconstruction teams now reaching out into the valleys, raids by Special Forces, which were supposed to deliver them greater freedom of movement, were not so assuredly doing this. There was another side to the decapitation missions. They often angered locals; leaders and fighters were taken out but soon replaced. According to one Australian engineer it was 'all a bit like mowing the grass'.

CHAPTER 9
CIVCAS

In October and November 2008, Special Forces Rotation VII packed up to surrender its now more comfortable barracks accommodation at Camp Russell. Australian Special Forces makes up about 5 per cent of the entire Army; to this point in Afghanistan it had carried at least 50 per cent of the load and suffered over 90 per cent of the casualties.

The earlier rotations of three-and-a-half months were now being lengthened; the punishing month-long patrols of 2006 and 2007 could not be easily sustained. To help ease the pressure Australia's 1 Commando Regiment, which had provided small groups to earlier rotations, would deploy a full company to operate through the supposedly quieter winter months. The notion of an off-season would prove another misconception born of the unusually cold winter of 2007–08.

Rotation VIII was principally made up of general Reserve soldiers and fell under the command of Special Operations, with the further sinew of Regulars through the ranks. It would be known as Force Element (FE) Charlie.

One of the many fault lines in this struggle is the long-established divide between the Regulars and Reserves. Reservists have endured the 'choco' and 'weekend warrior' taunts for generations, at the same time producing some of Australia's most famous soldiers.

Few Regulars will accept that Reservists have their level of training and many in Special Forces openly doubted the reservists could handle Afghanistan. Even fewer will concede civilian skills—drawn from the police forces, hospitals and universities—can complement operating capability as well as raise the general intelligence quotient. One young university graduate arriving with Rotation VIII told me: 'We had real jobs in the real world. But once on operations the distinction is not an issue. We were all getting shot at.'

At this time Reconstruction Task Force 4 (RTF4) was also packing up to return to Australia. For Captain Clare O'Neill and the engineers there was cause to believe they were making a difference. In 2006 she had stood at the edge of Camp Holland and looked out at a dark night, broken only by the pulse of tracers and the blaze of flares. Now a thousand lights broke the night. Tarin Kowt had schools, government premises, a hospital and a busy commercial centre.

'The bazaar was a bustling Asian marketplace,' Captain O'Neill told me. There were females on the streets, some of the older ones without *burka*s. You hear a lot of bad things and I went back thinking it would not have improved, but after two deployments there was optimism. It is hard to articulate, still small steps, but it's working.'

Two others, Sergeant Mark Taylor and Lance Corporal Rod Johnstone, distilled their experience of RTF4: 'One hundred and eighty days there, 120 of them outside the wire.' The Australians had empathy for the locals. 'We had been in East Timor. We hate seeing people bullied,' they said.

When they first went into the Chora Valley people ran away. 'Months later they would cheer and wave. They sway towards the winning side. After we employed them as labourers on construction projects, we would see them wearing new shoes and driving new tractors, which the Taliban would then steal. Out there it was as clear as day—people living like shit—but we did see a huge change in the way they lived.'

Communicating to distant Australia how steep the task had been and from how low a base the Australians had climbed had always been difficult. But by now, to anyone with experience enough to acquire the longer view, progress was remarkable. To first-timers arriving from Perth or Brisbane, the place was still a shit hole.

In October, Mentoring and Reconstruction Task Force 1 (MRTF1) transited in, replacing RTF4, which had suffered no losses. A new phase had begun, with a mission focus adjusting towards training and capacity building. This meant continuing the reconstruction work with a view to incremental transfer of skills and responsibility to the Government of the Republic of Afghanistan (GIRoA). Australians and anyone in the International Security Assistance Force (ISAF) knew that gains achieved so far would be lost in an instant if GIRoA could not stand and deliver.

Working with the Afghan National Army (ANA) is a story of pleasure and pain, too often the latter. Captain Paul Graham, who came to the Army as a seventeen-year-old in 1997, was now commanding an Operational Mentoring and Liaison Team (OMLT). His description of the ANA being 'like schoolkids' is one you hear many times. However, what Graham understood is what you also often hear—that these Afghans, soldiers and civilians, were not only the centre of the mission, they *were* the mission.

Graham encountered 'a short-term survival outlook. The ANA talked about crushing the Taliban, but were reluctant to do the hard work. We were anal about timing, ready to go on patrol as arranged at 0600, and at 0610 you were shaking them awake. They could be lazy and irrational, but at other times surprise you with what they could do.'

Twenty-five-year-old Private Lachlan Grono, with a degree in International Relations from Macquarie University, had joined the Army in the preceding year, 2007.[1] He found the ANA 'unusual people. It is hard to understand why people in a country in conflict join an army but are not that keen about constantly soldiering. They are happy to go out and crack off a few shots if they did not have to work too hard. Some are excellent, some a waste of time and there are a lot in the middle. A lot of them had a hatred of the Taliban, through personal rather than ideological experience. Friends and family having been killed or tortured is what motivated them.'

Major Josh Jardine, providing force protection to MRTF1, shared the same mixed view as Lachlan Grono and Paul Graham. He saw 'true professional soldiers under fire' and others who would 'go missing'. A constant worry for the Australians patrolling with the ANA was being hit by undisciplined fire from their allies.

Another worry was the ANA's treatment of locals. They could be as bad as the Taliban at taxing them, and generating animosity by stealing food and chickens when they searched the walled compounds. And coming generally from the north, most of the ANA's soldiers spoke Dari rather than Pashto, so sometimes the non-Pashto speakers would remain mute as they did not want to let on that this was the case.

Jardine recalls encountering a complexity that was uniquely Afghan. One of the building projects requested by the locals was a shopping bazaar at Sorkh Morghab, an area that had seen a lot of fighting in the previous two years. The project was recognised as being good for the local economy and evidence of ISAF spending crossing tribal barriers. But there were still problems: 'We built eighteen shops, but there were twenty-seven local tribal groups in the region, and each had to have their own shop.'

The objective of the Combined Task Force now deployed out in the valleys among the people was to dominate the area of operations, with the smack of hammer and nail continuing alongside the stutter of gunfire. The OMLTs, with Australians accompanying the ANA, would conduct clearance operations. With Australian infantry and cavalry armour providing a protective screen, they would enter and search compounds of interest.

As with just about everything pertaining to the mission, the procedure was delicate. A full body search and rifling through the winter storage would not seem the best path to winning hearts and minds. Whatever the problems with the ANA handling clearance operations, the locals soon made it clear they saw intrusion by their own countrymen as the lesser evil.

Local Afghans particularly hated the night raids and any proximity of the foreigners to adult females. One Australian medic moving to assist a local couple who had fallen from a motorbike had first to deal with the refusal by the husband to let him touch his severely injured wife.

Before heading to Afghanistan, every Australian soldier was extensively briefed on cultural sensitivity. They all carried a small Afghanistan handbook with sections on Islam and the people and a language and culture guide, for example telling them: 'A handshake is common among men, who tend to be expressive in greeting friends and may pat backs during an embrace. Lengthy verbal greetings are often accompanied by placing the right hand over the heart. A man does not shake hands with or otherwise touch a woman in public . . .'[2]

I saw Australians searching and interacting with Afghans many times, the locals responding with practised pragmatism, offering wrists and hands for cuffs and fingerprinting. The Australians seemed as courteous and respectful as circumstance allowed. One time I saw a soldier step into an irrigation channel and help a farmer clear a blockage. On numerous occasions Australian soldiers could be seen bantering with children.

All the same, there was criticism that at a deeper level, when it came to comprehending the undercurrents of power and retribution, the Australians were clueless. Daoud Mohammed, son of the Afghan leader killed by Special Air Service Regiment (SASR) in 2008, told *Four Corners*: 'At the beginning they did not know anything about the Afghan culture, its traditions and the tribal issues. They did not have a clue about anything.'[3]

Major David McCammon, deployed with MRTF1 after doing battle in Canberra as aid to Chief of Army Peter Leahy, described one telling incident at Patrol Base Locke. An improvised explosives device (IED) had killed an Afghan policeman and seriously wounded others. Americans, Dutch and about ten Australians were present when chemical spray pulled up traces of explosives on a suspected insurgent. After one of their men bled out, the Afghans wanted to kill the insurgent. There was a stand-off between the foreigners trying to protect the detainee and the Afghans intent on murdering him. Tension mounted and the Dutch started to back away, donning their body armour and helmets. At this point an

Australian cook dressed in footy shorts, T-shirt and thongs stepped up, and moving to the centre of the crowd yelled, 'Everyone settle the fuck down.'

The tension was broken and the insurgent hustled away. McCammon reflected on how lucky he was 'to have someone with common sense and maturity. He did not have to do it. I spoke to him later and he said he had a great time and that not every job gave him the opportunity to do that stuff.'

Since its first patrol, MRTF1 had encountered pot shots and skirmishing, but as the fighting season was supposed to wind down the troops in contact incidence actually intensified. Captain Paul Graham had averaged one contact per week when in late November 2008 he established an overwatch at Cemetery Hill West in the Chora Valley to assist a planned cordon and search operation. When the Australians had taken over nearby Forward Operating Base (FOB) Locke from the Dutch, according to Platoon Mentor Sergeant Adam West, their parting advice was: 'Don't patrol over that creek because the Taliban are there . . . So that is what we did.'

As the sun came up on 25 November, a local walking the hills spotted the movement of the Australians on Cemetery Hill West and began counting heads. 'He walked our position and reported back. They know our rules of engagement,' explained Captain Paul Graham.

Seeing they had the numbers and with time to form up, the Taliban attacked in groups from three directions. Captain Graham, commanding OMLT1, had to organise a complex defence strung out across two irrigation fields, interposing his platoons of ANA with difficulty.

Private Lachlan Grono remembers having 'dramas getting the ANA to move in the right direction and not shoot RPGs [rocket-propelled grenades] at us'. Caught in the open, the air was alive with bullets. Paul Graham saw a tree disintegrate and was knocked flat by the back blast of an RPG fired by an Afghan soldier standing too close. Although dazed, he held his wits. With Afghan interpreters monitoring the enemy frequency, Graham warned West of an impending attack.

Alerted by the dust raised when a PKM machine gun fired, Sergeant West saw his first Taliban, prone behind a bipod. He returned fire with greater accuracy. 'I have respect for them as fighters. They are not to be underestimated.'

Private Grono saw one man 'jump from behind a building, spray our position and go back behind the building. Then he dropped his weapon and came out to check his animals. There were less than polite requests to circumvent the ROE [rules of engagement], but everyone stuck to it.'

The Australians and ANA were outnumbered, the small overwatch group in danger of being overrun. They were forced to withdraw, hurriedly leaving valuable equipment such as night-vision goggles (NVG) behind.

Graham had confidence in his parched and weary men but struggled with the ANA. Two hours in, the shooting began to abate. The ANA pulled back, wanting to take a group of detainees with them. Paul Graham was sure they weren't Taliban, but a group of 'friendlies that had come for a look, and were now being followed by a procession of wailing women'.

He tried to rally the patrol to recover equipment left on the hill but the ANA commander refused, telling Graham his soldiers had exhausted their ammunition. 'Some of our guys were not keen either, but no one shirked. My heart was in my mouth when we stepped back in.'

Lieutenant Jamie Smith, over 1 kilometre away, moved his seventeen Afghan soldiers to marry up. With the physique of a basketball player, Smith had further cause to lament his size. Back at Royal Military College (RMC) during the Shaggy Ridge exercise the problem was hunger; now it was the large target he presented as he pushed towards the sound of battle. One enemy lined him up, but as Smith noted, 'I can't in all consciousness call him a sniper if he could not hit me from one hundred metres.'

By now most of the gear had been recovered, if not from the hill then from nearby compounds. Days later a puff jacket from one of the packs was spotted being worn by a local and swiftly retrieved.

Captain Graham, 'the grey man', had been part of the RMC class of 2000 with Captain James, who for his action in Khas Uruzgan two months earlier was awarded a Distinguished Service Medal. Those extensive RMC field drills must have had some benefit. In a later Queen's Birthday Honours List, Captain Paul Graham also received a DSM, as did Sergeant Adam West.

Extricating the patrol to safety during the fighting at Cemetery Hill West had been a high point for MRTF1. When asked about the down moments Jamie Smith says: 'Your low points are whenever there is a death.'

Special Forces soldiers would often camp in the patrol bases, and it was here at FOB Locke, close to the Cemetery Hill West action, that Jamie Smith ran into Michael Fussell, a fellow Lieutenant and a joint terminal attack controller (JTAC) from 4RAR (CDO), who was now seconded to 1 Commando Regiment. Having joined six years earlier, the 25-year-old Fussell was on his first tour of Afghanistan.

One week after Rotation VIII kicked off, on 26 November, Lieutenant Fussell was returning from a mission when he was hastily retasked to another. Intelligence had indicated a Taliban commander was laying up for the night in a compound in the Mirabad Valley near Nayak.

A satellite view of the Tarin Kowt bowl shows a wishbone-like river formation with the provincial centre at the junction. The river branching north is the Dorafshan, which flows past Chora through the Baluchi Valley. The branch pointing east is the Teri River or Rud, which flows through the Mirabad.

The routine was to march 5 kilometres or so, and 'kick the door in at 3 am to capture a Taliban, usually with no argument'. On this occasion the vehicles found their way to a high point in the *dascht* adjacent to the targeted compound before the patrol trekked in.

Setting off after midnight, in below freezing temperatures, the Australians worked their way towards the green zone. It was an inky night, a new moon providing little ambient luminosity. The insurgents mined ridgelines, often marking the paths with small cairns of stones, and ISAF intelligence indicated the area had been heavily sewn in order to protect the Taliban commander. Accordingly, there was concern among some of the experienced soldiers about the haste of the operation. The Incident Response Regiment (IRR) has ways of marking the trail, which can be followed with the help of NVG. 'We were very careful about treading in the footstep of the soldier in front; super anal about it,' said one.

The company-strength patrol was commanded by a Major, who had been promoted through the ranks of the Special Air Service Regiment. His second-in-command was a most interesting digger indeed, Captain Bronson Horan. A former member of US

Operational Detachment Alpha, he married an Australian soldier he met in Iraq, joined the Australian Army and was subsequently posted to 1 Commando.

The Officer Commanding (OC), Horan, and the Company Sergeant Major (CSM) were to the front; Fussell was eleventh in line. Though a highly competent soldier, having topped his JTAC class, he was not beret qualified, having only partially completed the Commando course.

The patrol was going at a faster than usual pace, to a point where track discipline was sometimes lost. The ten men in front were moving alongside the path, while further to the rear others took to following the person in front rather than the IRR-defined route.

At 0112 on 27 November, those towards the rear of the column heard a massive thud and saw sparks rise into the blackness. They knew what had happened, and were hoping the injuries were minor. But then they heard the dreaded 'one KIA' over the comms.

Fussell had stepped on a pressure plate. The CSM, a tactical response trained police officer from New South Wales, stunned by the blast, recovered his breath and took charge. Bronson Horan, immediately in front of Michael Fussell, was also hurt. Concussed, he got to his feet and went to work. (It was later determined he had suffered a cracked spine, brain injury and sensory defects.[4])

Fussell was placed on a stretcher. Two teams led by Sergeant John, who part owned a car repair business in Melbourne, cleared a tortuous route, skidding as they cross-grained the scree back to the vehicle drop-off point (VDO). Suspecting the Taliban would have heard the blast and might come to investigate, an ambush team remained. Over the ICOM Taliban were heard reporting they had 'got one'.

As a JTAC, Fussell carried sensitive documents and communication gear, some of which was yet to be recovered. Sergeant

John volunteered to return to collect the mission-essential equipment. In the course of doing so, a further IED was located. An explosive ordinance expert was called and yet another IED found. After sunrise a Taliban spotter was observed and shot by FE Charlie snipers.

Lieutenant Fussell's remains, draped in the national flag, arrived at Tarin Kowt soon after dawn. There was speculation the JTAC may have had more to concentrate on as he moved along the trail, his earpiece networked to a wider communication grid. There was no blame attached to the speculation; Fussell had not deviated from the path, and as every soldier in Afghanistan knows, but for a footstep they could share the same fate.

The loss, so early in the deployment, was a brutal blow on many levels. The OC, with leadership competence now brought into question, was returned to Australia. Many of the soldiers who were there thought the CSM who had taken charge was deserving of a medal, but this was not to be. Rotation VIII, with over three months to go, would suffer even more bad news.

One month later a stretcher would again be called for, this time by MRTF1. On 28 December Section Leader Corporal Leon Gray was on patrol with his under-strength team providing a protective screen for the OMLT engaged in a cordon and search operation about 1500 metres further down the Chora Valley.

Lieutenant Ashley Judd, in command, felt the full force of a well co-ordinated ambush. 'The two sections I had got separated.' Outnumbered and under heavy fire, they were almost twice overrun. According to Corporal Gray, 'We were caught in a bad spot in open ground. I had to get my guys behind a *quala*, so there was no choice but to close and dislodge them.'

Corporal Dan's medals. (Chris Masters)

Australian Recruit Training Centre tailor, Bub Noack. (Chris Masters)

Their new home. Over eleven weeks about 10 per cent of Kapooka recruits drop out. (Chris Masters)

At the half-way mark recruits visit the Australian War Memorial. (Chris Masters)

Graduation day at the Royal Military College. (Chris Masters)

Afghans welcome the building of the Talani School. (Chris Masters)

RTF2 plumber turned Warrant Officer, Brendan Johnson. (Chris Masters)

Jason and Susan Blain at the MTF1 homecoming. (Chris Masters)

Section Commander Corporal Adam Heemskirk contemplated getting out. (Australian Defence Force)

The dust of Uruzgan. (Chris Masters)

Captain Clare O'Neill, a young veteran of RTF1 and RTF4. (Australian Defence Force)

Lieutenant Ben Gooley, though surrounded, survived an ambush near Sorkh Morghab. (Australian Defence Force)

(Left) Troy Simmonds was a Private in Somalia in 1993 and (right) an SASR Patrol Commander in Afghanistan in 2008. (Courtesy of Troy Simmonds)

His weapon disabled, Troy Simmonds and SASR fought for their lives at Khas Uruzgan. (Courtesy of Troy Simmonds)

Patrol Base Wali on the edge of the green belt in the Mirabad Valley. (Neale Maude)

Captain Aaron Cimbaljevic is wounded by an IED strike near Sorkh Lez. (Courtesy of Aaron Cimbaljevic)

Warlord, Police Chief and ally, Matiullah Khan. (Australian Defence Force)

Captain John Crockett mentors the Afghan National Army. (Australian Defence Force)

The charm of army life at Patrol Base Wali. (Chris Masters)

The habs or hardened accommodation blocks at Patrol Base Atiq. (Chris Masters)

Major Jason Groat (right) as David Deitz receives his first stripe. (Chris Masters)

Special Forces arrive at the pivotal battle of Gizab. (Australian Defence Force)

Sapper Darren Smith (left) and Sapper Jacob Moerland. (Neale Maude)

The first patrol to depart Wali after Snowy and Smithy were killed. (Chris Masters)

Survivors of the fatal 2010 Blackhawk crash return to the sky. (Chris Masters)

Roll of Honour 2 Commando Regiment, Holsworthy, 2010. (Chris Masters)

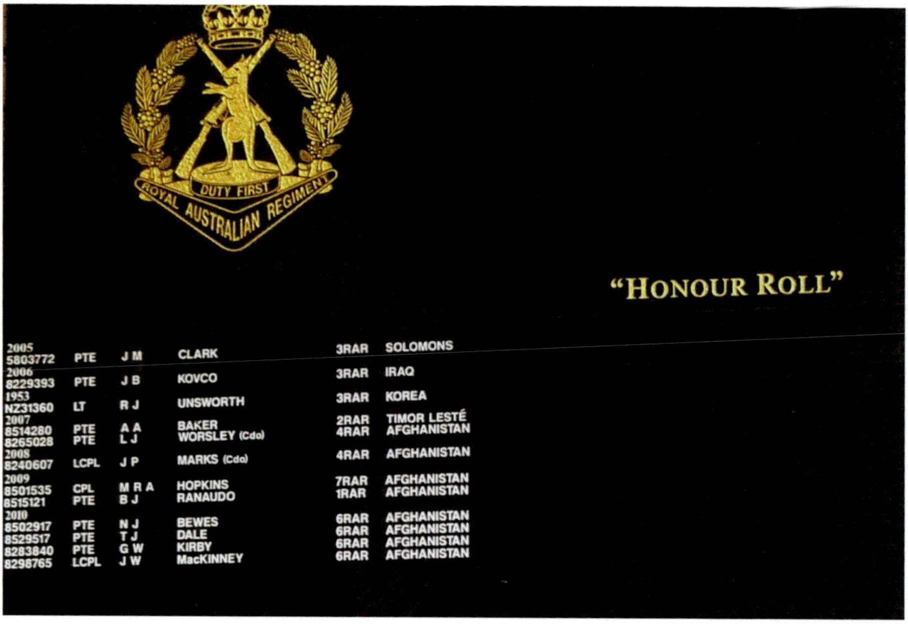

Honour Roll Gallipoli Barracks, Brisbane, 2010. (Chris Masters)

'Stonecutter 06'. Warrant Officer Kevin Dolan MG in the Mirabad. (Chris Masters)

A Dutch soldier biometrically 'enrols' an Afghan fighting age male (FAM). (Chris Masters)

FE Bravo. The Commandos are inserted in the hostile Chineh Kalay Valley. (Chris Masters)

Bram Connolly with Afghan locals. (Courtesy of Bram Connolly)

Bram Connolly (right) and Yankee Platoon prevailed at the 2010 battle of Zabat Kalay. (Courtesy of Bram Connolly)

Every soldier carries a radio. There was frantic communication; Gray describes it as 'like listening to a horse race'. The enemy's small combat teams kept moving, spraying the Australians with small arms and RPG fire. 'We were on the ground firing at where the noises came from. We caught fleeting glimpses at best, all fighting age males, beard and man dress, dark-coloured vest and turban, all the same.'

Lieutenant Judd 'had to find a way to get both elements together and break out. We ended up having to throw grenades.' Australian Private Mathew Pepi, in the other section, caught a round in one leg when moving off. It passed through the other leg, the hole on one surface 'big enough to put a fist in'. Another in Gray's section suffered fragmentation wounds to the cheek and back.

Leon Gray dragged the wounded Pepi 400 metres towards the safety of a watercourse. 'I was so fatigued. The belief is that a shot of adrenaline fuels fitness. It is not true. Two hours in I would almost rather get shot than continue running.' Afterwards, the section leader said: 'I could not be prouder of the way each soldier went. I had been waiting for a long time to fire my weapon. When it happens it seems the most natural thing in the world. It is surreal to be actually doing it, with the bullets coming past. Part of the brain is terrified, but as an infantryman it is the pinnacle of what we do.'

Corporal Gray would be awarded a Distinguished Service Medal for 'distinguished leadership in action while a Section Commander in 2 Platoon Combat Team Tusk, MRTF1'. Lieutenant Ashley Judd received a Commendation for Distinguished Service. He later reflected: 'Anzac Day has a tendency to elevate Australian soldiers to the super heroic. This misses the whole point. The thing of soldiers doing amazing things is not that they are super heroic, but they are normal blokes. They come from normal society. I saw acts of physical courage, I saw them going out to open ground to recover our wounded, fire going all around. Dragged him into an aqueduct, first aid half under water, tourniquet and bandage. Sounds like big talk but most would find the thought of letting down a team member worse than themselves getting harmed.'

The motivation to fight for the man alongside is not new. What was different about the mentoring work in Uruzgan, however, was that frequently the soldiers fighting alongside could not be relied on to return the commitment. On 4 January 2009, an OMLT operating from Patrol Base Buman (formerly Worsley) near Sorkh Morghab, 13 kilometres to the north of Tarin Kowt, discovered this—almost at the cost of their lives.

Lieutenant Ben Gooley and Sergeant Matt Lines were the only Australians on a cordon and search operation with eighteen ANA soldiers and two Afghan interpreters. The preference was to take six Australians, but manning restraints were becoming an increasing problem. The MRTF had a longer deployment than Special Forces and, unlike Special Forces, was granted leave generally at the halfway mark of the eight month tour. Out of country leave and an injury had thinned its ranks.

Two OMLT squads were patrollng west towards Kakarak when they crossed the Dorafshan River and sighted a Taliban spotter with an AK47 who took to his heels, disappearing into a *quala* complex. The Coalition team in pursuit began to take fire. The ANA returned fire and grabbed one of the locals. According to Lines, 'They [the ANA] were adamant it was him [the Taliban], but it was the wrong person. A poor farmer got bashed for no reason.' Even so locals were helpful, a boy coming forward to lead the OMLT platoon to where the shooter, weapons, a chest rig, magazines and a hand grenade could be found.

The ANA was ready to pack up and return to Buman, so Lieutenant Gooley had to persuade the reluctant ANA commander to continue with the original mission. Carrying maps that identified every single *quala* by number, the patrol proceeded in two files south along a narrow track hedged with mud walls. What they did not know was they were about to bump a Taliban *shura*, which was protected by a cordon of around 25 bodyguards.

Ben Gooley heard a loud crack, accompanied by a white flash, and was 'put down on my arse'. An RPG had soared between the two columns, exploding with a shower of dirt and rocks, somewhat extraordinarily missing everyone.

Two to three PKM machine guns then began an intermittent stammer, the trees alongside the track whipped by fire and the mud walls around them splintering. Gooley made a radio call: 'Buman, Buman. This is Oscar 29 Alpha. RPG strikes and multiple machine gun fire. Wait out.' He checked the GPS and communicated the grid reference. The lieutenant could see ANA soldiers lying prone all along the road. 'I thought everyone was dead.'

Matt Lines was about 25 metres in front but not in Gooley's line of sight. When the PKMs opened up the ANA soldier ahead of Lines was shot in the chest. The bullet had gone in above his chest plate and exited through his shoulder. Lines tried to apply a dressing but the soldier refused his ministrations.

The Taliban then moved to surround the column, shooting coming from two sides. Anxious to support his sergeant, Lieutenant Gooley grabbed the collar of an ANA soldier with a PKM and tried to drag him forward. But he 'curled into a foetal position' and could not be moved. 'Others were digging in with their eyelids.'

To Gooley's immense relief he began to hear the 'whump' of a 40 mm grenade. He knew Lines must have fired it, using the launcher attached to his Steyr. Reaching Lines on the radio, Gooley heard his sergeant tell him he was being 'whaled'. 'I'm getting smashed up here, boss.'

While the Taliban was scampering across rooftops and firing, the ANA, inert as 'sandbags', offered little to no resistance. Gooley crawled forward to a point where he could sight Lines' firing position. 'I could see the splash of rounds all around him.'

The Lieutenant was having trouble with radio communication but he was able to reach Patrol Base Buman where Private Ross, one of the few Indigenous members of the Australian Defence Force, was manning the radio. 'Rossy battle tracked the whole time. I was struggling to communicate with HQ. But Rossy organised a quick reaction force to come and help us.'

A Dutch Apache gunship arrived. The pilot would not fire, reporting he could see people running but could not see them firing weapons. According to Lieutenant Gooley, what saved them was Lines and the 40 mm. Popping up and firing accurately across two flanks, the high explosive rounds accounted for an estimated eight insurgents. He carried eleven rounds and at the end had just one remaining if a last stand was required.

Gooley was also busy with his Steyr, expending five-and-a-half of his ten magazines. 'I fired at three or four guys. I definitely saw some fall over but you can't always tell whether it was a kill.'

As another ANA unit jumped into the Ford Rangers and rushed to the aid of Oscar 29 Alpha, so too did an Australian combat team led by Lieutenant Tom Larter. With another soldier blinded by flying debris, the patrol began to withdraw, at which time some of the ANA soldiers finally began to fire their weapons. They were motivated in part by an interpreter who joined the fight after grabbing an AK47 that had been earlier confiscated. By the time the patrol reached better cover and reinforcements arrived, all the water was gone and Lines and Gooley were spent.

There would be some recrimination later that Gooley and Lines chose not to take with them another digger, who they considered to be short on the experience necessary to assume command if either were killed. But credit was also due to Sergeant Matt Lines, whose steady resistance in the first 20 minutes had prevented the squad being 'rolled over'. Later promoted to Warrant Officer, he was awarded a Medal for Gallantry.

This action, however, fought over three hours across the middle of the day, would be eclipsed a month later by another action, at Sorkh Morghab, a few kilometres further up the Baluchi Valley near Sajawul.

Patrol Base Qudus, built by RTF4 six months earlier, was on this day, 4 January, being used as a rest spot between missions by FE Charlie from 1 Commando Regiment. MRTF1 engineers, needing to move the container in which the Commandos had sheltered overnight, hustled one of the teams into the open, where it settled in stray patches of sunlight. The temperature in the middle of the day was around 10°C. Beyond undertaking preparations for that night's mission, FE Charlie was doing what soldiers mostly do: waiting.

At 1255 the patrol base came under indirect attack from 107 mm rockets, fired from the surrounding hills. One missile fell short, then there was a massive bang. The second penetrated a Hesco wall, struck a shipping container of water bottles and changed direction, exiting the container and exploding against the distant wall.

A second before as friends yarned, Private Greg Sher rose to his feet. The 107 mm rocket, notoriously inaccurate, this time found its mark. The popular soldier was killed in an instant. With no sign of life, the air medical evacuation was given low priority. The rocket's point of origin was soon identified, a spotter was sighted and the area engaged with mortar fire. Two men believed to have fired the rockets were later captured.

The greater issue of concern was that intercepted radio traffic picked up the enemy reporting it had killed a foreigner. The Australians deduced the only way this could have been known was if someone inside the base was in phone contact with the insurgents. (There was always concern that some members of the ANA were collaborating with the Taliban.)

When the Coalition loses one of its own, the battle generally stops and, as they put it, 'the jungle drums sound'. At Camp Holland and the outer patrol bases communications are closed down. The Australian Defence Force does not want to risk someone making a phone call home and passing on details before relatives can be informed.

On this weekend, Felix and Yvonne Sher had travelled from Melbourne to Daylesford for a break. On Monday at 3 am the phone rang, and Felix heard his other son Barry on the line. 'It's Greg. He was killed.' Stunned, the father asked: 'Where? How?' Barry replied: 'In Afghanistan, by a rocket.'

When the 30-year-old private deployed to Afghanistan the previous October, he had not told his parents. The news of his death came as a double shock.

The CSM and a padre were waiting when the Shers arrived home early that morning; Felix had set the GPS and 'followed it home'. The Army had tried without success to find a rabbi. The family asked for the Army to be told how Greg's remains were to be returned—he was not to be left alone.

Greg's father described his son as 'a protector, not an attacker'. The loss, so brutal, could never be recovered, but a community of the Shers' many friends was formed. 'We still keep in contact with his mates,' says Felix.[5]

Back at Camp Russell they were also suffering. FE Charlie, halfway through its rotation, had already endured two ramp ceremonies. And there were more operations to occupy the weeks ahead, one uncovering a major weapons workshop on the edge of Tarin Kowt.

On 7 January the Australians were engaged in an interdiction and disruption operation in the Baluchi Pass. An announcement soon after declared: 'Following receipt of positive identification and all necessary approvals, ISAF executed a precision air strike.'[6]

Facilitated by Special Forces, the strike killed Mullah Abdul Rasheed, a subordinate to a key leader in the Baluchi–Chora area. (Key leaders were commanders with direct links to Quetta.) Intelligence put Rasheed in charge of the rocket attack that had killed Private Sher.

Rasheed's death was announced on the day of Greg Sher's funeral in Melbourne. The Australian Defence Force, disinclined to revenge attacks, or at least admitting to them, came close when Chief of Defence Angus Houston, then visiting Tarin Kowt, told Special Forces: 'It is quite clear you made them pay for the death of a comrade.'[7]

The operations in the Baluchi–Chora region immediately following Greg Sher's death had not been as precise as ISAF wished. The indirect rocket attacks by the insurgents were met by indirect mortar fire by the Australians. The Australians, obliged to observe the strikes, did so, but for two bombs that landed over a ridgeline.[8]

On 5 January, a group of Afghans turned up at the patrol base seeking medical assistance and reporting that ten locals, including eight females, had been killed. Another inquiry was begun, ultimately concluding it could not determine whether the victims fell to Coalition or Taliban fire.

This was a common story throughout Afghanistan. In 2008, 1445 civilians had been killed, victims of either the Coalition or the insurgents. To the bereaved families the distinction was not as important as it was to the combatants. Proof that the lethal fragment came from an insurgent rocket rather than an ISAF mortar bomb did not improve regard for the foreigners. ISAF had failed a central objective to protect the population.

Throughout 2009 civilian casualties in Afghanistan were shown to have grown by 40 per cent. This had become a central issue in government, within ISAF, the Australian Forces and for all soldiers sitting in on mission-planning briefs.

For FE Charlie, 12 February dawned with another night raid scheduled, this one called Operation Pakula targeting insurgent leader Mullah Noorulla and compounds at Sorkh Morghab, near where Ben Gooley and Matt Lines had fought the month before. Twenty-four gunslingers from 1 Commando Regiment joined other personnel, including six ANA soldiers and interpreters, in an area that was officially classified at the time as denied to ISAF.

After midnight on 13 February a team entered a *quala* and detained a man who offered no resistance, but he turned out to not be the target. Mullah Noorullah was presumed to have fled. Acting on intelligence, the patrol commander ordered two teams to further search for weapons caches in a neighbouring compound.

It was 3 am when Sergeant John led his team 100 metres to the next compound. A motor mechanic and son of a Korean War veteran, he was on his first trip to Afghanistan after tours of Iraq, Bougainville and East Timor. He is the same man who returned to collect mission-sensitive equipment and documents after Michael Fussell was killed a month earlier.

The team began searching rooms. Some shoes indicating the presence of children were sighted outside one door. Further on, through NVG, one of the Commandos saw a man raise an AK47 and point it at the door toward the advancing column of soldiers. Lance Corporal Tim fired, wounding the man in the arm. He fired back and Tim dropped, struck by flying debris. Though only slightly injured, Sergeant John and the others to the rear thought Tim had been killed.

According to the soldiers, the ANA and an interpreter called out to the man with the weapon in Pashto, telling him: 'We are the security forces. Stop firing. Come out. We are conducting a search.' They were met, they say, with a burst of AK47 fire through the window.

Sergeant John was conditioned to take the initiative. He ordered Lance Corporal Dave, another experienced soldier, to throw the first grenade. The firing and yelling continued. Sergeant John ordered a second hand grenade thrown. After the blast and billow of smoke and dust, with ears still ringing, a wailing arose.

Amrullah Khan had been killed, along with his ten-year-old son and a teenage girl, a boy aged eleven and two infants, all members of the extended family. Three more children were wounded.

Amrullah's wife, Shapiro Khan, later said she heard noises and alerted her husband, who picked up his weapon. In Uruzgan, to the average farmer, an AK47 can be as common an implement as a scythe or spade. Shapiro insisted her husband was not Taliban, but a farmer trying to protect his family. The noise of the sudden, intense fighting within the small room may have meant he did not hear the soldiers calling him out.

When the Australians saw what had happened they were shaken. 'The back of the head felt like mush. The eyes of a dead child stared up.' The bodies were wrapped in blankets.

An unmanned aerial vehicle had traced the episode from the time the soldiers arrived at the second compound to when the firing stopped. There was an estimated 25 seconds between the first shot fired and the last grenade thrown.

The deaths were a cruel blow, to the family, the community and the mission. Honour payments of $1500 for each person killed were distributed by the Uruzgan governor. The wounded received $800. Beyond a moral obligation to try to do something, there was a further rationale that payments help avert the prospect of revenge attacks.

The family was understood to be angry at the Australians, but more so at the person who fed the intelligence that caused its compound to be targeted. Mullah Noorulla had a close escape. When the air medical evacuation Blackhawks arrived, his panicked voice was intercepted as they passed overhead.

Shortly after, an inquiry officer arrived at Camp Russell with a small team of investigators and set about interviewing witnesses. The Australian soldiers say they were co-operative, understanding the death of the civilians was tragic and a mistake. But they did not believe they had committed a crime, in that they were under fire and obliged to defend themselves.

Nineteen months after the deaths at Sorkh Morghab, Sergeant John and Lance Corporal Dave would be charged with manslaughter by the independent office of the Director of Military Prosecutions. Their Commanding Officer was also charged with breaching ISAF rules governing the entry of civilian compounds.

The case gained much greater coverage in Australia than had hundreds of similar preceding incidents in Afghanistan. In a battle space with no middle ground, debate surged to hysterical extremes. Some commentary and reporting condemned any scrutiny of the sacred digger, vilifying the Director of Military Prosecutions. Other reporting stretched for evidence of a war crime.

A first rule of war reporting is to maintain an eye on the primary victim. There was good sense in Defence taking a tough line on tough behaviour, and in media rising to the cause of the innocent. Both parties keep an eye on another line that can't be crossed: if the innocent become dominant and indiscriminate victims of war, it is clearly time to go home.

In March 2009, Sergeant John and Lance Corporal Dave did go home, along with the rest of FE Charlie.

Rotation VIII generated many shock waves. David McLure, an astute lawyer and a Major in the Army Reserve who had deployed with Rotation VI, took on the defence of Sergeant John. Major John Hyde defended Lance Corporal Dave. At the pre-trial hearings they asked the prosecutor to identify what alternative option was available, what negligence was demonstrated, and to whom soldiers in combat owe a duty of care.

The case was dismissed, as later was the charge against the Commanding Officer. The trial, like the battle at Sorkh Morghab, had descended into chaos. Sergeant John was most angry at the proposition that he and others on that mission felt no sorrow and remorse. The war always follows soldiers home, and this time it had done so with abnormal persistence.

There were many further formal inquiry hours devoted to weaknesses in preparation and leadership during that winter rotation.

Over time the Reserves would not deploy in as great a number, and more attention would be paid to ensuring leaders were properly prepared.

In March 2009, when Special Operation Task Group (SOTG) Rotation IX was arriving, MRTF1 was still trying to maintain a stable presence around the outer patrol bases. The Mentoring and Reconstruction Task Groups were not always fans of Special Forces; beyond conventional jealousies, they could sometimes feel up close the anger of a community after a raid had occurred.

The insurgency, settled among the people, meant targeting commonly occurred within close proximity to non-combatants. And whatever ISAF said about smart warfare and exact rules of engagement, as the incident at Sorkh Morghab showed, armed combat is also inherently reckless. The soldiers patrolling the irrigated fields for the sake of suppressing the insurgency and protecting the locals were vulnerable to IEDs and any local or imported fighter who sought to gain status by killing a foreigner.

On 13 March, the poppy and wheat crops were beginning to emerge and foliage was returning to the almond trees that proliferate the green belt at Kakarak, across the river from Sorkh Morghab. At 0900 a six-man Australian mentoring team had crossed the Dorafshan River and was moving through the fields in the company of a larger ANA patrol.

Just before 0930 the patrol saw the danger signs of women and children scurrying away, and at 0931 it came under fire from distances of 50 to 100 metres. Major David McCammon had joined the patrol to 'see how his teams were going . . . They [the insurgents] were prepositioned, attacking from three firing positions. Their use of ground is outstanding. They decide when and where to engage. While different to us in technique, they are not stupid. You quickly learn to tell the difference between farmers taking pot shots and the organised ones.'

These *were* the organised ones. Major McCammon and Lieutenant Jake Kleinman, to the rear of the patrol, were caught in the open. They felt the heat rise as further fire opened up from deeper to the west. Kleinman remembers being 'hammered'. Two years earlier at RMC he had been taught about the tactical pause, the importance of stopping and looking around. 'But there was no time. We did not take a breath. You are going at a million miles an hour. There is a time to fall apart. When you are in the middle of it is not the time.'

Recognising they were outnumbered, the Australians staged a fighting withdrawal. Kleinman was close enough to sight and shoot some of the enemy. Up ahead a group of Australian soldiers, among them Corporal Matthew Hopkins, raced for the cover of a compound. Well positioned behind a dirt mound at the eastern corner, Hopkins began to return fire. But then he suddenly stopped shooting.

Corporal Hopkins had been shot in the head. Without hesitation, medic Private David Cox sprinted 60 metres across open ground to render first aid. The radio call went in for air support and Medevac. A Dutch Apache appeared overhead but would not come close enough to fire. The Australians were far more impressed by the female American Special Forces pilot who, upon seeing they could not reach the assigned casualty evacuation point, put the Blackhawk's wheels down closer and within range of enemy fire.

Matthew Hopkins had been revived, but one hour on he showed no signs of life. The small Australian team, although distraught and exhausted, remained composed.

The Australians have mixed regard for their heavy body armour, which sometimes saves their lives and always weighs them down. During the battle one forward observer had gone down with heat exhaustion.

Lieutenant Kleinman couldn't speak more highly of his soldiers. 'They did everything required plus more. Private soldiers running sixty metres in open ground, Lance Corporals taking command. For all of them, the training kicks in. Great guys and fantastic soldiers.' Kleinman and McCammon, both later awarded Distinguished Service Medals, said much less about the ANA force, which remained inactive throughout the contact.

Corporal Leon Gray, who also fought with distinction in the Chora Valley action of December 2008, was close to Matthew Hopkins. 'I brought the casket back,' he said. 'Alex [Corporal Hopkins' son] has three hundred uncles now.'

The rise in civilian casualties brought changes to ISAF operating methodology. A new ISAF commander, US General Stanley McChrystal, took over in June 2009. He called for more judicious use of air power and a reduction in night raids. The two significant advantages held by the Coalition—the ability to strike from the air and own the night—would be therefore restrained. Coupled with an additional tithe of working with poorly trained partner soldiers, often unmotivated and sometimes outright treacherous, this meant Afghanistan did not get any easier. Anyone expecting otherwise was in the wrong place.

Soldiers, to a fault, are trained to remove from their vocabulary the words 'too hard'. Australian soldiers, having grown up with the legend of ancestors sticking it out against all odds at Gallipoli, were still keen to carry on. Even though they bitched about the ANA, rules of engagement and counter-insurgency, from many a conversation it was clear they also largely accepted a difficult deal.

Up close the Australians acknowledged the importance of the handover. Though the rules of engagement often frustrated them, they could see the point as well as take pride in adhering to the General McChrystal mantra of 'courageous restraint'. The counter-insurgency objective of standing between the population and the Taliban, while equally frustrating, was not a theory they could muse over while scanning a newspaper. It was a reality they lived with, and sometimes died by.

SOTG Rotation IX arrived, as usual, in stages and, as usual, went to work straight away. In one respect the tempo and challenges increased: SOTG was now extending operations beyond Uruzgan, and more often than not was partnered with Afghan forces. Showing an Afghan 'face' became a new refrain.

By now Special Forces in particular had experience to call upon. On his third tour, Sergeant Chook of 2 Commando Regiment (formerly 4RAR [CDO])[9] would encounter the most dramatic fighting to date. 'We went into northern Helmand. We fought for six days straight. We had indirect fire support. They had indirect fire support. They had heavy machine guns. We had heavy machine guns. It was large-scale offensive fighting.'

By crossing the border into Helmand, Australia embraced further risk. The southern province, with a heavier concentration of Taliban, had seriously taxed Coalition partners, the British losing seventeen soldiers killed in action in a single month.

Insurgent threat groups in Uruzgan, while operating largely in localised cells, had strong connections to larger groups. Taliban commanders in Uruzgan were used to slipping into Helmand for sanctuary, supplies and reinforcements. So in order to protect MRTF, Special Forces needed to stretch further.

Begun in March 2009, Operation Aabi Toorah aimed in a sense at cutting off at the pass the Taliban spring offensive. Afghan forces combined with British, American and Dutch forces; the Australians attacked the north Kijaki region.

Australia's first loss occurred before the campaign had barely begun. Force Element Echo, drawn from the Special Operations Incident Response Regiment, was clearing a route through Uruzgan's Chambarak Valley 50 kilometres north-west of Tarin Kowt. Early in the morning of 19 March one of the team found an IED, and Sergeant Brett Till was given the job of destroying it. He detonated an explosive charge without effect but, when moving back and kneeling to inspect the main charge, it exploded. At 0715 Sergeant Till suffered catastrophic injuries, becoming the tenth Australian soldier killed in action in Afghanistan.

Breanna Till, an art teacher, faced another battle. Pregnant at the time and caring for two children from her husband's previous marriage, she would now have to do so with the assistance of a meagre pension and the support of Legacy. Speaking later, the widow made this request: 'Don't use my lovely's death as a statistic or opportunity to push political agendas or argue the worth of our soldiers' role.'[10]

On 4 April Rotation IX came within a heartbeat of losing another soldier. Private Damien Thomlinson also suffered catastrophic injuries when in the middle of a night operation his special reconnaissance vehicle, a lightly protected Land Rover, drove over yet another IED.

With one leg blown from his body and another hanging by a thread, both arms broken and further significant injuries, the young Commando almost bled out, coming 'as close to death as could be'.[11] He was located in the dark by the sound of his breathing and saved only by his fitness and the combat first aid from other soldiers, including his close friend Private Scott Palmer.

The Australians also lost a Bushmaster after it tripped another IED. The better-protected vehicle took the punishment instead of its crew, but was damaged to a point that it had to be destroyed on site. The Australian Task Force encountered many more IEDs. On his second Afghanistan deployment, Corporal Dan counted more than 24. One soldier said it was almost pointless taking a vehicle because the constant mine detection meant they had to do so much walking.

The fighting wasn't all one-sided. The Australians also inflicted pain, confirming 87 enemies killed in action. On Anzac Day the Australian Defence Force proclaimed the excursion into northern Kijaki a 'rout', having taken the Taliban by 'surprise' and leaving its operations in 'disarray'.[12] The Kijaki fighting took the Australians a step away from irregular warfare.

For two weeks the Commandos worked their way into position and then fought for six straight days. Here the compounds were fortified with integrated defences: concreted gun positions, murder holes and defensive mines. 'If they had aircraft we would have been nigh on parity,' said one soldier.

Corporal Dan remembers enemy numbers being 'the heaviest I have ever seen. They were fully formed, and operated in depth, with mortar support and vehicle resupply.' He also observed the insurgents operating to 'gentleman's hours': fighting through the day, breaking for lunch and then resuming the attack, which would extend sometimes deep into the night.

In July 2009 MRTF1 transited out of Afghanistan. Commanded by a rangy Queensland bushie with an international pedigree, Lieutenant Colonel Shane Gabriel still drove a ute and spoke with a drawl when I met him. Prior to leading 7RAR to Afghanistan, he had experience with the British Army in Northern Ireland (before the ceasefire) and in Bosnia as a military observer.

Using words like 'gold dust' to describe the work he had seen, Gabriel believed freedom of movement for the Taliban had been curtailed. 'The local population became more secure. The significant patrolling tells them the insurgents are not as powerful.'

Unlike some of his colleagues, Lieutenant Colonel Gabriel believes the media should be out there telling the story of what Australia's soldiers are doing and achieving. He had allowed an ABC reporter, Thom Cookes, to follow his men into combat after Cookes failed to secure an embedding arrangement through Australian Defence Force in Canberra. According to Gabriel, 'The media has a right to be there. We have nothing to hide. It is not as if we go around burning villages and causing mayhem.'

In one area Gabriel was less happy with reporting of the war. Along with many of his men, he believed Australian media coverage consistently represented Special Forces as doing the fighting, ignoring the work of the Mentoring Task Forces. MRTF1 lost one soldier killed in action, and others returned to Australia with serious injuries. 'It could have been far worse. I am surprised some of my blokes are alive.'

The issue was alive within the ranks as well, with Major Jim Hammett challenging the Army's use of Infantry. In an article written for the *Australian Army Journal*, he asked: 'Have we entered an era that will foreshadow the decline of the Infantry Corps as the Army's fighting arm? Have the higher echelons of Special Forces shaped contemporary military and political thinking to a point where they alone are considered combat capable?'[13]

*

Midway through 2009, Lieutenant Colonel Peter Connolly led Australia's Second Mentoring and Reconstruction Task Force to relieve Shane Gabriel and MRTF1, continuing the mentoring work with the ANA's 4th Brigade. The 1RAR Battlegroup of 600 soldiers replaced the 7RAR Battlegroup. Again the Task Group was formed not only of Infantry but also other elements, notably from the Engineering and Armoured Corps.

There would, however, be a first on this tour; a female photographer was to accompany the men on patrol. 'When the boss was told a phot [photographer] was coming he said, what's his name?' Corporal Rachel Ingram recalls: 'When told Rachel, he said, "funny name for a bloke".'

Rachel, whose call sign was 'Snapshot', did not want to be treated differently. She accompanied the OMLTs patrolling through the Baluchi and Mirabad valleys, searching and clearing *quala*s. One patrol started at 0330 and finished at 2330.

Her gender was useful as MRTF2 assisted with preparation for the presidential election. Postponed by political disagreement until August, tension was high. With an expectation of attacks by suicide bombers, Rachel was able to help search the women at vehicle checkpoints. 'I was the first female soldier they had seen. They called me Miss Click-Click. Some were shaking, but when I touched them they calmed. Sometimes under the *burka*s I saw horrible injuries.'

Corporal Ingram caught a glimpse of a society over conditioned to violence, and over familiar with abuse of women. 'We took lollies for the kids. If we gave them to the girls the boys took them. I saw boys beating the girls.'

Rachel also saw children appropriated to the battlefield. On one patrol an alert Dutch Provincial Reconstruction Team officer saw a child acting out of the ordinary; kids don't usually sit still, but this one appeared to be positioned to signal when the soldiers arrived at a marker. Duly warned, the patrol Rachel was with backed off, waiting two hours in a cornfield as combat engineers probed the area. 'The EOD [Explosives Ordinance Disposal] found a twenty kilogram HE [high-explosive] charge containing live 7.62 rounds and ball bearings the size of marbles. It was cable initiated, a cord leading to a small hole in a *quala*. But the bomber got away.'

On 18 July Private Ben Ranaudo, a fresh faced 22 year old, was part of a cordon and search operation working from Combat Outpost Mashal in the Baluchi Valley, 27 kilometres north of Tarin Kowt. This time the IED caught the Australians and local nationals, detonating at 0647 near an aqueduct crossing point. Ranaudo, who had less than three years of soldiering, was instantly killed. His friend, Private Paul Warren, 'crawled for a while' searching for Ben, 'before I realised my leg was missing'.[14] An air medical evacuation in two flights carried the wounded private, his dead mate and three injured civilians, one of them a child, to Camp Holland.

Back in Australia, as with Damien Thomlinson, Paul Warren endured months of surgery and more months adapting to a prosthetic limb (one for Warren and two for Thomlinson). For Brett Till and Benjamin Ranaudo's families the grieving would last indefinitely.

By July 2009 4RAR (CDO) now 2 Commando Regiment had acquired a new role as well as a new name. Like the MRTF and others in SOTG, Corporal Dan became a mentor, the 'only white face' on some direct action missions.

The ANA soldiers, some of whom spoke good English, had been handpicked for Special Forces mentoring. They were given the same equipment as the Australians, and by Dan's account became so good he had nothing but confidence in them going into action. Dan observed how the Afghans could look at a mountain 'and see what we could not'. It was their country after all. He was impressed enough to begin to think 'this country has got a chance'. A number of other Australians witnessed much the same development.

This experience, however, was not always well shared. Other soldiers returning in 2009 gave accounts as varied as the uneven terrain. No one corner of Afghanistan mirrors with any reliability the story of another. Corporal Rachel Ingram described the ANA soldiers she worked with as 'like an under six soccer team with weapons'. On one patrol she saw an Afghan soldier hiding under a bush the RPGs he was supposed to be carrying. He looked at her and said: 'Too heavy.'

The Australians could also not help noticing Afghans skimming money, pinching and reselling petrol as well as smoking opium and marijuana. And homosexuality was formally condemned, but informally flaunted. The Australians became used to seeing ANA soldiers wearing eyeliner and nail polish; Thursday night was known as 'man love' night. The custom of commanders being attended by chai boys was not something they could readily tolerate.

Sergeant Adam West, a model of candour, told me: 'I honestly don't like the people. I don't agree with the way they live and their religious values. They lie, they cheat. I would not trust them as far as I could kick them. I would not leave any shiny, flashy kit about because it would be gone. But when five Australians and seventeen ANA are out there they are all you've got, so you have to trust them.'

Lieutenant Ben Gooley, who almost lost his life when the Afghans patrolling with him refused to fight, tried to see the bigger picture. 'You have to be realistic about the Afghan contribution. I don't think the less of them.'

The broader mission strained to focus on this bigger picture as the conflict approached its eighth year.

CHAPTER 10
'WE DIDN'T GET DRESSED UP FOR NOTHING'

You hear the throbbing of the Blackhawk's motors before you see it sweeping in across sparse scrubland. In the foreground is a mud brick *quala*. I watch from a safe distance, my attention drawn to a scurry of activity. Figures on the ground have also heard the helicopter, which becomes two and then another.

The first Blackhawk dips as if someone has thrown out an anchor, and settles about 400 metres from the *quala*. More figures scuttle from the open hatches before it touches ground. And within seconds, above the rotors, another sound arises—the rattle of gunfire.

The uniformed figures race from the Blackhawk as a man in robes climbs onto the *quala* roof, in one movement aiming and firing a rocket-propelled grenade towards the second helicopter which, unscathed, disgorges more troops.

By now the attackers have reached the gates of the compound. They do not stop. A white-robed fighter falls in the gateway. Shooting is heard for a few more minutes, and then as the echoes roll into the distant hills all that is audible is intermittent shouting.

When I advance to the compound I see what amounts to a crime scene. Soldiers are rounding up men, fingerprinting and photographing them and settling them with faces to the walls, hands cable tied. Women who have gathered in one of the rooms are moved to one side. They had been atop a concealed hatch, which is opened. More soldiers begin to probe the cellar.

This battle is the most detailed I've yet observed, for a simple reason. It has taken place in a barren corner of South Australia, at the Cultana training facility alongside the Spencer Gulf where the Australian Defence Force (ADF) has built a mini Uruzgan, complete with mud brick villages and Pashto-speaking locals. It did stop short of introducing the goats the locals wanted, for fear of them going feral. The site could come in handy to any future filmmaker scouting locations for an Afghanistan movie.

The scenario-training budget accommodates fees for extras and the casting could not be better. Afghan nationals, many of them recent arrivals to Australia, have been bussed in. Ironically, they take up residence not far from the old Baxter Detention Centre outside Port Augusta; it had housed some of them before it was closed in August 2007. Now it accommodates Special Forces soldiers engaged in mission rehearsal exercises before deployment to Afghanistan.

My access is a result of repeated requests to observe these missions from the start. The task forces form well before arrival in Afghanistan. Families of soldiers will often say that a tour is as much as doubled by the amount of time away training before they actually say goodbye.

A main aim of the mission rehearsal exercise is the infusion of corporate knowledge. The tour tempo is such that since Australia returned to Afghanistan in 2005, lessons were being learned and relearned. While the Australian public understandably sees the mission in Uruzgan as stuck fast in quicksand, the soldiers have an opposite view. To them the operations are dynamic and their enemy highly adaptive. The rehearsals are supposed to keep the reinforcement cycles in touch with every development.

Another objective is to fuse the elements that comprise the Task Force. The Infantry, Engineers, Armoured and Intelligence Corps, Headquarters Group and so on are brought together. So, too, does Special Operations forge its new Task Group comprising a troop from the Special Air Service Regiment (SASR) with a company of Commandos, a unit of the Incident Response Regiment and further support elements.

The soldiers won't always admit it, but they seem to love their toys and all the accoutrements. More than once I have heard them invoking the famous Braveheart line: 'We didn't get dressed up for nothing.'

Afghanistan is one of the toughest assignments on the media horizon. Just as a soldier climbs to an overwatch position prior to an operation, journalists try to do something similar. We strive for overview, which in Afghanistan is near impossible. You can't get a full picture sitting in on a press conference in Canberra any more than you can if you do find your way to a remote Uruzgan village and manage to question a local.

The truth is harder than usual to come by. Government and Defence fret over their hot issues briefs, and in doing so shape and misshape the truth. The Afghan villager does something similar. Only the superbly naive could expect more than a guarded response, if you do get an answer, on where they stand on the Taliban.

Following my first visit to Afghanistan in 2007, Chief of Defence Angus Houston expressed his frustration that the story of the mission was not getting through to the public. As a *Four Corners* reporter who pushed for long-form television coverage, I argued that such a complex story is not easily communicated through a series of 600 word newspaper articles, or 90 second television news reports.

At the time close-quarter media management by the ADF constrained coverage. News Limited reporter Ian McPhedran, with the experienced photojournalist Gary Ramage, had embedded with Mentoring and Reconstruction Task Force 2 (MRTF2) in 2009. So frustrated were they by the experience they wrote a report to the Defence Minister, complaining: 'The media should never be stopped from doing its job because a PR bureaucrat in Canberra has decided that nothing should move until the Minister has spoken to Parliament.'[1] McPhedran and Ramage had too much of their patience tested as they waited in patrol bases, restrained not only from the action but also from the story.

Like Ian McPhedran, I pleaded for improved access and the opportunity to build trust with the soldiers, a difficulty when contact is fleeting. It was on this basis that Angus Houston suggested I attend the mission rehearsal before joining the troops in theatre. He might have done so with trepidation. At the time the formerly tame subject of the mission rehearsal exercise had found its way to the top of the hot issues briefs. For one soldier, Cultana proved every bit as dangerous as Afghanistan.

On the night of 20 October 2009, Lance Corporal Mason Edwards, a thirty-year-old psychology graduate turned soldier preparing for his third tour of Afghanistan, became the victim of a fatal error. Edwards was shot in the head and a fellow Commando wounded. His team was in the wrong place, outside a building, when another team inside fired live rounds that penetrated the wall.[2] A series of inquiries found more flaws in mission preparation, but for Special Forces live fire would continue.

It was ironic that the death, in preparation for Special Operations Task Group (SOTG) Rotation XII, had occurred while Rotation X, still in theatre, would suffer no fatalities, the first SOTG to do so since Rotation IV in 2007. Some of the soldiers close to Mason Edwards wanted to come back early to attend the memorial services, but were told they still had a mission to complete.

No one saw the casualty record of Rotation X in the second half of 2009 as a result of anything but good luck. As with all deployments, there were plenty of close calls. Sergeant Brett Wood, wounded back in 2006, would keep from his partner Elvi the story of the two rounds deflected by his body armour during intense fighting in the Mirabad Valley.

There were more firsts for Rotation X. This was the primary deployment under the guise of 2 Commando Regiment and the initial deployment of Charlie Company, the Specialist Counter Terrorism unit that had until then formally remained in Australia on Tactical Assault Group (East) duties.

In Uruzgan, Charlie Company was able to sharpen its focus on man hunting, or the International Security Assistance Force's (ISAF) more tactful descriptor: counter leadership. The Mirabad Valley, which hugged Tarin Kowt's eastern fringe, was still a Taliban danger zone. Some high-value targets with strong influence on this region had taken to hiding out in Pakistan.

The targets were given code names frequently associated with weaponry. One such objective, considered responsible for many of the improvised explosive device (IED) attacks in the Mirabad area—such as the one that claimed the life of Lieutenant Michael Fussell—was vigorously pursued.

Having first spread the ink blots through the Baluchi and Chora valleys, ISAF was now turning to the Mirabad. Operation Castnet, as the name suggests, sought to gather in the objective along with other targets, such as objectives Switchblade and Quarterstaff. MRTF2 and the Afghan National Army (ANA), as touched on in the preceding chapter, joined the operation, staged with a further objective of establishing a more secure environment for the presidential election.

Between July and November ISAF fought a range of actions around Musazai and Sorkh Lez. The fighting, according to one four-tour veteran, was as fierce as ever seen. The insurgents, at first with confidence, grouped and engaged, attempting to outflank the Coalition forces.

The local fighters, operating in small groups, would carry limited ammunition, shoot from a well-concealed position in the green belt and then scoot. In doing so they would often hide one weapon before moving to another position, where they would resupply, collecting further weapons as well as additional ammunition.

The Australians responded with unanticipated vigour, determined to out-swarm the enemy. Over the ICOM Special Forces heard Taliban fighters crying out in panic as they in turn were outflanked.

The insurgents would not engage if the Coalition appeared in large numbers, which enabled an indelicate practice known to some as 'goat herding'. Using overwhelming force, ISAF would move through communities rounding up all the fighting age males. It hardly seemed the best way to meet the prime objective of winning the support of the population, but the locals did not always complain, some equally keen to remove troublemakers. And it sometimes worked.

After one such Castnet mission, early in August prior to the election, ISAF issued a press release revealing it had captured alive four of the targeted insurgent leaders. The ISAF capture and release policy meant persons under control could be held for no longer than 96 hours unless incriminating evidence was attached to the target. All four were handed on to the government of Afghanistan.

Charlie Company also crossed into Helmand and, as with Rotation IX, met more structured resistance, again in the Kijaki region. This time it travelled by helicopter, the Australians joining British and US Special Forces. The objective was again 'decapitation' of leadership, the various Special Forces Tier One operatives simultaneously targeting a range of leaders.

After a thirteen hour operation that killed nine insurgents, the Australians heard a message over the radio as they pulled back. Knowing the foreigners listened in, the Taliban announced 'this was the best fun we have had for a while. You are welcome back any time.'

Coalition forces now compromised an obligatory 30 per cent Afghan component. As with Rotation IX the Australians were impressed with handpicked ANA soldiers, but it was still a mixed story. During Ramadan the ANA would be sometimes taken along, but then left to wait under a tree. There was a practical concern that a weakened state, through lack of nourishment, could make them a liability. Conversely, because they were on a Jihad the Taliban were able to sidestep Ramadan strictures. Despite these problems, when the Australians left in November 2009 they had made many new friends, leaving behind gear such as boots for the not so well-equipped Afghans.

The Australian operations beyond Uruzgan were also advancing the reputation of Task Force 66. There was a lot of talk throughout the Coalition about the prowess of the Australians. I heard some of it, one American joking ISAF had become an acronym for 'I Saw Australians Fighting'.[3]

In November 2009 the winter rotation took over, again comprised principally of Reservists from 1 Commando Regiment. Force Element Charlie would be busy, determined to do more than 'give the vehicles a rest' as advised. According to one of the Commandos, 'we did a lot more counter-insurgency work', which meant 'talking our way out of a lot more battles'.

In northern Kandahar they entered country notorious for Taliban attacks. Taking the time to talk to elders, the Australians were told it was not the Taliban shooting at the foreigners but teenagers paid by drug traffickers protecting their businesses. One of the Commandos was moved by an account from one of the elders of a generation stunted by war. The man, who knew some English, lamented the fact that his grandchildren had no opportunity to learn anything but warfare and banditry. In tears he told the young Australian: 'We are becoming a nation of stupid people.'

In November 2009, the same month that Rotation XI arrived, I watch another battle. A mounted column of Australian soldiers in Bushmasters and light armoured vehicles is proceeding along a dirt track. As one Bushmaster draws level with an abandoned vehicle there is an explosion, followed by angry bursts of fire from the hills above.

One Australian soldier falls while running for cover. The machine gunner in the rear hatch of the Bushmaster struggles to return fire, his weapon repeatedly jamming. Pink smoke begins to swirl along the track, masking the action. Turning away from the smoke I see groups of uniformed men, in concentrated scrutiny, as if on the hill at the footy.

Not far distant is the equivalent of an outside broadcast van. Within it another group of soldiers peers into screens, punching in data on keyboards and calling instructions via radio. One of them is Major Simon Moore-Wilton, who had been awarded a Distinguished Service Medal for his part in a real life version of a similar battle in 2007. Also doing his bit to advance collective memory is Sergeant Michael Lyddiard, who survived an IED attack in the same year.

That was the idea of this staged battle on the Townsville High Range. Using an area similar at least in size to the Uruzgan area of operations, fighting already experienced was being electronically replicated. A force of 2000 was scattered among the gum trees; so too were 94 portaloos. Mock patrol bases and over 50 *qualas* were set up, mimicking those in the Baluchi Valley. A training audience acting as civilian, Taliban and ANA role players joined a battle group drawn in the main from Brisbane-based 6RAR. Mentoring Task Force One (MTF1) was preparing for its February 2010 deployment.

The R from MRTF had been removed. Reconstruction and development had become more the responsibility of AusAID. The Australian Federal Police were also now providing training support. For sometime there had been eagerness to take pressure off Defence and apply more of a whole of government approach to the mission. But as would be discovered, movement beyond Tarin Kowt without a mass of heavy weapons was still unwise.

On the Townsville High Range, soldiers got the best taste of battle the scenario trainers could manage, albeit without having to duck live bullets. Every soldier wore body armour fitted with electronic sensors, which determined whether they had been hit and if by enemy or friendly fire.

I watch as the soldier struck down early in the fighting is given first aid. An Army doctor advances from the surrounding scrub for the sake of a closer diagnosis, before offering advice to the crouched combat first aiders. Another observer trainer then appears with a small device known as a 'God gun'. When triggered, the soldier who suffered simulated gunshot wounds is simulated back to life in order to resume the exercise.

Major Jason Groat commands Mentoring Team Alpha. As is the way in the Army, I suspect he has been volunteered to look after me and the *Four Corners* crew of Neale Maude and Shane Munro. To a middle ranking officer, management of a media crew is a potential career killer.

We stay two nights on the High Range. Some of the soldiers are friendly, but most move for safer cover when I approach. In the fading light they warm a touch, amused by our novice efforts to erect the camp stretchers and operate the tiny key-like can opener sometimes known as Fred (Fucking Ridiculous Eating Device). Ration packs are broken out: baked beans, a muesli bar, tuna, freeze dried rice, biscuits, a tin of cheese, matches and a scouring pad they muse about using for roughage.

After the mission rehearsal, MTF1 will have time with their families over summer. Over in Uruzgan, MRTF2 is shivering through a white Christmas. Like the SOTG, the Task Force was pushing further into the Mirabad Valley. By December, Operation Baz Panje, in partnership with the ANA, uncovered 62 weapons caches.

In January 2010 members of Mentoring Team Alpha, bound for the Mirabad, gathers with family for a farewell parade and a barbeque within Gallipoli Barracks in Brisbane. Outside the front gate a pair of brave demonstrators hold high anti-war placards. Inside, Commanding Officer Lieutenant Colonel Jason Blain hands out 'For Our Families' badges. They bear the inscription: 'Our strength and support at home'. The new Commanding Officer, having once studied journalism, does not seem so troubled by the prospect of hosting a television crew. An important audience will be the 780 families of the servicemen and women about to depart. I don't understand this so well at the time but will come to see how right he is. I am yet to fully understand how much Australian soldiers prefer a third party explaining what they do rather than do it themselves.

There is a formal parade and speeches. The uniformed assembly is thanked for its service and wished a safe and speedy return. On the neighbouring recreation ground, sausages are being barbequed, splattered in red and wrapped in slices of white bread.

Squeezing close for photographs Private David Deitz, with his wife Kathy and two boys, tells me he had planned on getting out to finish his nursing degree. 'But I love the job, always have, I love being an Infantry soldier.' Heading off on his fourth overseas tour, Deitzy says, 'After this trip that is going to be it.'

In that same month I get a glimpse, if brief and choreographed, of the 6RAR-based Task Force's more clandestine partner force when I am invited without camera to attend a demonstration at Special Forces' new urban warfare training facility at Holsworthy in New South Wales. It is another live fire exercise. At this time, SOTG Rotation XII is preparing to relieve the 1 Commando winter rotation, another to bring everyone home without significant casualties.

On a back lot in an old barracks area is an urban battle block, and a mock village lined with shipping containers. There are street signs—Bank Street, Retail Street, Shop Road and so on—as well as men in black suits with guns. They burst from bullet-proof LandCruisers carrying suppressed M4s, a breaching ladder and chainsaw. One team blows the door of a mock embassy, and seconds later another team is seen on the roof. The embassy capitulates. I would, too.

They are impressive, like mythical warriors firing thunderbolts from their fingertips. At an indoor range lined with ballistic curtains, another team demonstrates its precision assault skills, weaving and firing and making a well-practised distinction between pop-up models of hostage and hostage takers.

The assault teams are close enough for empty cartridges to bounce off onlookers. Among the spectators are Duntroon cadets who have just finished the enervating Shaggy Ridge exercise. They still look a little pale.

While all soldiers are subjected to irregular weapons proficiency testing, Special Forces soldiers must be proficient at all times. To validate pistol use they are required, while wearing a gas mask, to enter a room and within two seconds twice hit a target the size of a teacup at a distance of 15 metres.

Despite the now more apparent danger of using real bullets, the live fire exercises are seen as vital. When conducting advance close quarter battle drills, Special Forces need to promote not only the feel of combat, but also situational awareness. One soldier explains it as like being on an Aussie Rules field where you develop a 360° sense of all that is around you, friend or foe, before committing ball (or in this case bullet).

The skills and weaponry on show build a picture of the soldier as a killing machine. After all, this is what many millions of taxpayer dollars trains them to do. But the Afghanistan mission was also calling for an opposite set of skills. An ISAF confidential directive from this period acknowledged the war was not going well. 'Nearly eight years of international presence has not brought the anticipated benefits. The Afghan people are sceptical and unwilling to commit active support to either side until convinced who will win.'

The report conceded the insurgency was better at adapting to local conditions: 'They claim to protect Afghan culture and religion . . . they use inappropriate ISAF actions to support their argument.' The ISAF saw its conflict 'as an argument with the insurgents for credibility', with the people as the audience.

The report also called for a change in the way the soldiers acted, thought and operated. 'A military force, culturally programmed to respond conventionally (and predictably) to insurgent attacks, is akin to a bull that repeatedly charges a matador's cape—only to tire and eventually be defeated by a much weaker opponent. This is predictable—the bull does what comes naturally. While a traditional military approach is instinctive, this behaviour is self-defeating.'[4] It cited examples of how the ISAF could anger locals by cutting down trees that provided a livelihood, and by responding to provocation designed to trigger violence and cause injury among the innocent.

While the ink blots of security were soaking further outward from Tarin Kowt, the locals were also fed up with foreigners entering their compounds uninvited. The destruction of poppy crops and blindfolding, handcuffing and dragging away their workforce could also play into enemy hands.

Sometimes disputes and compensation claims were impossible to arbitrate. A farmer would claim a vehicle destroyed in fighting had been co-opted by the Taliban. Others would say the man was an active Taliban supporter.

By 2010 Special Forces was expected to do more than just mow the grass and improve on the Russians, well remembered by survivors from the 1980s for shooting up everything.

The Cultana training range in South Australia might not seem an ideal location for a lesson in Uruzgan geopolitics, but after the staged raid a cast of locals still in costume oblige. Playing the part of the insurgent, the innocent, the tax collector or the cop is for them not much of a stretch—they have seen it all. In a mock marketplace selling counterfeit DVDs they gather, surrounding me with stories of a brother who had been executed, of a cycle of honour and revenge killings, as well as tribal bloodshed that has spilled over generations.

From the Hazara tribe, Sakhi had come from a village in Khas Uruzgan that had also been home to his father and grandfather. 'No go back Afghanistan,' he says. 'If go back Afghanistan, Taliban kill me.'

This group, now safe from all but simulated violence, prove to be most vocal supporters of the Australian mission. Their rudimentary English is enough to convey heartfelt gratitude, tinged with surprise that Australians would risk their own lives in such a place.

The Army requires a lot of paperwork; it seemed to go on for months. One of the forms to fill out is titled 'Proof of Life', in case we come to need those hostage rescue skills earlier

witnessed. We also had to complete a hostile environment course and medical checks.

Although we will be transported and accommodated by the ADF, the assignment is still expensive. It costs around $20,000 to insure the crew for the month we will be away. The ADF applies a maximum threat level classification to Afghanistan, awarding its personnel an additional $141.36 a day tax free. In contrast, the ABC asked that we take a reduced travel allowance, advancing the rationale that we would have no use for it. There are many reasons to explain why Afghanistan is under reported; this is one. The highly remunerated jobs in journalism are not generally associated with risk taking. And for the ABC, an additional cost came with the hiring of a separate crew to gather additional material not so easily reached from within the ADF perimeter.

On 18 May 2010 we gathered at Sydney airport to be met by an assigned escort officer, Major Andrew Sommerville. He had not been to Afghanistan before and had no experience of working with the media. Although his role was not clear, Andrew was personable and keen to help.

The chartered Strategic Airways flight to a 'secret location somewhere in the Middle East' via Darwin is crowded with young short-haired men wearing T-shirts revealing a mixed mosaic of sleeve tattoos, many returning after their relief out of country leave. This meant around eleven days back in Australia with families, and an accumulated week of travel on either side. Was it worthwhile giving yourself and your family a taste of being home to then have it snatched away? Some thought not. Others, particularly the 'singlies', chose to holiday out of country, say, in Europe.

Camp Mirage, a staging area leased by the Australian government and situated alongside a military airfield at Al Minhad in the United Arab Emirates, is more or less an open secret. It is also a 'furnace'. However, in the modern Army an air conditioner is generally never too far away. We have sheets and a pillow and are directed to huts marked 'Bourke', 'Bondi', 'Bundaberg', 'Kinglake' and 'Marysville'.

In a large mess hall, also air conditioned, a tall man directly in front of me in the breakfast queue appears familiar. Waiting his turn behind privates and Lance Corporals is Chief of Army, Lieutenant General Ken Gillespie. I am impressed, perhaps less by the absence of privilege as the way the other diners respond. Seeing nothing remarkable in this, they greet him with 'How ya going, sir?' before moving on.

In briefings we are told the Afghan National Police are still a 'brake on progress'. Recruited locally, they are particularly prone to family and tribal influence. The most effective way the Coalition had found to minimise corruption was to bypass government and work directly with locals. But the locals are still guarded with outsiders, preferring to deal with their own despite the corruption.

A young Lieutenant Colonel, Jason Logue, who first saw Afghanistan with Special Forces in 2005, introduces me to a military concept applicable to a battlefront littered with contradiction. 'The shooter-hugger transition', he explained, is something US Marines grappled with in Iraq, needing to switch from fight mode to support mode once they entered a village after the insurgents had left.

We are kitted with helmets and body armour and then spend a day on an IED training course. And there is a change from 2007; this time, the thinking is to not differentiate military camouflage. The non-combatant blue previously worn is now considered to draw rather than deviate fire.

The IED training is a grim affair. Part of it is familiarisation with how the roadside bombs are typically assembled and concealed. Walking the range behind an engineer with the face of a boy, his experienced eye is trained to see what to the rest of us is invisible: a faint thread of wire, a rock positioned as a marker.

Why is an IED made of fertiliser and old bits of plumbing and bike chain bits more frightening than military-grade explosives? Photographs of victims who appear to have fallen prey to a crazed butcher show horrible injuries. The clinically shining factory produced NATO ordinance must do much the same.

The tactical combat casualty course conducted by American ex-military contractors requires a mental and emotional leap. Here in the classroom or, as is explained, out there on the battlefield, there is no hiding down the back. There is no predicting who will be injured, and who else will be called on to provide trauma assistance.

We are taught the obligatory nine-liner code for calling an emergency evacuation and the basics such as how to apply the individually issued tourniquets and bandages. Then, in a darkened space, with the simulated sound of gunfire and amidst the wreckage of vehicles and blood-soaked dummies, we are each tested. The trainers are correctly uncompromising. News comes in of another IED strike on this same day.

As a journalist, professional detachment is essential, but detachment from reality disastrous. Complacency is something sensibly left behind.

CHAPTER 11
SNOWY AND SMITHY

The RAAF delivers us to Multinational Base Tarin Kowt, as it was now known, on Sunday 23 May 2010. Australia's reach and influence is still tiny, and the forthcoming Dutch withdrawal means the Australian Task Force, now climbing towards 1500 personnel, will be more thinly spread.

Neale Maude, Shane Munro and I are dropped at steel chalets resembling cell blocks, the reason for the hardened accommodation being the intermittent 107 mm rocket attacks. My block still bears scars along the lattice iron staircase from a hit two weeks earlier.

By this stage I have developed a mostly positive view of the Australian soldier, finding them generally to be more worldly and intelligent than most people seem to realise. I admire their honest capability as well as understated sense of duty. But this is not a romantic view. As we drag our bags from the back of a truck I see a digger living up to his name. He is sweating on a Sunday, shovelling dirt in baking heat because somebody has ordered him to do so. And in the welfare hut graffiti by the phone reads: 'I am the master of my fate. I am the captain of my soul. Then I joined the Army and they took it all away.'

The torment of company is one of many career-shortening features of service life. Accommodation is tight, so each of us is assigned not so much a room as a bed. Behind a bank vault-like door is a steel box with four bunks. There are no windows nor is there cupboard space. Shiftwork means someone is probably sleeping, so I try to be quiet and avoid stepping on the face of the soldier below as I haul myself onto a top bunk. There is more graffiti: 'Dear 6RAR. Enjoy getting fucked on, blown up and shot at just like we did. Love 1RAR.'

In the briefing room the Regimental Sergeant Major (RSM), Tiny Colman, looms on the stage like a circus strongman. Warrant Officers have a language of their own or, more to the point, speak the common language of the soldier. One example so far collected is of a large parade presided over by a RSM. In a pause before the ceremony resumes he bellows an instruction that the assembly is now permitted to 'Speak shit'.

Here, as we sit among new arrivals, Tiny lays down the law about uniform codes and banned goods with a practised mix of charm and intimidation. He does not like baseball caps: 'If I see you with one you will pay.' And he preaches abstinence: 'If you think you are going to smuggle alcohol in, fill your boots, I don't give a fuck. I love a challenge.'

The first sequence we film for our *Four Corners* report is of a ramp ceremony. At Camp Holland, standing deep in fine, grey dust, Afghan, Dutch and Australian soldiers line the roadside to the airport as another coffin makes its way home. For the Royal Netherlands Army it is the 24th. Corporal Luc Janzen was killed on 22 May when his thin-skinned Mercedes Benz four-wheel drive rolled over an improvised explosive device (IED) near Deh Rawood.

The ramp ceremony curiously calls to mind images of the Great War, when Australians were sometimes noted for standing a head taller than their British cousins. Here it is different. Looking along the columns, the Dutch, said to be from the tallest nation on earth, unmistakeably stand above the Australians and positively dwarf the Afghans.

We do not stay long in Tarin Kowt, and for this I am grateful. A decision has been made to send us forward to a new patrol base. And considering all the complaints from the previous year of the media being cotton wooled, we are instead heading for the badlands.

The active patrolling of the Mirabad by the Special Operations Task Group (SOTG), the Mentoring Task Force and the Afghan Security Forces in the preceding months is aimed at spreading Coalition influence up the valley, emulating the inch-by-inch gains in the neighbouring Baluchi and Chora valleys.

Mentoring Team Alpha, first met at the mission rehearsal six months earlier, now occupies two patrol bases in the Mirabad: Atiq, 8 kilometres from Tarin Kowt, and Wali, a further 8 kilometres distant. In Afghanistan 16 kilometres equates as another century.

We board a US Blackhawk helicopter. A door gunner scans the barren ridges as we clip low along the green belt. It takes minutes in a straight line to travel what could take nine hours in an armoured convoy, weaving through the *dascht*, avoiding choke points and set paths, with mine labs and sniffer dog on foot out front.

Patrol Base Wali is like a Wild West fort. In keeping with population-centric counter-insurgency operations it clings to the village of Nayak, on the northern edge of the green zone. On Cav Hill, perched above, is an Australian Light Armoured Vehicle (ASLAV) with an imposing 25 mm cannon, manned 24 hours a day and positioned for protection in case the insurgents attempt to swarm the ramparts.

Visible from the hill on the other side of the green zone, half a kilometre away, is another military outpost. It stands alongside a vehicle checkpoint manned by Afghan Security Forces with oversight from a section of Australians.

The 191 soldiers of Mentoring Team Alpha are split between the two bases, alongside companies of Afghan National Army (ANA) soldiers and a small Dutch Provincial Reconstruction Team (PRT). The Australian component at Wali is an amalgam of Infantry, Engineers and other specialists, one a Navy clearance diver, another a RAAF bomb disposal expert.

Company Sergeant Major Tas McGinley, last seen three years earlier, shows us to our quarters. Space is again an issue, so we are given one-man tents to erect out among the camel spiders. I draw a smaller version, and my bunk won't fit. Showing a bare trace of pity, Tas leads me to the neighbouring hab (hardened accommodation block), where I am able to 'hot bunk'. One of the sappers, Section Commander Corporal Jeremy Pahl, is taking his relief out of country leave.

The air-conditioned tent has space for about twelve bunks. Each area is customised, with towels and flags, pin-ups and empty mail cartons not yet ready to be thrown away; hung clothing forms meagre partitions. The smell is a musty mix of canvas, body odour and air conditioning. My new roomies, not much progressed from adolescence, live in the way of teenage boys. No mother's touch to be found here.

As I release the air valve on my tiny mattress, a small head appears to inspect and sniff this stranger. Herbie, the explosive detection dog (EDD), is being given a rest from the kennels. The next face to appear belongs to his handler, Sapper Darren Smith. At 25, he is a little older than most in the hab.

Shy and thoughtful, Sapper Smith is another example of a soldier not conforming to the stereotype. Although a 'reo', or reinforcement, Smithy has melded with the already formed group, his quick wit and easy nature deflecting relentless banter. He is keen for Herbie to do well.

The Officer Commanding, Major Jason Groat, emerges from the command post. We are welcome inside at any time and have an open invitation to every daily briefing. I am grateful and surprised. The job of the Mentoring Task Force (MTF) is to be an International Security Assistance Force (ISAF) beat cop. Major Jason Groat has eight months to make an impact on behaviour shaped by centuries. There is a lot of patrolling and trouble literally at the doorstep; in the week before our arrival two IEDs exploded 200 metres from the front gate, injuring ANA soldiers and a local teenager. But more immediately, we are distracted by a crackling noise.

Soldiers in shorts and T-shirts pull on body armour, pick up weapons and race for the parapets. We collect our gear and do likewise. Someone is taking pot shots; 25 to 30 rounds are fired. An Australian peering through telescopic sights tells me 'they often have a crack'. From somewhere out in the green it is as if we are being told, 'You might have moved in, but don't think the fight is over.'

It was not—there had been multiple troops in contact incidence since Mentoring Team Alpha arrived. One was on 23 March, when a mixed patrol of Australians and Afghans threaded single file and well spaced through a wheat field, heading west towards the village of Sorkh Lez. Captain Aaron Cimbaljevic was the 23rd man in a column of 26.

'Cimba', a former Australian Services rugby fullback, said the bomb blast was 'like being tackled by a dozen Pacific Islanders'.

It had been remotely detonated, the Taliban probably targeting the officers. Although no one wears conspicuous badges of rank in the field, the signaller's radio antenna, never too far from the commander, can be a give away.

On the ground bleeding and concussed, with a swallowed tongue and multiple fragmentation wounds, the nine liner was called in. The Blackhawk arrived, and 56 minutes on Cimba was on the operating table at Tarin Kowt. With wounds to his hand, face and hip and some ringing still in his ears, he was returned to Australia.

Eight days after the IED attack Cimba's mate 'Polly', Captain Callum Pollock, was shot in one of the many gun fights that erupt outside the wire. To the grand amusement of his fellows, the bullet exited close to his bum. There was ongoing debate about whether the Taliban or the ANA was responsible for the additional crease. By the time the *Four Corners* team arrived the two captains were back at work, recovered from their wounds and anxious to see the deployment through.

While Patrol Base Wali was a safe harbour, it was not meant to lock troops within. ISAF had advised: 'Get to know the neighbourhood. Learn who is the most successful farmer and why, who feels excluded and why, and which families are the most powerful and who they are united to by marriage. Be a positive force in the community, shield the people from harm, and foster normalcy.'[1]

Australian Special Forces Major Ian Langford noted at the time: 'Australian Infantry and Special Forces have a reputation amongst their foreign colleagues for having a specific and unique focus on ground patrolling and physical presence as a mechanism for establishing security, rather than through alternative methods such as "free fire zones" and through the application of firepower as a means to control and dominate key terrain.'[2]

On 29 May another patrol, this time from Mentoring Team Alpha's other Mirabad Valley base Atiq, heading east towards Sorkh Lez came under attack. The comparatively minor confrontation provides a telling close up of opposing forces, as well as a broader portrait of the nature of battle.

In preceding months the residents of the Mirabad had watched the foreigners come and take their young men away in the hope of identifying the enemies within. The enemy would then come and drop night letters threatening retribution for any collaboration. It is likely, however, that most residents preferred the foreigners and the government for beginning to deliver education, health care and at least the promise of public safety. PRTs were providing pipes and generators, seeds and funding to help stimulate the local economy and goodwill.

Locals had been sneaking into the patrol base at night to tell of Taliban recruiting young men and offering weapons and money. But they also required an accommodation with the Taliban because experience told them the insurgents would still be around when the outsiders were long gone. The outsiders also found it easy to reach their own accommodation, and to recognise without any words spoken how far a patrol should go before it sensibly returned to base.

To the consternation of the mentored Afghan soldiers, the Australians sometimes took the view that it was their job to press too far. That is what happened to the Atiq patrol. As it pushed beyond the village of Musazai, bullets and rockets began to streak across the river from the direction of a compound. The Australians were not allowed to shoot into the homes of villagers unless they were certain of where the attack emanated; sighting gun flashes from above a *quala* wall at a distance of 200 metres, the patrol returned fire. Once the shooting abated, it advanced on the ambush site to find a blood trail leading to an irrigation canal and one of the snipers shot through the eye. He was aged about sixteen or seventeen.

An older man appeared, presumed to be the father of the victim. He claimed the body without comment and the Coalition soldiers returned to their base. In subsequent days no locals came to the patrol base to complain. Villagers were observed on one of the hilltops conducting a funeral for two young men, the second fighter evidently having succumbed to wounds. Cemeteries with gravesites marked by clusters of sticks tied with rags were often seen on hilltops, the green ribbons denoting a martyr's death.

ISAF had been waiting a while for a tipping point, when the locals would turn on the Taliban. It came at last late in April 2010, and, as it happens, in the Australian area of operations. Gizab, in the north of the province, had long been known for its 'hot gates'—the fusillade of Taliban fire that could be anticipated upon approach.

The citizens of Gizab, some of them the oppressed Hazara tribe sick of being taxed and robbed, gathered up weapons and began arresting Taliban. When shooting followed, they called for reinforcements. The American Operational Detachment Alpha, a twelve-man A team of Special Forces soldiers operating close by, could not get there in time because of a swollen river. But the Australian Special Forces swooped in, according to Matiullah Khan, arriving 'within half an hour'.

MK, as Khan is known throughout Uruzgan, was proving as influential as he is controversial. To some in ISAF, MK represented another tipping point: no one worked the levers of power in the province quite so well as he did. The Lord of the Highways (another soubriquet) ran a protection racket. According to a US House of Representatives report of the time: 'Every contractor assigned to take U.S. supplies to Uruzgan exclusively uses Matiullah's security services at a cost between $1,500 and $3,000 per truck, per mission.'[3]

The local warlord had been working with the SASR and US Special Forces for some time. Efforts were being made to legitimise him by making him police chief and drawing him more clearly into the clutches of the Government of the Republic of Afghanistan. The background machinations helped deliver the Gizab dividend.

MK's 2000-strong private army became the Provincial Police Reserve (PPR), which helped hunt the Taliban from Gizab. 'We and Australia together,' MK said, 'and also Americans, penetrated the locals and we helped them to arrest the Taliban leaders.'[4]

ISAF was delighted. The local Taliban commander, Mullah Atiqullah, and two of his deputies were captured. The *Washington Post* reported a US commander citing the mutiny at Gizab as 'perhaps the most important thing that has happened in southern Afghanistan this year'.[5]

While some other villages followed suit, the revolt of the 'Gizab Good Guys' did not reach as far as hoped. And nor perhaps had Coalition influence, with local factors probably at least as instrumental in the success. Still, for the SASR in particular, Gizab was a notable victory.

In other respects the SOTG's Rotation XII seemed blighted. Weeks earlier, on 10 April, one of the Commandos, Private Steve, went to the shooting range alongside Camp Russell to test his 40 mm grenade launcher. A round fell short, a splinter of shrapnel striking another Commando in the face. The wound was fortunately slight, but the outcome severe.

Since Mason Edwards' death during preparation for this rotation, concern about weapons discipline had heightened. Private Steve had tested his grenade launcher without authorisation, and would later face a court martial; he was charged with grievous bodily harm and unauthorised discharge of a weapon.[6]

On 28 April there was more trouble for 2 Commando when Private Daniel, also from Alpha Company, was found unconscious in his shared room. Protein supplements, in common use, were discovered along with pills and white powder, and a toxicology test detected traces of opiates. There was suspicion of illegal drug use.

Soldiers in Afghanistan have significant exposure to masses of raw heroin and marijuana, often recovered from caches and easily purloined. Within an extreme body conscious environment, steroid abuse was an even more pressing concern. Banned supplements could be purchased by mail order. One American had already overdosed at Tarin Kowt, his body returned to the US without the tribute of a ramp ceremony.

Private Daniel was flown to Germany for treatment, and then returned to Australia. Up until this point the Commando had a strong reputation, having been awarded a Commendation for Gallantry after rescuing a comrade during Rotation VI. The incident cast a large shadow over the regiment back in Australia and at Camp Holland.

On the night before the private was found unconscious, there had been (to use the vernacular) a 'piss up'. Within the Camp Russell enclave there was particular consideration for Special Forces, for whom greater discretionary use of alcohol was allowed. The rationale was that intense combat experiences called for opportunities to decompress, as long as the soldiers were sensible and didn't overdo it. However, management could have been better, with resentment already on the rise. Soldiers walking the dirt road outside Camp Russell did not take well to Special Forces guys sitting above the Hesco on home-renovated balconies, kicking back with a beer.

The inquiry into Private Daniel's alleged drug overdose took two years to complete, with no charge being laid. The Commando had choked on his vomit after a bout of heavy drinking. The trace of opiate in his system was consistent with medication used to revive him.

The dust kicked up by the incident further hardened existing resentment. Alcohol restriction across the entire Australian deployment was strengthened, and 300 Special Forces soldiers were subjected to drug tests. Within Camp Russell, long simmering animosity between the Commandos and the SASR ignited, with misgivings about Commandos behaving like cowboys gaining currency. Some of Force Element Alpha declared they would not work with the boys from Bravo.

Not that the charge sheet of the SASR could be seen as spotless. On Rotation X, one of its members was returned to Australia after setting a booby trap in the ready room, annoyed that other members of the team appeared to be interfering with his gear. The Nico distraction grenade found its mark, splinters from the shredded benchtop slightly injuring another trooper.

Out in the valleys where the MTF was scattered, there were also problems. One soldier was returned after his girlfriend ended their relationship over the phone and he began talking about turning his weapon on himself.

For our first patrol, an information operation, we take the back gate. It is a neighbourhood watch patrol, at night, towards Sorkh Lez; the

Taliban have been distributing 'night letters'. One of the interpreters, after introducing himself as a 'motherfucker Afghan rock star', translates a letter that has been recovered. It threatens a local farmer because of his 'good relations with the Americans and the National Army'. The Taliban make clear its intention to find the farmer and 'cut out your abdomen, brain and knees and kill you'.

Major Jason Groat wants the insurgents and the locals to know that the Taliban don't own the night. Ninety-five per cent of the patrolling is dismounted and we thread through fields, avoiding the footpads where IEDs are more likely placed. We cross many irrigation canals, but getting your feet wet has an upside: the Taliban has not yet figured out a way to manufacture a waterproof mine.

It is peaceably quiet. The rustle of wheat stalks, the bark of a dog, the trickle of irrigation. We are advised to keep a safe distance and watch out for kite strings, which are sometimes used to trigger the bombs. I can make out some of our soldiers via the moonlight and the green glow of their night-vision goggles. Locals, too, are seen, illuminated by camp fire. They often work their fields at night, when it is cooler. We slump in a wet paddock and watch until distracted by the brilliance of the night sky, so clear we can follow the arc of satellites. Before midnight we head back, pausing 400 metres from the base to advise of our approach so the ANA soldiers don't shoot at us.

There have been many patrols, 500 so far, after four months. In the same period, 75 weapons caches have been found. Jason Groat strains for the long game, seeking out local leaders and settling down with chai to ask about maybe building an all-weather river crossing or paving a section of road.

Sometimes we are greeted as friends; sometimes the farmers remonstrate about the soldiers having shot an angry guard dog or damaged crops as they cross the fields. The soldiers in turn explain they needed to avoid the footpads, as the laying of IEDs is a risk to themselves as well as the locals. At times the patrols target suspected caches, or operate to disrupt freedom of movement for the insurgents; sometimes it is for key leadership engagement and medical civil aid programs (MEDCAPs).

ISAF has found one of the most useful weapons delivered to these remote communities is through MEDCAPs. A young Lance Corporal, Joel Hughes Brown (anyone in the Army with a double barrel surname is inevitably known as 'Two Dads'), assists in these programs. He reports chronic health problems; the children are generally riddled with intestinal worms.

The locals' conditioning to routine violence has influenced the medic's understanding of the environment. 'You come back a little more crazy and develop a dark sense of humour. When I see kids hurt it shatters me. Kids don't deserve to be stabbed or shot.' Joel has just treated a fourteen-year-old boy with stab wounds to his head, inflicted by his brother. 'They escalate from zero to a one hundred per cent. A petty squabble turned to the brother trying to cut off his ear with a blunt knife. The father intervened and raced him to me.' There are many such stories.

While it also advances risk, an important dividend from all this engagement is an improvement in information flow. MTF1 lifts the volume and reach of patrols, with the sappers conventionally leading the way. Smithy moves forward as Herbie bounds back and forth, seeming to live for these moments out there with the boys. Snowy, distinctive even under his helmet for his shock of white hair and beard, is never far distant. Their call sign is 'Echo One One Alpha'.

The engineers are accompanied by the gunslingers, a section of Infantry providing force protection led by Corporal Brian Jenkins.

India One Two is a very tight group, each a component of a living whole: a machine gunner, a medic, a signaller and a scout. They have trained together for eighteen months. A glimpse inside their hab reveals no partitions.

The gunslingers sometimes get into gun fights, particularly when they press far. The insurgents will instigate 'come ons', usually from a distance, trying to draw the soldiers onto mined ground. They tell me the Taliban is 'good at what they do. They have been doing it for centuries. They are not afraid to die.'

An old hand is in attendance. Call sign 'Stonecutter 06', is the joint terminal attack controller and Alpha Company's most active patroller—not bad for a forty-eight year old. Warrant Officer Kevin Dolan, who has seen fighting in Northern Ireland, Kosovo and Iraq, transferred from the British Army Royal Marines prior to mandatory retirement. He tells me the constant nature of the combat here makes it 'the worst I have seen in thirty years of Army life'.

When Alpha Company arrived in February an icy wind howled through Wali, the temperature falling to –17°C. Now in May it is nudging 50°C. Standing at the back gate watching the gunslingers return heaving 40 kilogram loads I see Jorgo, a tall red-headed private, pitch over. He is carrying the heavy electronic counter measures pack and not wanting to ask anyone else to carry the load, he had waited until the gunslingers were home before collapsing.

The ANA, isolated in its own corner of the base, is joined with most patrols. Mentor liaison officer Captain John Crockett runs an energetic and impassioned defence of the Afghans; he says you can't expect them to operate to the level of the Australians because they have neither the education nor training. This is the same in the Australian Army, where different units, such as Special Forces, have different levels of training.

I see the ANA's reputed observational strengths up close. On a patrol, one of the Afghan engineers spots a thread of wire in a rock wall. (The Taliban often secrete the IED charge, but wait until a target approaches before connecting the battery pack.) A decision is made to 'BIP' it, that is, blow the IED in place. Sitting behind a low wall about 200 metres away we hear a dull thud, the sluggish ignition of non-military grade explosives. A plume of white smoke spirals skyward as we are showered with rocks and dirt.

There have also been non-combat problems with the ANA soldiers. The Australian medics at Wali have treated them for opiate overdose and sexually transmitted diseases. One soldier tells me 'you can't make this shit up' as he relates a story of an ANA soldier returning to base reporting he had suffered a broken jaw after being attacked by a demon. He later adjusted the story to say he had been attacked by two genies—a female one with fangs, and a male one with a beard. 'I am happy to report his jaw is okay and the straitjacket fits well,' the soldier says.

Efforts are made to integrate both camps. Cookie Corporal Peter Barber puts on a curry night. The ANA soldiers bring out a range of coloured rugs and Cookie lays down steaming plates. Lieutenant Sediqullah, an ANA officer from Kabul, tells me with some sincerity and a little English that his service is for the sake of the next generation.

The engineers' gift for diplomacy is apparent. They have a regular chai session in one of the ANA huts, where war stories are exchanged via the common language of the soldier.

Twenty-one-year-old Snowy Moerland stars; a rare eccentric, a living tonic, he is resistant to uniformity. He is also fearless, not the least for caring nothing for how he is viewed.

That afternoon Snowy was seen swinging a pick outside the hab in order to dig foundations for an extension. The hard-packed earth reminded him of his mother Sandy's block at Gayndah in Queensland.

The sappers from 2 Engineering Company soon forget I am there when we settle down for the night. I love listening to their jousting and sense a rare bond every bit as strong as that within a good marriage. Behind the barrage of sledging you know they are looking out for one another, proving how much punishment they can take. It is when they stop paying out on one another that they start to worry.

Snowy and his mates play 'Tour of Duty', a video game simulating combat, before heading off to do the real thing. From the neighbouring ANA lines the drone of Muslim prayers joins with the battlefield sound effects in the hab. 'Reo cunt.' Sound effect explosion. 'That weapon is gay.' Sound effect machine-gun fire. 'You're a fucking retard.' Sound effect missile strike. 'Wicked.' 'Jerk.' More sound effects. 'You can't get inside my head, boy.' 'Ha, ha, ha, eat a dick.'

We are frequently up before dawn. Racing to dress in the dark, I smash my watch; Afghanistan is tough on stuff. On 2 June we have our longest patrol, a mobile one, with a sleep-out in the *dascht*. The Bushmaster containing the film crew, call sign (they joke) 'Kodak One Two', has Jason Groat at his customary lookout post, standing in the rear hatch. David Deitz, Deitzy, is the driver. Older than most of the Australians in Wali, he has resisted all threats of promotion and is relied upon for his understated common sense.

I am up front with a view of impossible terrain. We first ford the river then gun it up a severe slope, cresting, crashing down and tilting mightily as we negotiate a crater. There are intermittent glimpses of the ASLAV in front, appearing and disappearing through swirls of dust. This goes on for five hours.

We emerge feeling seasick in a desert. It is approaching last light as we make camp at an overwatch alongside the hamlet of Musazai. A Dutch Special Forces team is in place with sniper rifles and a spotting scope. Unlike their Australian counterparts, the camera does not bother them.

A *shura* is planned for tomorrow. Some heavyweight government and ISAF delegates are arriving to negotiate the building of another patrol base; it will stand between Wali and Atiq, challenging what has been the potent influence of the Taliban at Musazai and Sorkh Lez.

In the last light Corporal Pahl takes his section down to check the ground around where the *shura* is planned. Sure enough, a call comes back to say they have found something. Another IED is blown in place.

When dawn breaks I watch a battle unfold, the like of which I have never before seen. Yet it is one that typifies military operations in Afghanistan: massive resources range against a village and a mindset. An unmanned aerial vehicle (UAV) buzzes like a lawnmower in the sky, and helicopters duck back and forth. At times like this the insurgents are expected to lob a few rockets in, but they will be less inclined to do so if someone is watching.

Another armoured convoy arrives from Tarin Kowt along Route Wale, the Bushmaster in the lead pushing a mine roller exerting 14 tonnes of pressure.

A tarpaulin is erected and Afghan rugs are laid out. It takes a little while, but older men with long beards appear and settle. The plates have been forgotten, so ration tin lids are found and loaded with fruit. The locals are intrigued by the pineapple and kiwi fruit.

The Australian Commanding Officer, Lieutenant Colonel Jason Blain, makes his case. He knows there will be Taliban or Taliban sympathisers in the audience; it would not be otherwise. Beyond providing security, the building of the patrol base will generate income and work. The foreigners expect they will be charged three times the going rate—that too would not be otherwise.

Jason Blain is also playing a long game; this is an arm wrestle for support of the local population. The Musazai base is being deliberately located to straddle a tribal boundary separating two Gilzai tribes, the Hotak and Toki. The corruption and tribal machinations come with the territory. The pragmatism on show is part of the search for 'workable transition concepts'.

Through an interpreter I ask one of the village elders for his view on the presence of the foreigners. Predictably, I am told the Taliban come from outside and are unwelcome. He also says the soldiers can add to the risk, making many locals fearful of leaving their *qualas*, particularly at night.

A UAV sights a group of young men gathering what appears to be a cache of weapons. Columns of Australian soldiers move in to form a protective perimeter. There is the sound of one shot from an AK47, like a full stop firmly stamped on the day. Someone will later boast about driving the foreigners out, but the base at Musazai will go ahead.

Back at Wali I seek out the Dutch PRT. The common complaints about the Dutch being standoffish don't seem to apply here—once barriers are overcome, people are found to be people. At Wali you are never too far from anyone and, as it happens, the Dutch have a stunningly effective winner of hearts: a young female soldier, the only woman in the entire camp. About the same age as most of the diggers and sharing their interest in music, movies and video games, the signaller is never short of friends. Many of them are doe eyed and, by the estimation of the older hands, over-primed with optimism.

Lieutenant Jasper Jansen runs the Mirabad PRT, which has done a lot of work putting in small hydro-electric power plants that have also proved to be heart winners. He says: 'We don't choose sides. If the project is worthwhile we do it. We try to be fair, and we know they can be Taliban, but if it is a good project we do it. We gain ground if they know the PRT has funded it.'

So what about the vision of progress through the prism of those who live around Tarin Kowt?[7] The tribal enemies of the warlord Matiullah Khan say MK is out to help his bank account and not Uruzgan, that he will further divide the population, that he manipulates intelligence to prosecute his own war, and that the Australians are wrong to side with him. Some locals speak highly of the Dutch approach to development and scorn the Australians; others do the opposite.

At street level there is annoyance at the way the military convoys slow traffic and act like they own the place. Some locals proffer conspiratorial views that the foreigners secretly plant the roadside bombs and instigate much of the violence blamed on the Taliban. If there is a uniform view it is that most of the trouble being endured is influenced by outsiders motivated by the meddling interests of Pakistan, Iran and the United States. Many locals contend that Uruzgan was safer when the Taliban ruled—before the infidels came.

One father who has lost a son caught in the crossfire when the Afghan National Police and ANA took to shooting at one another observes wearily: 'I don't know why the foreigners have come. They say they have come for the security of our homeland. What is their purpose? I haven't seen it. Only the people who work for the government know why the foreigners have come.' Abdul Bari speaks for many when he says that the $31.9 million Australia is spending in Tarin Kowt in 2010 has neither liberated nor captured him. 'I don't have enemies. I haven't hurt anyone. The Taliban are my one eye and the government is my other eye.'

Part of our time in the Mirabad is spent at Patrol Base Atiq. Closer to Tarin Kowt and established for longer, it tells a story a touch more encouraging. Accumulated wisdom now sees it as poorly located, atop a hill and some distance from the people. When it was built there were security advantages, but now it can't claim to afford close protection to friends, and enemies easily observe all comings and goings.

Life inside the base has disadvantages, too. Water has to be carted in. Showering is limited to those returning from patrols. Sewage is a problem, dealt with by virtue of a fuel can and match. Burning the shitters is one of the unpleasant duties confronting the good soldiers of Atiq. On the upside, when you do go outside the locals are friendlier.

Our longest patrol is back towards the proposed location for a new Forward Operating Base. Crossing some of the muddy fields is like wading through quicksand, our boots gaining weight with every step.

One group of farmers is making hay. They wave, and we chat. The kids hustle us for pencils, paper and water. Here some profit from development dollars is more evident—the ink blot has seeped this far. While Wali is still in the 'Clear' phase of the Clear, Hold and Build strategy, Atiq is more in 'Hold' territory.

After yarning with a group of farmers, one carrying a load of hay twice his size, Captain Spencer Milburn explains the difficulties encountered when the ink runs out. The Gilzai tribe, he says, are less eager to take money because being seen spending conspicuously carries too much danger.

While it is true that the closer to Tarin Kowt the safer the ground, the security bubble can burst in an instant. Indeed, while at Atiq we hear the now familiar crump of a detonating IED. On a water collection mission, the ANA has hit a roadside bomb. A Ford Ranger arrives back at base, its windscreen caved in. One soldier limps off toward the clinic with Australian Warrant Officer Richard Van de Leur in earnest pursuit, questioning the wisdom of returning to the same point where water was collected the day before.

Atiq reconnects me with more uncommon soldiers. Corporal Adam Heemskirk, last found under a tree discussing whether or not he should get out of the Army, has received a box of goodies from home. 'My wife and son are very good to me,' he says as he unpacks pineapple juice, pasta and a book, *The Tall Man* by Chloe Hooper.

Private Sam Drake, last seen at Kapooka when he was the oldest recruit by seven years, is getting on fine with the younger soldiers. Known to them as 'Drakey', 'Snake' or the 'Old Man', he is proud of 'helping one of the younger blokes over a *quala* wall'.

Sergeant Kyle Faram, wounded in the action that killed his friend Jason Marks, is back in the field. A bone graft helped him recover, but a medical reclassification meant he could not rejoin the Commandos. Faz says he misses them.

As we talk outside the hab, a pet goat climbs onto the table and attempts to consume a pair of scissors. The engineers had purchased

Conan, intending to put him on a plate, but their hearts softened. The goat now roams the camp, butting soldiers and grazing on cigarette butts and Red Bull cans.

Back at Patrol Base Wali, Cookie has prepared fried chicken and potato wedges. The officers wait until the men and solo female are fed. As we queue we collect bottled water from the fridge, which has a sign scrawled with a marker pen: 'Take one out, put one in. Not fucking hard.'

The Officer Commanding (OC), Major Groat, and the Company Sergeant Major, Tas McGinley, are often seen in a huddle tuned in to a peculiar wavelength, monitoring the morale of the men and the mission. The soldiers are kept busy—peeling potatoes, carrying water bottles, shifting rocks to secure a tarpaulin, sweeping and cleaning.

The OC and his Warrant Officer agonise over route selection and patrolling patterns. 'You don't see it, you feel it,' they try to explain. They are both rigid and relaxed. When the sections return, there will be no yelling in their ear about hair length and Army standard of dress.

Jason Groat has lent me a spare watch, which I rarely consult. You start to operate to an alternative timetable, sleeping when you are tired, eating when you are hungry and washing when you remember. Life outside is set aside.

I am hot bedding again. A bunk has become available alongside Snowy Moerland.

It is 7 June at 0300 and lights come on. I hear some movement in the hab, and go back to sleep. A full-strength patrol with the sappers in the lead is heading west towards Sorkh Lez on an IED disruption mission. A few hours later, Jason Groat wants to do another meet and greet, trying to sort out the proposed all-weather river crossing. At dawn we wade across the Teri Rud, heading east.

I am a little awkward about admitting how much I enjoy this. It is perilous; it is pastoral. The soft light turns the wheat fields to gold. Then the stutter of the personal radios signals a halt as ANA engineers detect a metal signature through the headphones. It is not yet hot, and there will be pause to rest as they probe a wheel rut. I settle in the shade and begin to scribble. The senses are stimulated and the senses are soothed. Humans are not designed to stay indoors.

Major Groat does not have a lot of luck persuading the land-owner about the river crossing. While the locals are becoming more co-operative, it does not pay to be too visible about it. By mid morning we head back to base. Along the way the radio tells us the other patrol has had success uncovering four weapons caches around Sorkh Lez.

At 1113 we hear that awful sound, a sickening thud. Looking out across the green zone, a column of white smoke lifts through the clear air. We hurry to the command post. The radio is alive. The faces are dead, colour drained away. 'Casevac nine liner . . . Category Alpha . . . be advised EDD deceased . . . arterial bleeding . . . Mike 875 no vital signs.'

Snowy and Smithy had been checking the footpads on the way back to base, and Snowy had found something. Smithy and Herbie the dog came forward to help when the IED exploded. The smoke had not cleared as the signaller called in the report. Stonecutter took charge, checking for secondary explosives while combat first aid was applied. Snowy had been killed and so, too, Herbie. Still alive, Smithy tried to get to his feet and go back to work, then he began to tell the others how much he loved his wife and son.

Two Blackhawks appeared above. On the way back to Tarin Kowt, Smithy died.

The news sweeps through the base as a rare shower of rain wets the earth. Cameraman Neale Maude and sound recordist Shane Munro make a good decision to leave our camera gear stacked in a corner. We will wait for a better moment before asking how people feel.

It is as bleak a time as I have known in many years of reporting, and also a time of privilege. In the next hours and days we witness intense comradeship and loss, something not normally shared with outsiders. The risks soldiers take are mostly on behalf of one another, so when one is killed all through the ranks a part of each of them also dies.

The Dutch female signaller, Sharon Frowijn, is sobbing without restraint. There are plenty of red eyes. Jason Groat confirms the deaths, and Tas McGinley tells the assembled company that they will be back at work tomorrow. We watch him lead the patrol.

Snowy and Smithy are the twelfth and thirteenth Australian soldiers respectively killed in action in Afghanistan. At the Tarin Kowt ramp ceremony on 9 June, uniforms of the United States, the Netherlands, Singapore and Denmark merge with green and desert camouflage. The dogs, Tank, Harry and Bundy, are also there. So too are the Special Forces soldiers from just across the Hesco at Camp Russell. What I don't know at the time is how busy they are, and how far they have extended the envelope of risk. At this time Rotation XII, in its last month in theatre, is engaged in a series of offences on the Shah Wali Kot region of northern Kandahar.

Half an hour in a helicopter from Camp Holland is country that has seen little if any Coalition presence. Remote communities linked by roads that are more like goat tracks make ideal hideaways for the Taliban leadership in Pakistan to connect with active insurgent networks in southern Afghanistan.

The day after the ramp ceremony, the Commandos (Force Element Bravo) head for the Shinazaf Valley. The next day four US Blackhawks carrying Force Element Alpha, 25 members of 3 Squadron SASR and five Afghans from the partner police force bear down on the village of Tizak.

A common tactic after placing different squads in position is to buzz the location to block insurgents when they 'squirt'. The SASR, in smaller numbers, are on a kill capture mission targeting Taliban leaders. The expectation is that the Commando action will pull them onto the communication grid.

What is not anticipated is enemy strength around Tizak. On his fifth Afghanistan rotation, Corporal Ben Roberts-Smith is part of an air mobile sniper team providing the ground assault force with airborne fire support. His fight begins while still in the air, the Blackhawk yawing to give him a stable firing platform as enemy machine-gun bullets batter the helicopter and rockets pass close below.

Though outnumbered, the SASR refuses to abandon either the target or the initiative. RS, as Roberts-Smith is known, all 2 metres of him, goes forward. In combat reminiscent of the feats of Albert Jacka at Gallipoli, he overwhelms one machine-gun post and then another. It is another of many actions in Afghanistan, fought among people, that calls for precision as well as aggression.

In a strip of fig orchards and green fields pocked with brown compounds around the village of Tizak, 72 insurgents are counted dead. The photographing and biometric testing begins. Ten of them are medium-value targets, and the costs are comparatively slight—one trooper from the SASR and an Afghan policeman are evacuated with wounds. It is learned later that the high-value target sought had also been wounded and did not recover, so the ISAF and the Americans are well pleased. The Taliban's command and control structure in the area has been destroyed.

Ben Roberts-Smith, already awarded a Medal for Gallantry for fighting in 2006, would receive the Victoria Cross for his significant role in this important battle. The son of a Major General and Queen's Counsel and brother of an opera singer, he exemplifies the extraordinary strengths found among the other ranks of the Australian Army.

When Chief of Army Ken Gillespie later travelled to Perth to inform Roberts-Smith and his family of the award, his wife Emma Roberts-Smith, after hearing the reading of the citation, turned to her husband and said, 'You did what? I am very proud of you, but don't do that again.'

While the battle at Tizak was a high, a dismal low was soon to follow. Ten days later Force Element Bravo returned to Shah Wali Kot to attack an IED training area on one of the final missions for Rotation XII. A wing of US Blackhawks hugged the flat desert as they sped through the night. One of the ten Australian Commandos on board, peering through his night-vision goggles, saw how close they were to the ground, instinctively bracing.

That action might have saved his life. At 0339 on Monday 21 June, his Blackhawk clipped the ground at 150 knots. The crew, though experienced and having flown the route before, lost co-ordination in hazy visibility. Crew in the other Blackhawks saw the burst and tumble of flame, and immediately turned to assist.

On the ground the Commandos heard calls for help. The wounded were still harnessed to their seats. A defensive cordon was established and treatment begun. Private Scott Palmer and Private Tim Aplin were killed in the crash, along with a US crewman. Private Ben Chuck, having suffered catastrophic wounds, died on the way to hospital.

In what became Joint Task Force 633's blackest day so far, all eleven survivors sustained injuries, at least three of the seven wounded Commandos facing a life or death struggle. One of those sent for treatment at Landstuhl military hospital in Germany was Private Steve, who had accidentally wounded another soldier in the range incident of 10 April. All he remembers of the crash is 'lying on the ground, smelling smoke, hearing yelling and feeling intense pain'.

Less than three weeks later, on 10 July, another Australian is killed in action. Private Nathan Bewes from 6RAR had been operating from Patrol Base Mirwais in the Chora Valley. Not far from the base, Private Bewes and another soldier from MTF1 were struck down by an IED. Nathan Bewes did not make it alive back to Tarin Kowt.

By August, SOTG Rotation XIII had arrived to move into Camp Russell and resume operations in northern Kandahar. While being Australia's most highly trained soldiers, the SASR was still at times dependent on a measure of luck.

Jason Brown, at 29, was on his first tour of Afghanistan. On 13 August on a disruption operation close to last light, his small patrol entered orchard country, moving through the thickest vegetation they had yet seen. From within 3 metres Trooper Brown was struck by a burst of fire from a belt-fed machine gun. The patrol, unable to sight its assailant, returned fire and lobbed grenades into the thicket while moving its fallen comrade to safer cover. An Apache gunship poured more fire into the thicket. One enemy machine gunner was killed; Trooper Brown was declared dead upon arrival at Kandahar airfield.

Reflecting on his action in neighbouring country two months earlier, Corporal Ben Roberts-Smith saw that without luck 'you won't live long. Who that first burst might hit is a matter of luck.'[8] It does not matter how good a soldier you may be.

SASR Sergeant Dave would be awarded a Star of Gallantry for his response to the attack. According to an unconfirmed account, he rushed to assist and was shot as well, rounds hitting his body armour, dropping and stunning him. When the enemy came forward to finish him, the Sergeant regained composure and killed them.

The good fortune that marched in step with the Australians for the first months of 2010 had by mid year deserted them. Three more coffins would precede the return of MTF1 to Australia.

On 20 August Private Grant Kirby and Private Tomas Dale were in an overwatch position in the Baluchi Valley when they stepped from their Bushmaster and began exercising in an area already cleared for IEDs. By now ISAF was aware the Taliban had access to low-metallic bomb-making components, which may have been the explanation for the presence of a concealed mine that killed both soldiers.

Four days later a battle occurred in Uruzgan, the like of which many thought had been consigned to the past. 6RAR's Delta Company (famed for the Battle of Long Tan) led an ANA-partnered patrol from Forward Operating Base Anar Joy near Deh Rawood. It had taken the area over from the departing Dutch and French, and began probing untested ground.

At Derapet the Taliban attacked in depth and in numbers, using fighting pits and spotters. The insurgents must have been confident, as they were heard on the ICOM rejecting an offer of reinforcements.

Not until a weight of fire from ASLAVs, air support from an ISAF Mirage, accurate artillery fire and determined resistance on the ground occurred did the shooting abate three hours later. And during the battle another air medical evacuation was requested. Early in the contact, while leading his section, Lance Corporal Jared MacKinney was fatally shot.

MTF1 returned to Australia in October, and in eight months suffered six combat deaths. Lieutenant Colonel Jason Blain thought the savage spike in casualties was partly explained by the additional ground the Task Force sought to control. 6RAR would win a rare Meritorious Unit Citation. Blain was proud of the gains, which could not be written as vividly as losses inscribed in blood.

An interview recorded for *Four Corners* with one of the young soldiers did seem to cut through back in Australia, where rhetoric from ministers and generals often failed. 'It's obvious that they need help here,' Private James Smith said. 'If we leave, all the work done, for all those years, will go to nothing. The Taliban will take over and it will be worth nothing. The lives that we've lost and the injuries will be worth nothing.'[9]

A little while earlier Private Smith was blown up by an IED, one of 40 of MTF1's battle casualties. Like Captain Cimbaljevic and Captain Pollock, after treatment he asked to be returned to the Mirabad.

It would be easy to see that the soldiers' rationale for staying the course is about protecting an emotional investment, but that is not all the truth. They also see a practical return from years of risk, labour and sacrifice.

During his time at Tarin Kowt, Lieutenant Colonel Jason Blain opened two new schools. Across the province there were now 250 schools catering for 50,000 children. There was a vast improvement in access to health care. Vaccination rates for children had risen from 30 per cent to 90 per cent. Gizab was wrested from the Taliban. A paved road now reached to Chora. An enormous distance had been covered since the reconstruction programs began a few years earlier.

Jason Blain also counted gains in the improved capability of the ANA. Having government soldiers stationed throughout Uruzgan would have been unthinkable three years earlier. He also saw evidence that ISAF's arm wrestle for the support of the population was working, if still in patches. A community such as Chora, desperately fought over in 2006 and 2007, was now considered to be friendly, although no one could fail to notice that the Taliban strategy was also winning. In Uruzgan, even in the safer areas, every inch of ground was still contested.

On 21 June 2010, the day the Blackhawk went down, killing three more Australians, a survey was released showing the push to bring the diggers home had grown to 61 per cent.[10]

CHAPTER 12
ANZAC DAY

My view of Anzac Day changed through the course of writing this book. For most of my years I have been less than a fan.

Born three years after the end of World War II, I am of the generation that stood and clapped when Alan Seymour's challenge to the sacred occasion, *The One Day of the Year*, was staged in 1960. Soon after, some of us marched in protest as others were conscripted to join another war, in Vietnam, that also served to revile and divide the nation.

I had never quite signed on to the foundation myth—that on 25 April 1915 Australia was forged in the crucible of war at Gallipoli. And when a new generation revived the pilgrimages in the 1990s I was puzzled, and even a little worried, that no one seemed to be able to precisely define the honest significance of the Gallipoli campaign.

Two circumstances adjusted my perceptions. One came about as the result of research into the interwar years undertaken for a television series. Many hours were spent reeling through archival footage of Anzac Day in the 1920s and 1930s. At times I was absorbed into the past, taken to occasions when the keening drowned the sermons and rhetoric. Watching the old footage, I saw a contrast to modern, often-buoyant coverage of 25 April, as stark as what black is to white.

Australia was then soaked in grief. For every day from 25 April 1915 onward, close to 50 Australians died—and this, in population terms, from a nation smaller than contemporary Victoria. When the crowds turned out in suits and hats and sorrow, they did so in tribute to citizens who had laughed, loved and lived alongside them.

Following the Anzac Day services in 1927, John Curtin, a future famous wartime prime minister with a firm anti-war pedigree, advanced a cautionary observation. 'Their sacrifice was not to the god of war, but to the fairer goddess of peace, and while they remember the day it is because of memories of pals who died, and not because they desire to perpetuate war or any remembrance of it.'[1]

While in the interim Australia had not found a way to outlaw war, Australians had come a long way in developing an intolerance of casualties. The next time in my life when Anzac Day had feeling such as that ingrained in fading and flickering celluloid was 25 April 2011. I had been invited to 2 Commando's Dawn Service at Holsworthy.

You see few outsiders at Special Forces functions, and to this point no media. My invitations were some time in coming; it is pointless to attempt to broker co-operation for something like this through the Defence media office. The only way to prise open the gate was to go to someone with a master key—for me, that meant Special Operations Command, the Defence Minister or the Chief of Defence.

On 14 December 2010, the Chief of Defence Force (CDF),

Angus Houston, again looked down with a faint smile as I made perhaps too vehement a pitch; I can at times be a little over earnest. He had asked if I was interested in further reporting on the Australian Defence Force in Afghanistan. Like many reporters, I had pressed for years for access to the Special Operations Task Group and did so once more.

I did think it wrong that for most of ten years at least half of Australia's Afghanistan story had gone untold. It was not a surprise that Australians opposed the war when so much reporting was of Australians as victims. I could see no good reason why the other story, of the fight being taken to the Taliban, remained so determinedly off limits. This was not the case with other nations' reporting, particularly American. I put it to the Chief that constant rejection of access to Australia's Special Forces only generated suspicion that many a skeleton rattled behind the cloak of operational security.

Angus Houston had, I am sure, heard it all before. Like most of my mob I liked him very much. He had gained respect for his principled truth telling when dealing with the hot button issue of 2001, rejecting before a Senate inquiry the government's claim that asylum seekers had thrown their children overboard.

He held on to that respect through two difficult terms as CDF. And at the December meeting he offered some trust in return. Angus Houston told me he would support the first Australian Special Forces embed, a trust that could be understood as being aligned with an expectation I would 'do the right thing' and not offend. I always countered this proposition by making clear my position was to retain editorial authority.

I am sure I was trusted because my *Four Corners* reports to this point had not offended. I was not compliant, but had merely reported what I had seen. The only agreement I had made was that if our filming betrayed tactics, techniques and procedures that could threaten lives, we would not use it if I was persuaded this was so.

The only material censored in the 2010 *Four Corners* reports were code and call sign details picked up on whiteboards in the background of the command post when the news came through that sappers Darren Smith and Jacob Moerland had been cut down by an improvised explosive device (IED). As I continued to laboriously negotiate access to Special Forces, there would be a further caveat: that I respect the protected identity status of members.

There is only one way to maintain trust, and that is to earn it. If the diggers don't want to play, you don't get far. Before embedding I would take all opportunities to make myself known to them.

Which is how I came to be walking through the dark at Holsworthy prior to the Dawn Service wearing a wrist bracelet given to me by 6RAR. The event was at first heard rather than seen. The clip of high heels mixed with the voices of children, bleary-eyed and wondering why they had been woken in the middle of the night.

There is light rain and the scent of Bundaberg rum, and enough light now to see alongside the throngs of wives, partners and children the men in suits queuing at the brew stand. The rum, I presume, improves the appeal of the Nescafe.

You can tell everyone is close by the way they huddle. And you can tell this is important. Umbrellas lift as the drizzle thickens. The soft roar of distant jet engines signals the end of the airport curfew and the beginning of speeches.

Lieutenant Colonel Craig, the Commanding Officer of the 2 Commando Regiment in 2011, delivers words that are concise and eloquent. My epiphany comes in exposure to this direct, unforced commemoration. Here the losses are personal and the tears are not yet dry. Mingling in the crowd among the men and women, as in that archival footage, is the debt of survival.

With the intonation of the Lord's Prayer and the refrain 'Lest we forget' there is a primal growl. To this point the regiment, 4RAR (CDO), now 2 Commando Regiment, had lost seven of its own.

The mood changes as if a switch is flicked. The odd long neck can be seen semi concealed in the curled grip of comrades; it is not yet 7 am. There is another remarkable event to witness. I had heard a little of the famous 'H' and now was to meet him. The Warrant Officer Commando, mentioned in an earlier chapter for his actions in Afghanistan in 2006 while attached to American Special Forces, receives a US Bronze Star. His wife and children stand close and proud. I am not able to interview him; it is not the time, anyway.

Medals are everywhere as groups now head to town for the march. In Hyde Park, there is the scent of rosemary as we pass the trimmed hedges.

The diggers have their favorite meeting places, pubs and rituals. Generations merge; old buggers in suits, young buggers in suits. Corporal Dan calls Anzac Day the digger's birthday.

At a crowded pub well before midday it is twenty deep at the bar. There's a lot of drinking, but no fights as far as I can see. What I do see is welcome courtesy and generosity. I am glad of the introductions.

After attending the Commandos' Martin Place service, Elvi Wood makes her way home. One month earlier her husband Sergeant Brett Wood had left for his third tour of Afghanistan. There is a five hour time difference and Elvi is in transit when Brett calls after taking part in his Dawn Service at Tarin Kowt. He read the honour roll and was about to enjoy the beer ration broken out on this day. It was a short conversation, which Elvi will have cause to remember.

Months earlier, on 20 November 2010, Neale Maude, Shane Munro and I had been invited to 6RAR's welcome home in Brisbane. That day also began around dawn with Warrant Officer Tas McGinley walking Alpha Company up to the Royal Australian Regiment National memorial at Gallipoli Barracks, where the names of lost comrades had been newly inscribed.

Tas had more cause for despondence. This day was his last commanding these men, the best he ever worked with. 'It was a massive trip, fellas. It got hard. But you blokes kicked it . . . We need to look after each other still,' he said as they headed into town. 'The only thing I ask is drink piss and don't fight.'

In loose order they move towards Enoggera Station for a train to the march in the city. The crowd is hospitable. There are one or two strident flag wavers, but mostly the tribute is measured and sincere. Opposition to the Afghanistan war is not quite as strong in Queensland as it is in other states. But more to the point, the public here and elsewhere object with greater discrimination than was the case in the Vietnam years. While there are probably plenty in the crowd who opposed the war, no visible blame is directed at the soldiers. 'Good on you, diggers.' 'Well done, boys.'

Beyond the six locally based soldiers killed from one deployment in 2010, 40 were also wounded. On 18 May, Captain Matt Middleton had been thrown from the hatch of his Bushmaster when it struck an IED. It was his birthday, which he says 'was a blast'. Roadside bombs twice struck Sapper Michael Clarke, who is pushed along in a wheelchair. His father tells of the family's gratitude that the news received was bad instead of unbearable.

After the parade I share a hug with Sandy Moerland, Jacob's mum, on the grounds where the battle group was seen off exactly nine months earlier. Occasions such as this— homecomings, Anzac Day, reunions and the like—are harder for some. Corporal Jeremy Pahl sports a new tattoo to honour his lost mates and the engineers have a new dog named DJ, in memory of Darren and Jacob.

It should not be thought they don't grasp the evil of war; they know it better than most. But ask them if they would go again, and they say: 'Tomorrow', 'In a heartbeat', 'Can't fucking wait'. Maybe it's the allure of risk, the guilt of survival, even the money. They say it is because they are soldiers and it is what they train for. 'You would not go to teacher's college and not teach.' The war zone is also their home.

In the Special Forces community the ardour for action is accentuated. There are now soldiers with eight or nine rotations behind them, and they line up for more. Some return and negotiate a transfer to another company so they can jump the queue, to be back at Camp Russell within months.

It is not so easy for the injured. Of the 168 casualties sustained to this point, Special Forces bear the brunt. Having trained for years to achieve optimum condition, the news that they can't be considered combat fit is commonly and vigorously denied.

The survivors of the 2010 Blackhawk crash have found it particularly hard. Sergeant Pete sustained a severe fracture to his right leg, which suffered a further massive laceration when his rifle cut deep into it. His left kneecap had been broken, and so too his pelvis. Most of his right ribs were smashed, his right arm fractured and his back broken. His face had been cracked in three places and he incurred a bleed to his frontal lobe. Pete also wanted to go back, and had fought with amazing determination to prove his fitness.

Most if not all of the seven survivors were at first thought to be in need of palliative care for the rest of their lives. For some, a career in the Army let alone the Commandos was clearly over. Lieutenant Colonel Craig says the hair stood up on his neck as he watched them fight for their careers.

The small Special Forces community was also struck by the response of the other victims of the accident, the wives, partners and families of the survivors. With teenagers to manage, the wife of the critically injured team leader, who had sustained a severe brain injury, would make the trip to hospital to be with her husband every day.

Young signaller Gary Wilson would not be able to return to active duty or retain his protected identity status. His left foot had been crushed, every bone broken; his knee, hip, ribs and forearm, nose and brain were also damaged. 'Willo' was in a coma for two months. On his return to Australia the grim prognosis was that only 10 per cent of victims with injuries such as his wake from such a coma.

Gary's fiancée, Renee, had more optimism. So too did the Governor General Quentin Bryce when she visited him and the other survivors. And Gary did wake; the first word he uttered was 'ouch'. His initial conscious thought was that the Taliban had captured him, and then he recognised the Aussie twang in the nurses' voices.

Gary and Renee, having earlier postponed their wedding, married on 2 April 2011. When they later attended a reception in aid of medical research at Admiralty House, Quentin Bryce was moved when she saw Gary go over to some of the medical scientists and say: 'I offer myself to you as research.' At their last meeting he had been swathed in bandages.

Signaller Wilson's comrade Private Steve also maintained the fight for his career against painful odds. As he was recovering from head trauma, spinal fractures, two breaks to his right leg and ankle, a punctured lung and more, the young Commando received news that the Director of Military Prosecutions had charged him with unauthorised discharge of a weapon and grievous bodily harm (GBH) over the range incident that preceded the Blackhawk crash.

Steve and his fiancée Kate were as traumatised by the GBH charge as they were by the injuries. Kate was puzzled by how Steve's employer could have it both ways, using him to fight while initiating a prosecution that could end his career. 'If what he did was so bad, why was he not reprimanded immediately or sent home or kept on base? Hence he would not have been involved in the crash and God only knows how many other missions he was involved in after the incident.'

Kate was earlier flown to Landstuhl Hospital in Germany to be with Steve. When first informed of the crash, she threw up. 'You wait for these calls. It is always in the back of your mind. And then he deteriorated when in Germany. His mum and I were flown there. The Army was fabulous. I did not even have a passport, but they got me there in twenty-four hours.'

After recovering consciousness, Kate's 26-year-old fiancé first thought he had lost his legs in an IED strike. When assured otherwise, he asked what had happened to his team. Steve broke down, thinking all had been killed. Three was bad enough.

This is something Kate understood on her way to Germany. 'The girlfriends are kept out of a lot. I was torn between my own situation and a worse situation for a girlfriend whose partner was killed.'

When she arrived at Landstuhl, Steve was grieving for Tim Aplin, Ben Chuck and Scott Palmer but he was positive. 'His mates were paying out on one another, playing practical jokes. They were all black and blue passing notes . . . It is their way of saying I love you, mate.'

Kate and Steve were also later married. And represented by Major David McLure before his court martial, Steve received a verdict of conviction without punishment. Perhaps it was seen that there had been punishment enough.

Private Steve battled to prove his fitness, declaring after a spinal fusion operation that he was prepared to put on a full pack and parachute jump to prove the doctors wrong. Kate, living with this on a daily basis, was now allied to his will. 'When they get home they want to go again. My friends can't believe it when I say I want him to go back. I want it because I know it would make him whole again.'

The Sher family in Melbourne would never again be whole, but in a sense their son Greg endured. Within the trunk Felix Sher received containing his son's possessions was a book, *Anatomy of Courage* by Lord Moran. And within the book he found a series of quotes highlighted by Greg.

At another Anzac Day service Felix Sher, who had migrated from South Africa, read some of the thoughts that helped form Greg Sher's rationale for risk. 'A few men had the stuff of leadership in them, they were like life rafts to which the rest of humanity clung for support and for hope.' 'In the presence of danger man often finds salvation in action.' 'Only by the birth of a proper attitude to danger can we hope to discipline the frailty of flesh.'

Greg loved Australia and loved the Commandos. 'He was

attracted to the discipline, the physical side and the camaraderie. He loved his home life as well,' Felix told me. He thought the Australian media did not understand our military culture. 'Greg was not an attacker. He was a protector.'

Many of these stories of getting on with life are demonstrative of the heroic reasoning people are forced to find to go with those deeper reservoirs of physical strength. It is obviously easier to identify with the stories of inspirational struggle and success than it is to tell the stories of morbid, bitter, remorseless failure and heartache.

Major General John Cantwell, Commander of Australia's Afghanistan mission in 2010, had said on *Four Corners*: 'We cannot underestimate the damage that we might be doing to our people through constant stress. We must do everything we can to help them out psychologically, with medical care, with everything. These people are putting their lives on the line. They do this without question. They don't flinch, and when they're hurt, when they're hurting, as they will down the years, we've got to step up as a society and keep looking after them.'[2]

At the time, then Chief of Army Lieutenant General Ken Gillespie launched an initiative—'Dents in the Soul'—aimed at dealing with and destigmatising post traumatic stress disorder (PTSD). This was an issue close to John Cantwell's somewhat dented soul; he would write his own book, *Exit Wounds*, outing himself as a sufferer of PTSD. And, clearly, part of General Cantwell's ongoing anguish was linked to the loss of ten soldiers during this time of command.

Soon after Mentoring Task Force 1 returned and a day after the Brisbane welcome home, Alpha Company got together on the roof of the Fox Hotel on the city's South Bank. They had talked about it for months. Unusually, and to the trepidation of some of their superiors, I was invited along with Neale and Shane.

There is no avoiding the obvious; we could no longer pretend to be dispassionate observers. When the media deploys among soldiers, the soldiers take us under their wing. In doing so they increase risk to themselves and lessen it for us. Dependence gives rise to obligation—and, besides, we made friends.

While I accept I won't convince everyone, I did not see this process as one that bankrupted all trace of objectivity. I don't see emotional objectivity as a goal anyway. I want to be connected. I want to care. And I don't see myself shedding practised editorial judgement. Here in the pub or out there beyond the wire, if I see something they would rather I not report but it is judged to be important and of public interest, I say I will report it.

At the Fox, Warrant Officer Stonecutter Kevin Dolan arrives with the Officer Commanding, Major Jason Groat. Jason Groat would be awarded a Distinguished Service Medal and Kevin Dolan a Medal for Gallantry, one of five conferred to MTF1. In the end Combat Team Alpha had undertaken 1300 patrols. On his own, Stonecutter covered 1350 kilometres. He witnessed ten IED strikes, four within 10 metres, and 37 troops in contact incidences. After the fatal attack on 7 June at Sorkh Lez, he saw Taliban aggression ramped up. Alpha Company was up against a new type of fighter—Taliban sporting gold watches and running shoes, probably from outside the region, were stamping a claim of ownership on the valley.

The Special Air Service Regiment also got stuck in, and captured the bomb maker who killed Snowy and Smithy. By the time it returned, Alpha Company saw the arm wrestle for the support of the population in the Mirabad swinging its way.

As the boys with warrior tatts and their girlfriends in impossibly tight skirts make the most of the day, a few of us slip away. Neale, Shane and I, with Major Jason Groat, Captain Aaron Cimbaljevic, Lance Corporal David Deitz and partners head off for a meal. You do notice from time to time company is kept without regard for rank.

Back in June 'Deitzy', long threatened with promotion, had a stripe forced on him by Major General John Cantwell. Now we find a restaurant by the river. It is a warm night. And just like the IEDs, you can never quite tell when the shrapnel of memory will strike.

Cimba is talking about being blown up. He is laughing. It triggers something in Deitzy, who had been on the same patrol. Lance Corporal Deitz begins to sob, not for himself but for the near death of a friend. Her husband's face streaked with tears, Kathy moves to comfort him.

CHAPTER 13
THE AFGHAN WAY

Framed on the wall in the Afghan police barracks inside Camp Russell is a quote from Lawrence of Arabia.

> Better they do it tolerably than that you do it perfectly, it is their way and you are here to help them, not win for them. Actually, also under the very odd condition we work in, your practical work will not be as good as perhaps you think it is. It may take them longer and it may not be as good as you think, but if it is theirs it will be better.[1]

A one-man mentoring task force to Arab Bedouins during World War I, this pillar of wisdom resonated a century on among the tribes of Uruzgan.

The year 2010 was supposed to have been pivotal. The United States had begun a surge, delivering 68,000 more troops to Afghanistan. By year's end almost 400,000 military personnel stood against the Taliban. Afghan National Police numbers had grown to 115,000, and the Afghan National Army (ANA) was now 134,000 strong.

Australia was one of 47 countries battling to civilise a country with more pride than faith in the concept of nationhood. Unlike many Coalition allies Australia stood close to the fire, the worst fighting and the heaviest casualties occurring in International Security Assistance Force (ISAF) Regional Command South.

While to outsiders Afghanistan could seem like one vast graveyard, in many of the provinces, particularly in the north, there was much less violence. Indeed, there were places like Herat where a foreigner could settle with a cold drink, watch the world go by and feel well distant from a war.

You would not sensibly do that at Tarin Kowt, Kandahar or Lashkar Gah. In 2010, and on their way out of the troubled southwest region, the Canadians began to transfer Kandahar to the Americans. The lack of a clear objective and definable measures of success, as well as 2000 casualties (including 158 soldiers killed), had eroded public and political support in Canada.

By August 2010 the Dutch also had enough. I watched the early stages of the handover at Camp Holland, a pull-out that would increase responsibility for the Australians. While the United States took on the leadership role for what was now called Combined Team Uruzgan (CTU), the bulk of local knowledge, as best it could be claimed, was drawn from Australia's five year investment.

Among the diggers you did not need to excavate hard to hear an unflattering account of the Dutch. Many thought an army with not one but two unions, as well as earrings and all that long hair, a touch strange. Stories of Dutch soldiers not actively patrolling or providing aggressive air support had done the rounds of Uruzgan. One Australian told me she found the Dutch so rude she came to prefer working with the Afghans. Corporal Leon

Gray DSM thought them 'a bit weird. They did not have the same enthusiasm as the Australian soldier, who busted his nut to get over there. We did our own PR to explain we don't bash our wives, but it didn't work.'

However, plenty of Australians saw plenty of pluses in working with the Dutch. Lieutenant Colonel Jason Blain, who presided over the handover, later reflected: 'The Dutch are interesting. I enjoyed the Dutch. A lot diss on the Dutch as soft and weak. I tell you my experience is they focused on getting out there and achieving results. An interesting lot who don't want to be seen so much as professional soldiers.'

The lighter touch of the Dutch would be missed in an environment where military force alone has so persistently failed. On principle they resisted the formal appointment of Matiullah Khan (MK) as police chief because of his human rights record, expressing a practical concern that MK's endorsement could spill his many tribal enemies into the ranks of the insurgency. The Dutch also took a dim view of their convoys being discriminately hammered when travelling north from Kandahar along the main supply channel, Route Bear.

Jason Blain also admired the Americans, who were not used to seeing wars fought with a lighter touch. Although CTU Commander, US Colonel James Creighton, also opposed the endorsement of Matiullah Khan, it would come to be. Internal pragmatism that saw no one with power in this province as coming without a past would trump external principle.

MK had support in Kabul, as well as among many in Special Forces. Australia came to see the glass half full, believing the new police chief, who could neither read nor write, could be drawn into the folds of the Government of the Republic of Afghanistan

(GIRoA) and legitimacy. The Australian Defence Force, like Lawrence of Arabia, was aligning to cultural norms.

Lieutenant Colonel Blain respected the serious effort applied by the United States and Colonel James Creighton who, after doing fifteen months at the International Security Assistance Force (ISAF), accepted a twelve month extension to his tour without hesitation. The Americans were deploying for more than twice the duration of Australians tours, and their losses had climbed to over 1000 dead. 'This is the nature of the way they see themselves as soldiers dedicated to the job and the nation, far more than we are,' Jason Blain explained. 'That does not mean they are better soldiers for it.'

Midway through 2010, and prior to the Dutch departure, President Obama transferred command of US and NATO forces to General David Petraeus. The toppling of his predecessor General Stanley McChrystal is revealing of the potentially volatile mix of media and military. Fallout is unsurprising when a culture devoted to secrecy merges with another devoted to openness. McChrystal had taken a risk allowing *Rolling Stone* reporter Michael Hastings into the inner sanctum of his command. When the General and his aides openly criticised political masters such as President Obama as well as allies such as the French, Hastings reported their comments in his profile 'The Runaway General'.

General Petraeus, the architect of the surge in Iraq in 2007, brought to the Afghanistan mission a refined focus he called 'comprehensive counter-insurgency'. The 'Clear, Hold, Build' strategy would not so much change as integrate and strengthen to become 'Shield, Build and Shape'.

At a media conference in Australia in September 2010 Chief of the Defence Force Angus Houston asked the public for patience, explaining 'progress in counter-insurgency is gradual—achieved through small advances day by day and village by village . . . In General Petraeus we have the right leader with the right strategy, who has now the required resources to deliver the required outcome.'[2]

It made little sense for the Coalition to tell the world exactly when it planned to leave, thereby informing the Taliban how long it had to wait them out, but an exit strategy was also well overdue. And the squeeze on the Taliban needed to be matched by a squeeze on the GIRoA to seriously, and with a sense of urgency, embrace transition. President Obama announced that a gradual drawdown would begin in July 2011. Australia's plan was to be out by 2014.

So the new pivotal year became 2011, and a war without end or clear objective in sight at last had something. To the Australians on the ground, what this meant was doing their best to train up Afghan National Security Forces (ANSF) to take over the Hold function. The first Australians to transition out would be those with the population protection role.

Raising the capability of the ANSF was still a painfully slow process, and more mentoring task forces would be required. As Major General John Cantwell told me: 'I wish it was better. I do wish the government of Afghanistan was more active, more able to deliver on its promises. It confronts challenges at a distance. It confronts the way that this country is divided by geography. Tiny communities in valleys remote from Kabul don't care what is happening in the capital. They do care about what is happening in their village and in their valley and not much else. So it is very hard for the Afghan government to reach those people and convince them that change is coming their way. It is critical, though, that they do that. We can only do so much in a military sense.'[3]

A glaring example of the obstacles to capacity building could be seen every day while walking the gravel courtyards of Camp Holland. The Australian Federal Police (AFP) stood out in their immaculate sky blue uniforms as something of an anachronism. They had an important role training local Afghan police.

By now the accepted wisdom in ISAF saw the best classroom as being the battlefield; low literacy levels and high practical demands counted against theoretical training. While it was clearly in the interests of their safety and not always to their liking, after a massive endeavour to make secure the Uruzgan area of operations, the highly trained AFP officers were not allowed outside the gate. 'Typical government window dressing,' one officer grumbled.

By 2011 Mentoring Task Force 2 (MTF2) was in place, and outside the gate was still a dangerous place. The Darwin-based 1 Combat Engineer Regiment, working with 5RAR, suffered two killed in actions in the space of a month. On 2 February, combat engineer Corporal Richard Atkinson was killed by an improvised explosive device (IED) and another soldier seriously wounded. Twenty-two-year-old Corporal Atkinson was leading his section on a clearance mission in the active Tangi Valley near Deh Rawood, where months earlier Lance Corporal Jared MacKinney had been shot. He had been in the Army four years.

On 20 February, Sapper Jamie Larcombe, another combat engineer, was felled by a bullet in the Mirabad Valley. The Charmestan area, to the east of Patrol Base Wali, was sometimes seen as Coalition friendly but, like everywhere else, it could turn nasty in an instant. The Australian engineer and an Afghan interpreter were killed early in the contact. Jamie was 21 and had been in the Army for three years.

There were also plenty of near misses. One 5RAR machine gunner exchanged 7.62 mm fire with an enemy PKM machine gun. The Australian's MAG58 was struck on the flash suppressor, according to the young private, dropping him back 'on his arse'.[4]

To provide comprehensive security in these scattered, isolated valleys, an army the size of China's was needed. The available alternative was the one being pursued by training up the ANA 4th Brigade. While the Afghans tended to say they were already capable of taking over if given the foreigners' weapons and equipment, the foreigners were not nearly so confident.

Across the HESCO at Camp Russell, Special Forces also had an uneven relationship with its partner force. Some saw it had gone backwards. The old system of selecting the best from the ANA *kandaks* (or battalions) had given way to working with Matiullah Khan's Provincial Response Company (PRC).

Locally recruited PRC gunmen certainly knew this country well, but they were also entwined in lantana-like enmities and allegiances. The alliance with the former warlord cum police chief advanced the fear of Coalition forces that they were being drawn into a private war. When Special Forces soldiers made ready for an operation and heard PRC mobile phones chirping, there was a further fear the Taliban or someone else was being tipped off.

After MTF2 transited in, Special Operations Task Group (SOTG) Rotation XIII, having suffered the loss of Trooper Jason Brown, quickly regained the initiative. Fighting in the Shah Wali Kot region was intense and effective, while battles in the Gumbad Valley and at Zabat Kalay, dealt with in a later chapter, saw some of the most dramatic fighting yet involving Australians in Afghanistan.

*

The 1 Commando Reserves again endured the winter shift, Rotation XIV taking over in November. Accompanying Force Element (FE) Charlie was a small contingent of Special Air Service Regiment (SASR) and the Incident Response Regiment (IRR). 1 Commando again resisted a role some saw them as being better suited for: simply holding the fort. In 100 days it conducted more than 80 operations, capturing three insurgent leaders.

The Reservists noted a change to operating procedures. There was no more 'banging in' the doors of compounds late at night; the soldiers would instead assemble before dawn and call out occupants after first light. The local PRC security force partners were noticeably different to former ANA partners, with one FE Charlie member stating that during a cordon and search 'we would stop to let them pray literally outside the walls'.

Rotation XIV also stretched its legs working down into the hotter Shah Wali Kot region, although 'hot' is hardly the right word considering every inch of ground at that time of year was blanketed in snow. One mobile patrol to the Zampto Valley, its vehicles forming a defensive harbour, got into a fight that was something of a micro version of the Battle of the Bulge.

The patrol members rated the insurgents who closed in on them for their toughness. The Taliban enduring the cold, as they commonly do, talked themselves up over the ICOM. When the weather closed in the insurgents were heard further encouraging the attack, as the 'infidels' would not be able to call in air support.

When the attack came it was fierce. The war cry of 'Allahu Akbar' signalled commencement of fire. PKMs opened up. A rocket-propelled grenade (RPG) streaked between two Bushmasters:

one round skidded off a soldier's helmet, another slammed into a breastplate. Yet another struck directly the magazine front of a Commando's M4. The patrol fought its way out, with one soldier wounded.

As with the previous FE Charlie Rotation, no Australians were killed in action—but they did come close. On 28 January 2011 in Kandahar, IRR Sapper Lazarus Louis was shot twice while searching a tunnel system for caches. Cramped in the tunnel, his weapon was passed to a comrade when it discharged.

A Reservist with a background in emergency services helped get the sapper out and combat first aid kept him breathing, before doctors brought him back to life in Tarin Kowt. Lazarus later told the *Herald Sun* of his bitterness at feeling betrayed by Defence, Ian McPhedran reporting he 'feels stripped of his confidence, vulnerable and angry with the Army he once loved'.[5] Lazarus Louis' story was a small indicator that within the bristling FEs Alpha, Bravo, Charlie and Echo, mateship and harmony had its limits.

For the rest of 2011 the mission for SOTG remained much the same. FE Alpha, the SASR, would conduct kill capture missions in pursuit of insurgent leaders. FE Bravo, the Commandos, would conduct larger company strength clearing operations. FE Charlie would in future return as replacements instead of (as formerly) in company strength. And FE Echo, though wearying, would carry on its crucial role of probing the invisible front line.

The biggest change came with the new United States partnering. Out on the ramp at Tarin Kowt now were more rotary wing assets than the entire Australian Army could muster at home. When intelligence identified targets entering the area of operations, a team in a helicopter could be on them in minutes;

previously a vehicle-mounted operation would have taken days to cover the same distance, by which time the target was generally gone and the route home freshly sowed with IEDs.

In spring, Rotation XV arrived and was welcomed by the start of the fighting season. On 8 April, Daad, the senior insurgent commander for the Char Chineh district, was captured when compounds in the Khod Valley were cleared. Later that month another target was killed, the incident highlighting the fraught nature of assassination programs, sanctioned by the state, in collaboration with doubtful allies.

Local businessman Hayat Ustad had a warehouse within walking distance of the Multinational Base Tarin Kowt. It was suggested he had influential links to the insurgency and was responsible for arms smuggling and IED construction. On the afternoon of 29 April the SASR went after him, and Ustad was shot and killed.

Four Corners later broadcast allegations from locals that Ustad was unarmed at the time and was murdered. Doubt was also cast on the proposition that he was linked to the insurgents. Uruzgan governor Mohammed Omar Shirzad reported no such knowledge. A local senator believed business rivals had manipulated ISAF for the sake of taking out a competitor.[6]

The SASR remained tight lipped but angry, saying Ustad was fired upon in self-defence after he drew a Makarov pistol. There were witnesses to corroborate this account and, further, the governor's office had signed off on the warrant. The proposition that a prominent businessman might work both sides of the street was to the SASR less a surprise than another cultural norm.

During the winter watch of 2009–2010 Rotation XI also discovered a large cache of 107 mm rockets used to attack Camp

Holland, again within walking distance of the base, and again at the premises of a local VIP. [7]

Soon after the killing of Hayat Ustad came what would have been seen back at the start as the biggest breakthrough of the war. On 1 May 2011 US Seal Team 6 Red Squadron went after the man at the very top of the joint priority effects list (JPEL). Members of the Naval Special Warfare Development Group (DEVGRU), with whom Australian Warrant Officer H had worked back in 2006, were selected for the mission.

CIA satellites had finally tracked down the Al Qaeda leader in Abbottabad, Pakistan, in a middle-class neighbourhood close to a local military academy. This time there would be no disputing the state-sanctioned assassination. President Obama ordered that Osama Bin Laden, the architect of the September 11 attacks, be killed.

The DEVGRU team fought a short action before reaching its target, code named Crankshaft. Bin Laden was unarmed when a Seal with a suppressed Colt M4 shot twice. 'Geronimo', the code for the successful completion of the mission, was transmitted by radio to the White House.

In Uruzgan, where Australian Special Forces operated just up the hill from another Seal team, the war was far from over. The rhetoric still proclaimed the mission was first about eliminating the sanctuaries of global terrorists, but it had been a while since the Australians had seen themselves slugging it out with Al Qaeda.

The war had morphed into something else. The battle now was to protect a hard-fought investment, to ensure a departure with as much honour intact as possible, to shape something of benefit from the mire, and to leave the area having done more good than harm.

For some time now the struggle had been less for military victory than it had been for ascendancy.

Out in the patrol bases it was harder to sense the surge towards victory, but in Special Forces it was different. Within the close international Tier One community, particularly among the Americans, the death of bin Laden was a milestone, the raid one of many on that night. The decapitation missions were relentless. There was plenty of intelligence telling the Coalition that insurgent leaders avoided entering Afghanistan, and Uruzgan in particular. Continued pressure on the Taliban leadership would hunt them closer to the negotiating table.

However, critics saw the missions achieving the opposite, with targeting errors murdering progress. And decapitating the Hydra-headed insurgent leadership risked further radicalisation. Cut one head off and a nastier one, more resistant to reconciliation, grew back.

I spoke with many Australian Special Forces officers about the controversial JPEL. They did not see it as a hit list, and further considered the common 'kill capture' descriptor misleading—85 per cent of targets were captured rather than killed. And JPEL is about effects rather than targeting. 'There is a range of methods used such as information operations where we seek to shape a target to do something different so that other Taliban mistrust him and believe he is working with the Coalition,' a SASR commander explained. While individuals were targeted, other effects might be shutting down a drug laboratory, cutting off revenue or destroying a communications repeater.

But make no mistake: these Special Forces soldiers, well educated and accepting of the counter-insurgency heart-winning principles, were clear eyed and unhesitant about the other objective of putting bullets through the hearts of extremists. As one told me, 'The blood tax of war does not change. Irreconcilables need to be killed.'

In turn, the soldiers expected and received no mercy from the enemy. On Sunday 22 May 2011, Charlie Company of 2 Commando Regiment, last in theatre in 2009, was back in Helmand forming FE Bravo of SOTG. At first light, two platoons began clearance operations in the Kijaki district. Sergeant Brett Wood's platoon approached the village of Keshmesh Khan, while the other platoon came under heavy fire. Sergeant Wood's platoon, manoeuvring to support, was also engaged.

The Taliban cleverly employed the *karez*—a series of underground irrigation channels—to navigate the battlefield, popping up to fire through mouse holes. The Commandos fought back using the same mouse holes. The fighting went on for 41 hours; during its course, an IED factory was found and destroyed. By the next day, Monday 23 May, FE Bravo was calling for the air medical evacuation choppers to attend to the wounded.

Brett Wood had raced to provide covering fire, sprinting through a compound alleyway. The action is captured on helmet cam: the soldier ahead with camera running turns a corner and is enveloped in dust and debris. He had stepped over the IED and turns back after the bomb detonates. Behind him Sergeant Wood, who had dodged many bullets, is not so fortunate. There are two further wounded. You can hear the shock and pain in the voices of his team.

It was also heard a hemisphere away. Elvi Wood's earlier Anzac Day conversation with her husband belonged to an established pattern. It was not difficult for loved ones at home to figure when an operation was on as the phone stopped ringing. Worry would then intensify but Brett and Elvi, like many others, found a way to manage. 'We had our code words like: I will be busy tonight.'

Before the operation, after midnight on Sunday Sydney time, the phone did ring. Elvi was half asleep. Brett said he was tired and would be 'busy'. Many of the soldiers made further plans in consideration of their loved ones, with the real prospect of not coming back. Letters would be written and left with the padre. In Brett Wood's case there were particularised instructions that in communicating the dreadful news someone in the notification team should be known to Elvi. When that awful news did come through in the early hours of Tuesday it was decided not to wake her, and to wait for morning.

The doorbell rang. 'I expected the worst but you don't believe it when it happens. I turned on the porch light and saw a guy in uniform and I closed the door. The friend said, "Elvi, you have to open the door." . . . There is no easy way.' Brett's mother Alison Jones had the same experience: 'When you open the door and you see who is there . . . I just knew.'[8]

Warrant Officer H read a funeral oration before Brett Wood's family, the 2 Commando Regiment, the Chief of Defence and the Prime Minister. He gave an insider's description of the 'seldom understood' warrior: 'For a warrior it is a disgrace for the men around him to show more valour than he. He will strive to surpass his fellow operators time and again. Is it his lust for glory? No! It is for the silent respect of the man next to him—the nod we give as we pass each other.' H saw his close friend Brett as the epitome of the warrior.

The Helmand operations continued and the costs mounted to a point where the middle months of 2011 saw some shaking of resolve. The rationale for attacking Taliban sanctuaries outside Uruzgan was that doing so helped improve security within the province. The Taliban, with a good grasp of ISAF areas of operation and reach of air medical evacuation capability, organised its distribution and supply cells accordingly.

On the night of 6 June, Rotation XV lost another soldier. At twenty-three, Sapper Rowan Robinson was young for Special Forces. He had joined the IRR the year before, and two years prior to that I had interviewed him for this book.

After they received the unbearable news, parents Marie and Peter, sister Rachel and brothers Ben and Troy felt the ebb of sadness and pride. 'He took his work very seriously, knowing he was responsible for the lives of those who followed him through dangerous ground. He knew the risk of his job and accepted it. It's harder for us to accept he has been taken from us before his time, but we know he died protecting his mates and doing a job that he loved, a job for which he was greatly respected by the people who served by his side.'[9]

Rowan died of his wounds during a helicopter extraction to Tarin Kowt. He had been shot while moving to provide cover in an overwatch position at Moshtarak near Baghran in Helmand, another Taliban hot spot. Before he fell, Rowan and his team uncovered the largest weapons cache of the year: 70 anti-personnel mines, 20 RPG warheads, 2000 rounds of ammunition, grenades, mortar rounds, rifles and drugs. Too much to cart back while a battle was blazing, the cache was blown in place. Fellow soldiers exhibited remarkable bravery in recovering the body from ground that was like a sniper range.

I do remember that young man from our brief meeting at Lavarack Barracks at Townsville in 2008. He was like a poster boy for the Army: cheerful, brimming with life, eager to return after his first tour of Afghanistan the year before, telling me, 'I would definitely go back. I feel like I am achieving something.'

In the IRR barracks at Camp Russell, in the recreation room out the back is a tribute to Brett Till, killed on his way in to Helmand in 2009; and now there is another to young Rowan Robinson. One IRR sergeant told me: 'You definitely know everyone who gets killed through the tours, whether they are on your rotation or not. It's worse when you are on their rotation because we do work closely to the call signs, so everyone knows each other.'

Weeks later in Camp Russell they were given to wondering whether Canberra might call a halt to the out-of-province excursions, particularly after 4 July. On that day, at Baghran, close to where Brett Wood and Rowan Robinson lost their lives, Sergeant Todd Langley was shot and killed.

'Todd in Contact' was another soldiers' soldier with an uncanny knack for getting into action and instinctively knowing how to respond. He was on his fifth tour of Afghanistan, another decorated team leader from the 2 Commando Regiment. Thirty-five years old, Sergeant Langley was also a father of four. He became the 28th Australian soldier killed in Afghanistan.

In the preceding week within hours of one another came two more deaths. Lieutenant Marcus Case, formerly of 1 Commando and now with the 6th Aviation Regiment, died of wounds following the crash of a RAAF Chinook on 30 May. He was three weeks into his first Afghanistan tour when the Australian CH47 began 'porpoising', pitching and weaving until control was lost. Lieutenant Case, at the rear riding the ramp, fell while still attached by a strap; the double rotor helicopter hit the ground and burned. The accident occurred hours into a flight to the eastern Zabul province.

The other death earlier on that day, neither accidental nor combat related, was in all respects menacing. Lance Corporal Andrew

Jones, the cook at Combat Outpost Mashal in the Baluchi Valley, was popular for more than his culinary skills. 'Fair dinkum' is how the others described the 25 year old, on his first Afghanistan tour.

MTF2 was now in its seventh month, the soldiers at Combat Outpost (COP) Mashal due to begin movement home in ten days. Lance Corporal Jones had risen after a joint patrol had gone out in time to prepare breakfast for its return. He headed for the toilet unarmed, wearing shorts and a T-shirt.

Shafied Ullah was manning one of the guard towers at the time. He was new to the ANA, in uniform for four months and with only nine days at Mashal, and he was alone. The soldier sharing guard duty had also headed to the toilet.

As Lance Corporal Jones approached, Shafied Ullah aimed his M16 and fired a short burst. There is no evidence demonstrating the men knew one another. Shafied Ullah jumped the wall and took off, leaving his rifle behind. The other guard, racing to the sound of the fire, picked up the discarded M16 and fired off more rounds at his fleeing comrade.

It was Australia's first 'green on blue' killing. American and British soldiers had died at the hands of Afghan allies, so fear of such an occurrence had simmered for some time; Australians deploying through had by now accumulated reams of stories of anxious moments.

At nearby Patrol Base Buman during Rotation XI, FE Charlie had a frightening close call when the young ANA commander refused to allow the partnered Commando and PRC patrol to enter the base; ANA soldiers from out of province were sometimes hostile to the local Popalzai-dominated PRC. Weapons were drawn and trigger fingers poised, so the Australians cautiously withdrew.

On another occasion after an argument on the shooting range at Tarin Kowt, an American soldier shot an ANA soldier in the face after the Afghan cocked his weapon. Some Coalition soldiers made sure they carried a pistol when working with the ANA, however, it is only fair to say there were also plenty of Coalition soldiers who did feel safe among the ANA.

Corporal Dan from 2 Commando, after working closely with a more experienced and motivated ANA cohort, noticed 'they could not abide insults', that foreigners' condescension towards their lesser capability would offend. A myriad of cultural sensitivities, the prospect of plotting revenge because of the death of a family member, the opportunity for reward and status bestowed by the Taliban—all were potential explanations for the growing numbers of 'green on blue' killings.[10]

At COP Mashal in preceding weeks there had been no obvious or unusual anxiety. Now tension and mistrust mounted, but it did so alongside recognition that many ANA soldiers were also distressed and intent on tracking down Shafied Ullah.

Andrew Jones was dead by the time he arrived at Tarin Kowt; Shafied Ullah was dead three weeks later when a US and Afghan Special Forces team, including one Australian SF soldier on an exchange program, tracked him down and shot him in his home province of Khost. After as thorough an inquiry as possible was undertaken back in Australia, thousands of kilometres distant, the Department of Defence determined 'that the motive for Shafied Ullah shooting LCPL Jones is unable to be determined'.[11]

The best that might be deduced is that the working relationship was at all times brittle and unpredictable. If the Taliban stood directly behind the killing—and no such evidence was found—there is no doubt it had discovered a powerful and potentially decisive weapon.

Another lethal weapon was suicide bombing. And on 28 July busy Tarin Kowt, now commonly proclaimed as living proof of improved prosperity and security, took a massive strike to the heart.

Rotation XVI of SOTG was now in place, the handover occurring on 11 June 2011. One member of the rotation to definitely qualify as an uncommon soldier is a nurse, Captain Sam. Trained to deal with battle injuries sustained by soldiers, she was on duty that day.

'I remember turning around and seeing little bodies being carried in, just covered in blood. The most horrific injuries I have seen over here. When you see the bodies ripped apart . . . mainly kids, six Category A . . .' Coping strategies for dealing with injuries to civilians, often children, was something she had to find for herself. 'We worked around the clock and saved a lot of lives that day,' she says with evident pride, closing the subject.

The devastation had occurred in the middle of a busy Thursday, the suicide bombers staging simultaneous attacks on the compounds of the governor and deputy governor, as well as on Police Chief Matiullah Khan. The Taliban killed eighteen people, twelve of whom were children. All attackers, including seven suicide bombers, died as well.

Children had helped one of the suicide bombers push his car after it broke down near the maternity hospital alongside the compound of Governor Omar Shirzad, the main target. The building in front housing the deputy governor, Khodai Rahim Khan, was left battle scarred but standing, Khan having picked up a weapon to fight back. The bombers attacking Matiullah Khan blew themselves up when American soldiers intervened.

Locals were so angry at the bombers, recruited from outside the province, that they kicked their dead bodies off the roof and withheld normal burial rites. Among the civilian dead was Omeid Khpalwak, a journalist who worked at the local radio station as well as with foreign reporters. In the melee, a US soldier is believed to have fired the fatal shot, mistaking the reporter for a suicide bomber.

Afghanistan saw another day of death with victory impossible to claim, least of all for the Taliban. Lieutenant Colonel Chris Smith, Commanding MTF3, looked upon it as a disaster for the insurgents, who hit none of their targets. An expensive action to mount, at an estimated cost of $100,000, it should have been a PR catastrophe for the Taliban. But the propaganda war was aimed more at a distant public—in Afghanistan and in far-off nations where good citizens kept wondering why lives were still being wasted in this god-awful place.

Locally, anger and blame was dispersed as indiscriminately as shrapnel: in the direction of the attackers, at Pakistan, at the foreigners for attracting violence, and Kabul for failing to protect them. Captain Sam was surprised there was not more anger about the injuries to the children. 'I don't know who they blame.'

CHAPTER 14
CAMP RUSSELL

I had thought I would not go back; I was already too old for it. Out at Patrol Base Wali in 2010 an Afghan soldier took one look at me and told the translator I was past my use by date. There was that, and the last sight of my wife in the kitchen crying.

But time had passed. Having puzzled so much about why the soldiers go back, I should be better capable of explaining my own reasons. As for them, it mostly came down to doing my job. Besides, Angus Houston had come through. The first media embed with Australian Special Forces was set down for the second part of 2011.

The advent of Ramadan in August pushed the trip back to September. The month-long period of fasting during the ninth month of the Islamic year is supposed to lessen activity. International Security Assistance Force (ISAF) soldiers carried an information card instructing them not to offer food and drink between dawn and sunset, nor enter sacred sites or display skin. The ISAF counselled that Afghans would likely become more irritable because of the fasting and that their unwillingness to converse or participate should be respected.

As in winter, though, the Taliban was not of a mind to completely shut up shop. Patrol Base Anaconda in Khas Uruzgan, near where Trooper Mark Donaldson won a Victoria Cross, was the setting for a night patrol due to be completed before the post dawn fast. On 22 August, 2RAR sniper Private Matthew Lambert was part of an Australian, US and Afghan patrol when fatally wounded by an improvised explosive device (IED). The bomb also inflicted serious injuries on an American soldier. As described in Chapter 1, Corporal Dan was on the ramp at Tarin Kowt at the time with 2 Commando about to go into a related action, confronting a large force of Taliban at nearby Ashre Kalay.

Working with Mathew Marsic and Kim Butler, a new documentary crew from Network Ten, we were joined at Sydney airport on 6 September by a team from Defence—Sergeant Brent Tero, Leading Aircraftman Leigh Cameron and Lieutenant Adrian Miller—who were assigned to work alongside us. Special Forces get into a lot of trouble, so the plan was for the Defence team to undertake the higher risk work.

On 8 September, once off the lumbering C130, we are moved into Camp Russell. The atmosphere shifts straightaway; there is directness and determination when dealing with Special Forces. They don't like to waste time and do like to shortcut the laborious processes that are a feature of the bigger army.

Special Forces soldiers have a strong cultural aversion to publicity and recognition. It is in their soul and it is to their credit. There are also practical considerations of protected identity. I would not be in Camp Russell if I did not accept a further limit of disguising the names and faces of most of the personnel.

The soldiers have a range of roles beyond deployment to a battle zone. One company is permanently assigned to counter-terrorism work, and all of its members could at sometime undertake mission sensitive work. There is also concern that if their identities are known while they are away, then families at home could be targeted. Back in Australia, legal action had commenced against a couple following the receipt of offensive material sent to families of soldiers who had been killed.

Making a television documentary about subjects we could never properly get to know was a greater than usual challenge. But these conventionally secretive operations had importance and appeal that would hopefully rise above the imposed limits.

Inside Camp Russell we move into a hardened transit accommodation block. Rocket attacks are no less regular and fortunately no more accurate than usual. The rhythm of Special Forces is more constant; I am surprised at the momentum of operations. I would see soldiers in at breakfast, grimy and yet to remove the war paint from a night mission, *Play School* somewhat incongruously on TV in the background. And later I watch the same team gearing up for another operation. There is much less foot patrolling; by far, most of the missions are airborne.

My years spent poking about barracks and battlefields are helpful. I had crossed paths with some familiar faces, including Commanding Officer Lieutenant Colonel Gerry. He was one of the supporters of improved media coverage, so it is a little easier to mutually align what they call the left and right of arc to understand what we can and can't do.

Covering Force Element (FE) Alpha, Special Air Service Regiment (SASR) would be tough. They were polite in conveying a nonetheless clear impression of not wanting us around. I had heard a lot about their Officer Commanding (OC), Major James

DSM, who had fought in Khas Uruzgan with Troy Simmonds and Mark Donaldson in 2008. People had been saying since his Royal Military College (RMC) days he would be a future Chief of Army. Once I met him it would not have surprised me if he went on to run BHP, the CSIRO and the Commonwealth Bank while winning a grand final, a Nobel Prize and the heart of Cate Blanchett. Indeed, in no time I came to figure Major James might make a better go of my job; it turns out that at university he majored in English Literature.

'Martac' is a term used to describe getting into the mindset of an alien culture and winning them over. Major James martaced me. He worked out a program, including being allowed out on missions and into the top secret special operations command and control element, that meant I would be happy gaining coverage, and that coverage could be managed if not controlled.

SASR was already busy. Its counter leadership program had chalked up some sizeable 'jackpots', as they are known. Earlier in the year a high-value target code named Wiggum was tracked to a Kuchi camp in Uruzgan. His capture was notable most of all for the weapon used, the rotor blades of a US Blackhawk helicopter.

When Wiggum left the camp on his motorbike he made the mistake of thinking 50cc and two wheels could outrun a 4000 horsepower twin-turbo four-blade helicopter. As he jolted across country the US Army pilot, Warrant Officer Shane Ushman, drew close enough to enable the rotor wash to topple him from the bike. The SASR team on board bundled Wiggum into the helicopter and flew him back to Tarin Kowt.

While counter-insurgency had adjusted the role of the SASR in Afghanistan, Major James explained they still used the 'mark one' eyeball to conduct traditional strategic reconnaissance, putting their own people on the ground within sight and listening range of the targets. We accompany teams on quad bikes on US Sugarbear CH47s as far as the drop-off points. The bikes are good for keeping off tracks that can be carpeted with IEDs. These teams will be out for a while.

In the old days it was sometimes said the SASR failed if it got into a fight, and this largely held true today. In the five months before our arrival the SASR had gone without a night raid and six weeks without firing a shot. 'The shot you don't fire is more important than the one you do,' Major James tells me.

On 10 September there was another 'jackpot', this time far from bloodless, when the SASR went after a joint priority effects list (JPEL) target, Mullah Abdul Qadir, code named JDAM. Mullah Abdul Qadir had been active for two to three years. He commanded a cell of 30 fighters in Khas Uruzgan, the area where Private Matthew Lambert had been killed on 22 August, and was also known as a master bomb maker. 'This particular insurgent commander presented and we conducted a time-sensitive operation against him,' explained Major James.

Swift access to the US helicopters made a massive difference to the Special Forces' success rate, vastly adjusting in their favour the loss exchange ratio. The helicopters covered the 80 kilometres to the target within minutes, dropping right on top of a *shura* attended by JDAM. He was chased to a creek line, where he went into hiding in a cornfield. There he was flushed out by an SASR German shepherd attack dog, Kuga, and forced to flee, firing as he did so using an AKS74 (a lighter specialist version of the more common AK47). Four bullets hit Kuga. The wounded dog swam back across the creek to Corporal John, its handler. JDAM fell along with five of his men.

Kuga was rushed by helicopter to Tarin Kowt and then on to a veterinary hospital in Germany. Though fierce, the fighting dogs commonly used by Special Forces units are fondly regarded as fellow comrades in arms. More than a few members of 1 Squadron SASR took a keen interest in Kuga's recovery. A year later Kuga's replacement, Quake, would be killed in an attack on an insurgent bomb training and manufacturing operation.

After the operation against JDAM Corporal Stuart showed me what had been recovered. There was a quantity of drugs, an AMD65 (a Hungarian manufactured weapon that is standard issue for the partner force), communications equipment and the AKS74, which was a rarity and therefore something of a status symbol indicating its owner was of high rank.

Corporal Stuart is a good example of the other, more scholarly face of the SASR. The regiment values an ability for thinking as well as for fighting. Entering the Army as a private soldier, he had been hand picked and trained as an intelligence analyst. Stuart is at his desk from 0500 often until late at night in the Special Operations Command and Control Element (SOCCE) nerve centre, right alongside the aircrew ready room. Words and pictures course in from all points of the area of operations (AO). Unmanned aerial vehicle (UAV) feeds appear on large monitors. The real time images can be relayed to a joint terminal attack controller (JTAC) in the field. The desk-bound operator chasing and processing the imagery is a beret-qualified Special Forces soldier with 'battlefield sensibility'.

Analysts like Stuart develop familiarity with patterns of behaviour; he spends long hours absorbing the chatter. 'They do have signatures. We basically follow them, validate them, identify them and wait for the trigger. You need tactical patience, but we get a breakthrough almost daily,' he says. Major James, in an 'overwatch' position in the corner, reckons 75 per cent of the work is analysis and 25 per cent is prosecution.

The SASR sees much of its strength as being in diversity; not all its members come from the Army. I am often told about the rocket scientist who joined, and the F18 pilot. A super fit former rugby league player, Mick passed his selection course after a term as an airport guard with the RAAF. At the sharp end, he says it is not too complicated. 'I think when you are forced to make the decision you just know whether someone is a bad guy or not.' And they are not all Australian born. There are two Kiwis, and the inevitable British accent cuts through.

After a while I am amused by some of the regiments' stealth. FE Alpha soldiers have a habit of jumping out of shadows, passing snippets of information and then vanishing. 'You know those RAAF Chinooks that have been turned on?' one says. 'That only happened after you arrived.' While they are the least welcoming, I don't hold it against them.

In the mess each FE has its special place. The FE Alpha SASR crew tends to sit outside keeping to themselves. FE Bravo, the Commando crew, is inside close to the widescreen television; they are also tight. The support staff and Incident Response Regiment (IRR) are more inclined to mingle.

FE Alpha and FE Bravo speak well of FE Echo, respected for being out there in front. Commando Private Dave summarises: 'On our last rotation you'd do a job one day and chill out the next day. The IRR was out there in front every single day. Never rest, always clearing the way for us. We're out there actively seeking the enemy, they're out there actively finding the unseen enemy, IEDs and booby traps. Such cool, calm and collected dudes. Look fear in the face every day and get on with it.'

The engineers are required to be as combat fit as the other FE, and they see a lot of action. Captain Ricky, with all of the physique and none of the brashness of an Olympic swimmer, explains they are more integrated than mentoring task force (MTF) sappers. And on the rivalry between Alpha and Bravo? 'We are fence sitters.'

One member of Echo who would win any popularity contest paws down is the explosives detection dog (EDD) Joe. A floppy eared cross-cocker spaniel, Joe loves nothing better than getting out there on patrol. His handler Corporal Bart tells me the dogs have to have the 'correct engaged and eager' personality. Only 10 per cent make the grade.

Joe is a veteran, now on his second rotation. The IRR has already lost one dog, Lucky, which 'done the mad dash' when the sappers came under heavy fire. They don't want to lose Joe, and they are not alone. Defence media in Canberra trembles when there is a further canine loss, the in-trays filling with animal lovers' distress and disapproval.

The story of breaking the ice with the Commandos is similar to that with Infantry from the task forces. The Commandos default position is to keep a distance. Like the SASR, they are not used to an audience and have learned to gain satisfaction from doing their best out of the public eye. But, once we get to know them, it is clear they have a story to tell.

The nature of the Commandos' role to disrupt enemy sanctuaries means they have had an impact on the Afghanistan battlefield much greater than is recognised back at home. Unlike the SASR, they move in force and have a greater 'dwell' capacity. For years now, whenever these bearded devils turn up the Taliban suffers serious hurt. But because 2 Commando Regiment is a relatively new entity, the chronicling of its achievements sometimes goes awry, with its SASR rivals often being credited.

The mix of type A personalities does generate friction. At their worst the FEs are like head-butting bikie gangs. I am surprised at how deep feelings run, with Alpha and Bravo skirmishing for years. Echo and Charlie, the Reserve element, can also feel aggrieved—they get sick of the 'Choco' slurs, such as being told they are there just to mind the vehicles. The IRR, which would soon be rebadged as the Special Operations Engineer Regiment, suffers the 'just fucking support staff' and 'can't navigate for shit' jibes.

When it matters they do come together—when casualties occur the blood flows as if from one. The observation applies to all within Task Force 66; there is less delineation between the 'fobbits' who stay on base and those who reach beyond the wire.

Outside Camp Russell there is amusement sometimes about the swagger developed by clerks and IT specialists attached to Special Forces. I see little of it. The high tempo of operations and the connectedness of the base to the field is such that you can almost see the operations staff—hunched over consoles and tuned in to the action—duck at the fire they're tracking.

The main operations centre is behind hardened doors in the headquarters building. Personnel often walk past sporting knitted beanies supplied by the grannies of Australia, hundreds of which are provided in care packages. In the main corridor is a display case full of blinged-up captured weapons. Nearby is a Roll of Honour with pictures and the names of Special Forces soldiers killed in action. It occupies an entire wall. Of the 28 names noted to this point, more than half come from the Special Operations Task Group (SOTG).

Captain Ilana Napier, an intelligence analyst in an adjacent office, says she worries. 'I don't know whether it is because you know them, because you work with them or it is a female genetic thing. It is always tense when there is an incident on outside the wire. Everyone picks up on that emotion.' Major Chris tells me, 'We have lost colleagues whose mannerisms we can still remember.'

In the flight line before an operation, I watch the Commanding Officer Lieutenant Colonel Gerry, Company Sergeant Major Pup and others from Headquarters come out to farewell the Commandos going into action. Not much is said, but a lot could be distilled in the handshakes.

Returning to base with the SOTG media officer Simone Heyer on the night of 10 September, we hear a siren sound. Electronic detectors have picked up an indirect fire signature and have automatically activated a warning, which gives us six seconds to find somewhere safe. Simone jams on the brakes and tells us to get out and lie prone on the ground. We do so, and I hear Simone utter: 'Shit, shit, shit.' There is no fear for herself in her voice; more dread at the prospect of losing a media crew.

The next noise is like a plane crash. Two 107 mm rockets strike hundreds of metres away on the edge of the flight line. No damage is done. The insurgents are aiming at their terror weapon, the helicopters. Captain Napier says there are plenty of close call stories 'about people who decided to go for a piss or a smoke and the rocket has landed in their bed space'.

Later that night we accompany the Commandos, who are dropped on the mountain near Kakarak where Corporal Matthew Hopkins lost his life in March 2009. Alongside the Char Chineh Valley, the sniper team departs the ramp while we return in the CH47 to a comfortable bed. Tomorrow is a big day.

*

At Camp Holland there is a morning service to mark the tenth anniversary of the attacks on the United States that had brought us all here. Yesterday, when the war began. The chaplain begins: 'Gracious Lord, we pause for a moment to reflect upon our past and to reflect upon this day ten years ago.'

Why are we still here? If you look back without taking in the intervening space, it is hard to find a coherent answer. The initial motivation was clear enough. A lot of effort ensued, in the early stages too much of it misdirected. Painful lessons, many still to learn. Blood, sacrifice and progress too. Now, after a period the equivalent of two world wars, we are protecting a costly investment.

The 2001 attacks on lower Manhattan, Washington and Pennsylvania claimed 3000 lives from 90 countries. Midway through 2011, Coalition casualties in Afghanistan alone climbed past that number.

The US Combined Team Uruzgan commander Colonel Bob Akam speaks of the connection to the 'here and now where the enemy was born'. For the Americans, this is personal. Undisguised and unfazed by the camera, Sergeant James Hinchey says he was a senior in high school in Montana and joined because of 11 September. Sergeant 1st Class Phillip Mandrell had barely heard of Afghanistan and could never have anticipated his boots being on this ground. 'It shattered the peace. Just about everyone took it personal.' Master Sergeant Lawrence Ebert says: 'It brought our country together. It brought a lot of nations together.' He singles out Australia. 'We say all the time we are brothers by choice with the Australians.' The Australians notice on occasions that, to their principal ally, this can seem like a holy war.

Out in the field the Afghan National Security Force (ANSF) is conducting a large push through the Char Chineh Valley. Corporal Dan is in his ghillie suit in overwatch. CH47s drop a larger team in the valley. We again watch them spring from the back after the RAAF gunners spray suppressing fire. There is some reciprocal sniping from a distant tree line and rocket-propelled grenades (RPGs) speculatively launched as the helicopters make the return fifteen minute journey.

The idea is to open the gates for the ANSF to sweep ahead. Joe the EDD darts about as the IRR searches compounds, now largely empty; locals have come to know the drill. The large-scale disruption exercise is partly designed to activate a 'squirt': the hurried relocation of Taliban leaders.

And it happens. Two armed insurgents are heard reporting the disposition of the Coalition. The voice and visual recognition signatures are validated, and the UAV tracks them leaving a compound. An MQ-9 Reaper drone moves into position, authority to engage is approved and a $70,000 Hellfire missile released.

Corporal Dan says, 'That's when the teams on the ground identified children had moved into the engagement area and that's when we made the call to pull that rocket off station.' The UAV catches the image of children appearing from behind a wall, and observes the Hellfire swing away and crash into an empty field. It also catches the targets bolting. There is disappointment they get away, but unusually the footage is made available.

It seems strange, but in journalism you do better reporting the stuff-ups; a story of civilian casualties will travel further than a story of a tragedy averted. Reporting of the latter risks accusations of toady compliance. The Australians are eager to demonstrate they take care, and that above the chaos and tragedy you can find discipline and restraint.

The second in command, Major Graham, says of the soldiers who made the call: 'They do measure up. They are all very well aware, very mature. They know what we are here to do and what we are here to avoid.'

Bravo returned with a small quantity of weapons, IED components and 3 kilograms of opium resin. They counted four enemy killed. Sixteen detainees were brought back, one of them wounded. They reported that the ANSF, which had planned the mission, performed well.

Soon after there was a sense that Bravo was readying for something big. American civilians were noticed around Camp Russell; the US Drug Enforcement Agency (DEA) had arrived. Afghanistan regional director Mike Marsac and his assistant director, Keith Bishop (a famed former NFL star who excited attention among the Americans), could be found in the mess. The Americans would sometimes wangle an overnighter at Camp Russell, because they say the food is the best in theatre. Some of them, pilots in particular, came to share our transit block.

The enabling arrangement worked well for both the Australians and the Americans because assets were allocated on the basis of success. The 4 x 2 rotary wing package of four Blackhawks and two Apaches was readily attached to the SASR, because the Australians got results. The same went for the Sugarbears, the Chinooks and other transport helicopters. The US DEA preferred to work with Australian Commandos for the same reason.

The DEA has access to a mass of aerial assets, some of it 2000 kilometres up there in geosynchronous orbit but, as Mike Marsac explained, all intelligence gathered so far could not identify a distinction between the Taliban and the narco-traffickers. The intelligence gathered gave rise to what came to be known as a counter nexus program.

For years the ISAF had been searching for a way to combat Afghanistan's massive drug trade without a counter-productive impact on the security mission. The bulldozing of poppy fields had driven too many angry farmers into the ranks of the enemy. Corrupt government officials had an interest in protecting wealthy traffickers, who paid them off. They could then direct eradication programs towards the fields of those without the influence and wealth to bribe. Some poor farmers, lent money to grow crops by criminals, would find themselves unable to cover their debt after their crops were destroyed. One way to work off the liability was to do whatever the Taliban decreed.

What the nexus targeting delivered was more precisely directed pain. The DEA's immense intelligence-gathering capability was used to identify when a major batch of heroin would be cooked. It then needed the combat power to strike swiftly, taking out the laboratory and the drugs and millions of dollars worth of buying power used to furnish foreign bank accounts and holiday homes as well as an insurgency.

The idea was to strike at the nexus of crime and terrorism. Over the years the soldiers on the ground had many times bumped enemy territory that as much resembled a narco-state as a Taliban sanctuary. The drug lords shared with insurgent leaders a motivation to resist the rise of a functioning government with police, courts and a prisons system that actually worked.

When DEA intelligence indicated the drugs were ready to be cooked, which meant the principals of the operation would be in place, two armies made ready for battle. The insurgents cum drug traffickers assembled a protective screen around the factory, while at Tarin Kowt units of the DEA, the Afghan equivalent National Interdiction Unit (NIU) and Commandos board two C130s.

On 17 September the units head for Helmand. They then move on to Baghran, where three Special Forces soldiers had been killed a year earlier. The DEA had also suffered casualties in the same area. As the heavily armed Australians, Americans and Afghans take their bench seats, crammed and clipped into the C130s, they know they are in for a fight.

After being dropped by helicopter into a heavily wooded area, the teams disperse to surround the bush factory. Corporal Dan's sniper team is a distance back, acting as a blocking force. In the early hours the assaulters go in, immediately meeting resistance. Sighting something that looks like a hide through his night-vision goggles, Private Dave probes further. One insurgent goes for his weapon and is killed. The other man surrenders.

At dawn the IRR finds the lab and begins laying explosive charges. Resistance ramps up, the insurgents fighting to save the lab. Some are close, and they know how to shoot. The engineers switch to fighting mode. Their helmet cameras record the whiz and crack of bullets snapping the foliage all around. A marksman is close.

Commando Corporal Liney feels a pinch and notices he can't move his arm. When he experiences stomach pains, he reports he has been hit. 'Gunshot wound, India upper arm . . .' The operations room at Camp Russell is battle tracking on rigid alert. They learn an interpreter and NIU officer are wounded as well, and also another Commando. The Casevac is called in.

Further out, reinforcements race to join the fight. Corporal Dan's sniper team kills seven. Back at the bush factory, above the roar of gunfire and shouting comes the thump of high explosives detonating. The drug lab goes up in smoke. It is a multi-million dollar loss to the Taliban: 2780 kilograms of morphine base, 16,297 litres of morphine solution, 15 kilograms of wet opium, 4 kilograms of heroin and a mass of chemicals had been found. The laboratory equipment, including wet and dry presses, are destroyed; thirteen enemy are killed in action, and one wounded fighter is detained.

Corporal Liney, along with the other wounded, is taken to a British medical facility at Camp Bastion and then returned to Australia, where he makes a good recovery. Another soldier winged in the fighting will see the mission through. When I seek him out for a television interview, he gives the proposition some thought and declines, not wanting his school teacher fiancée to learn of the injury until he gets back.

In a conflict where success is difficult to measure, the Baghran raid delivers a strong result. Lieutenant Colonel Gerry, visibly relieved to have Bravo back, said it was the biggest drug seizure involving Australians in five years. Major Graham tells me the lab had been busted after the farmers were paid. 'To avoid having an adverse effect on their livelihood, we try to target between the selling and the distribution.'

Another raid soon after is on Langar in the Chineh Kalay Valley. Padre Sanderson unnerves me a touch when he asks whether I would like to write a letter for my wife and family.

Again the snipers go in early to set up observation posts. Trekking in, Corporal Dan reflects on the death of Jason Marks two years earlier on this very ground. His team climbs into over-watch and takes cover.

The next morning Bravo and an Afghan partner force are dropped 500 metres from a compound. There had been some talk of taking the camera along to cover a *shura*, but the Commandos tell me it is not what they usually do. On the way in intelligence comes through locating a Taliban commander at a motorcycle shop, and the mission focus is redirected in an instant.

When we leave the CH47s there is a sprint to the compound as the target squirts. Defence cameraman Brent Tero and I are suddenly in a race, the Commandos yelling instructions to closely follow in their footsteps. I am blowing like a draught horse by the time we arrive.

The compound is searched. The main target has taken off on a motorbike, but another 'jackpot'—a suspected Taliban bomb maker—is identified and detained. While the women move into a room to the rear of the compound, Afghan police explore the interior; meanwhile, the IRR and the EDD Joe probe the tunnels and storage rooms.

I go for a wander, much to the annoyance of my personal protector Lance Corporal Gatts. We find some local men standing outside watching, affable and unperturbed. They seem like ordinary farmers caught in the middle, and this is what they tell me. Lance Corporal Gatts and the interpreter are of a different view.

Soon after, detonators and ammunition are found and the farmers are also taken into custody. A shotgun is discovered but left behind; Afghan police are helping themselves to a barrel of fruit. The Commandos on the roof are alert and peering through telescopic sights and binoculars. A child herding goats has sprung the sniper team; ICOM chatter indicates there may be an attempt to encircle them. A drone comes on station to engage if the Taliban threaten. All this is monitored by a JTAC hunched over a small tablet computer.

We all get away safely, and there is a rush back to the helicopters. Night-vision goggles are donned as darkness falls. Inside the CH47 the persons under control (PUCs) sit blindfolded and manacled. They will be moved to a detention centre at Camp Russell, where the media is usually kept well distant. They will be given fresh clothing if needed, fed, questioned and released with 500 Afghanis in cash after 72 hours if there is insufficient evidence to charge them. Corporal Dan says they don't abuse the PUCs, offering a more pragmatic than principled rationale: 'We are not likely to get much out of them if we mistreat them.'

The SOTG is better known for wielding a big stick than for treading softly. Out the back of the camp is a training compound where the SOTG rule of law cell functions. There I find Clay Safford, a Baltimore police detective and reservist with the Naval Criminal Investigative Service. '*The Wire* meets NCIS,' I remark. I think he had heard it before.

Petty Officer Safford is taking a group of Afghan magistrates through a basic evidence collection and handling course. 'I am seeing progress,' he assures me. The SOTG legal officer, Major Nathan Clark-Hong, acknowledges the difficulties, considering the grade one equivalent literacy rate of police in particular.

Progress across this particular battlefield is inch by inch, using show and tell scenario training and a lot of repetition. Major Clark-Hong says the magistrates are not opposed to the infidels telling them what to do, and that since the training began local conviction rates had climbed from 10 per cent to 30 per cent.

Not far away, Commander Gavan Ryan of the Australian Federal Police (AFP) is also doing what he can to deliver rule of law to a society that has been lawless for centuries. He has a good CV for it, having formerly run the Purana Task Force investigating Melbourne's gangland murders.

Ryan laughs when I ask which is the hotter war zone. 'Probably Purana.' Commander Ryan says the five years he spent chasing murderers and drug dealers has left his tank empty. 'But we got 'em, mate.' Of Afghanistan, he says it is slow going but 'it is a worthwhile cause, and at the end of the day the people want peace the same as us'.

The AFP boss recognises the soldiers are doing the evidence collection work that should be the province of police, in executing warrants and linking evidence to a suspect. But he accepts the limit imposed on his force of staying off the battlefield. 'It is high-risk work and it is more their domain.'

After two years in Afghanistan, Gavan Ryan sees success taking more time and patience than was called for in the probing of Melbourne's underbelly. In teaching the basic patrolman's course to uneducated villagers, the first lessons are in basic literacy. And when investigating violence, a tapestry of motive and manipulation needs to be confronted. 'You will find that a local accused of having links to the insurgency simply drives a truck that someone else sees as competition.'

After years of processing PUCs and all manner of biometric enrolment, a huge database has accumulated that more and more delivers evidence to connect a culprit to a crime. One of many examples is of fingerprint evidence recovered from an IED found in Kandahar in November 2010. Later, a young man, Rahmatullah, was detained in possession of IED components and the fingerprint evidence matched. In 2011, he was sentenced to nine years' prison.

There is also no denying the frustration that claws at every gain. More than one high-value target captured by a previous rotation after much planning, endeavour and risk would turn up again in the Mirabad or Chora, having bribed their way out of prison. In fact, getting out of prison in Afghanistan could be a lot less complicated than getting in. In April 2010 the Taliban, with some likely help from insiders, broke almost 500 prisoners out of Kandahar's Sarposa Prison. It did so by building a tunnel that was used to just about empty the political wing of the prison.

At Camp Russell the SOTG partners with the Special Response Team (SRT), an Afghan police unit drawn from Matiullah Khan's forces and positioned under the broader umbrella of his Provincial Response Company. This partnership provides more challenges, so American advisers work closely with the police chief.

The SOTG worked to acculturate the SRT to principles the Australians could live with, some members of the SRT even being given a trip to Australia to help improve the relationship. Exercise 'Leadership Look' saw six SRT Reservists take part in Australian mission rehearsals in 2010.

After reporting the training trip, *The Age* newspaper asked the Australian Defence Force (ADF): 'Does the department have any concerns about allegations that Matiullah Khan is involved in corruption and human rights abuses in Uruzgan province?' The ADF responded by pointing out it engaged with many influential figures, including Matiullah Khan. 'It is important the ADF works within the cultural norms of Afghanistan.' With regard to the preservation of principle: 'The Australian Government has made clear its expectations of the Afghan Government in relation to combating corruption and human rights abuses.' Defence again asked for time and patience.[1]

At ground level it was far from easy. The SOTG came to know well the SRT, as its required participation rate on operations was set to climb from 33 per cent to 50 per cent. The SOTG saw the SRT as being often brave, aware of its environment and bearing a hatred of the Taliban. SASR Sergeant Dave, with eight trips to Afghanistan, had daily contact.

Defence and the SASR, often notoriously tight lipped and controlling, was anything but as we accompanied Sergeant Dave to his morning meeting with the Afghans. No one stood off camera massaging and manipulating responses. The SRT, each member paid $10 to $15 a day, was half an hour late, something Sergeant Dave had come to expect.

He introduced me to SRT commander Usman, who had taken part in the training mission in Australia. Sergeant Dave was refreshingly candid about challenges to ethical conduct on the battlefield. 'We had twelve detainees the other day and Usman knew they were Taliban, and he wanted to kill them right then and there. I said, "No, you can't". If we catch a Taliban he'll come back here and go to gaol for a few years, but if he is caught they will kill him regardless of whether he is armed or not armed. We're governed by rules where these guys have their rules, different to ours.'[2]

Warrant Officer Griff of the IRR explained how the task force, after finding that navigating the high moral ground was impractical, had come to negotiate a compromise course. 'I guess at the end of the day if I prefer not to work with them, Afghanistan will never be its own country. I am happy to work with them, I have been left alone with them providing security and I trust them.'

I tried to interview Matiullah Khan but, unhappy with the way he was being reported in Australia, the illiterate police chief kept his distance. An American liaison team that was never far from his side was also unusually media shy. Lieutenant Colonel Gerry assured me the Australians could see the razor sharp double edges of the partnership, and took care to ensure it would not be wielded on MK's behalf.

It seemed the collective view was to treat MK and the SRT with the same prudence called for when a convoy bears down on a choke point. Interaction had gradually improved when the Australians found ways to make the training enjoyable, avoided admonishing trainees and allowed them to more often take the lead.

I had admired what I saw as patient, good-natured tolerance when observing a difficult partnering arrangement on previous trips, and thought much the same around here. That is, if you could avoid noticing the T-shirts. At Camp Russell dress codes and cultural sensitivity did not always align. The '72 Virgins dating service. We'll hook you up' inscribed alongside the sniper scope motif is at least clever. But there were plenty of others: 'I kill terrorists', 'Trample the weak, hurdle the dead', 'There are problems only Heckler and Koch can solve'. Army standards of dress and Special Forces have never been an easy fit.

As Corporal Dan explained, at one level Camp Russell is 'the ultimate man camp'. There were Amazon purchases by the truckload and freezers full of ice cream. Camaraderie: 'How's it going?' 'All good.' When you are on base, time is often your own and clocks are of little account. I enjoyed this myself, taking the 'llds' (little lie downs) whenever I felt like it, be it 0600 or 1600. And each rotation left its magazines and books behind, with trunks of them in the recreation room: *Top Gear*, *The New Yorker*, *Women's Weekly*, Stephen King, Bill Bryson and Hilary Mantel.

I would see a young soldier sitting down to breakfast having learned that overnight he had killed a Taliban at close quarters, and all that appeared to occupy him was his large bowl of cereal. What I couldn't miss was the soldiers' sense of being on the winning side. You don't get that elsewhere.

At home the impression so often is of Australians as victims: another digger killed, another limbless veteran returns, another suicide bomb attack. But in Camp Russell, they had good reason to believe they were doing what soldiers do—killing the enemy. All manner of human and electronic intelligence demonstrated they had unnerved the insurgency to a point where fewer targets were showing up.

On 6 October we began the long journey home. I knew we only had part of a story. In Afghanistan, you tend to see only pieces at a time. Even though the war was now in its eleventh year, even this fragment of Australian Special Forces at work was well overdue in the telling.

Not long home, this conflict's death rattle was again heard, and the casualty count again rose. On 29 October Afghan soldier Darwish Khan murdered Lance Corporal Luke Gavin, Corporal Ashley Birt and Captain Bryce Duffy. A weekly parade had just finished, and the Australians were walking away when Darwish Khan turned a machine gun on the group, killing the three soldiers and wounding seven.

After hitting the ground, survivor Corporal Nathan Searle turned his Steyr on the Afghan and killed him. The Australians were occupying a new patrol base in Shah Wali Kot, where they were mentoring Afghan National Army (ANA) soldiers, including Khan. As with the murder of Lance Corporal Andrew Jones at Patrol Base Mashal in May, in the aftermath was mistrust and bewilderment. The ANA soldier appeared to be on a mission of martyrdom, but beyond that no motive was certain.

Ten days later there was another burst of gunfire and foreboding at another new patrol base in the eastern Mirabad. An ANA soldier opened fire with a rifle and an RPG, wounding several of his comrades as well as three Australians. The attacker then jumped in a vehicle and escaped.

Afghan soldiers had shot fourteen Australian allies in five months. It was as though Afghanistan was telling us it was time to leave.

CHAPTER 15
MAJOR BRAM

When I meet Bram Connolly, he looks like he could be joining the Army. His demeanour is still fresh and young. He is fit and athletic. Everything about him, words and thoughts included, communicate vigour and enthusiasm. The clear eyes and civility put in mind a life ahead instead of the one behind.

Far from joining the Army, he has just left Special Forces, which is why I can name him. And already he has a great story; from beginning to end, Bram Connolly's career has spanned Australia's new world of warfare.

Aged nineteen and with two years in the Army, he deployed to Somalia on the first of a series of peacekeeping missions that would characterise the nature and rhythm of Australian international defence operations for the next twenty years. The veterans of Vietnam were largely gone from the Army by the time Afghanistan rolled around. Looking back, you see the changing of the generational guard. The current Chief of the Defence Force, David Hurley, led the Somalia mission as a Lieutenant Colonel.

Other figures you have come to know through this book were also there. Major General John Caligari was David Hurley's operations officer. Major Mick Moon went as a company commander. Troy Simmonds, whose career also encompasses this period, deployed as a private alongside Bram Connolly.

Major John Caligari was on Magnetic Island just before Christmas 1992 when his holiday leave was cancelled and he found he had to get a company from 1RAR ready to relocate to Somalia within ten days. Private Troy Simmonds was at Strathalbyn in South Australia on Christmas leave with his family when the telegram arrived summonsing a return to Townsville.

Part of a United Nations stabilisation mission, Operation Solace saw a 1000-strong Australian battle group transported by ship and air to the Horn of Africa to help secure the distribution of aid after civil war and drought rendered Somalia lawless and Baidoa a refugee city. The experience of arriving in January 1993 would be described as a return to the Dark Ages, and bear similarities to the Afghan fields of fire twenty years on.

For Private Bram Connolly this was the highlight of his life thus far. As a number two scout he carried a then brand new Steyr behind another private, 'a country boy with an incredible ability to see and hear everything in front of us'.

The Australians deployed alongside the Americans, at first taking over the defence of an airfield. John Caligari won't forget hearing the strains of 'Waltzing Matilda' whenever the Stars and Stripes were lowered. The Marines unit had made it their regimental tune after serving in the Pacific in World War II. However, relations weren't always so smooth. Troy Simmonds recalls walking around the airfield camp and spotting several US non-commissioned officers roughing up a Somali boy, 'pushing him into a hole and shovelling dirt over him'. The Australians rushed to intervene and were told 'to get lost, that he was a thief, and they were teaching him a lesson'.

There was also the media to contend with. Australia was deploying at battalion strength for the first time in twenty years, so a scrum of reporters and cameras, seemingly sometimes in equal numbers to the soldiers, accompanied the early patrols.

Local security forces became a management nightmare as well. Employed by the aid agencies to provide protection, they stole supplies and used their weapons to menace the powerless. John Caligari had to counter aid agency pressure to supply security licences to guards 'who became the enemy at night'.

With only basic night-vision equipment, the Australians had to learn new techniques for unfamiliar urban patrolling on the run. The rules of engagement were defensive, allowing them the use of lethal force if they believed their lives were threatened. While hunting for Somali bandits, Private Connolly would often feel the hairs stand up on the back of his neck—and a responsibility for the soldier alongside.

General Caligari acknowledges 'we did kill people we should not have, including civilians'. One man was fatally shot when he pulled a pistol that proved to be a replica. The fighting called for critical split second decisions from junior soldiers. The era of the strategic corporal was upon us.

Perhaps the greatest burden on the Australians was their rising anger at the behaviour of Somali males, who they considered murderous thugs. 'We found that the Somalis didn't share the same conventions of right and wrong, or treat fellow humans with care and compassion,' Troy Simmonds explained. 'As a race we thought they were jack. When we provided security at a food distribution point we would often see an elderly woman struggling with a forty-five kilogram bag of grain, while her fit husband and sons would stroll behind her striking her on the rear with a cane like a draught horse.' John Caligari acknowledges that 'Some soldiers had to be removed because they developed racist attitudes.'

Within the nascent deployment inexperience showed. The Australians were not shy about wielding pick handles in order to restrain a mob. And unauthorised discharges were common. According to Troy Simmonds, 'This was caused largely because of extreme fatigue, lack of concentration but also the fact that back then Australian soldiers were not accustomed to carrying a loaded weapon all the time.' Preparation and training on rules of engagement and the law of armed conflict run by legal officer Mike Kelly (who would go on to become a federal MP) had of necessity been rushed.

Commanding Officer David Hurley was dubbed 'the Padre' by his men 'because of his quiet, gentle manner and very non-infantry appearance'. He urged his troops to resist provocation, stick to the rules and demonstrate courageous restraint, which would be called for time and again. 'He issued formal warnings that any Australian who was found guilty of physically abusing Somali citizens would be punished and sent back to Australia in disgrace.'[1] This was astute leadership.

A powerful example of how common soldiers can inflict uncommon harm upon national reputation came from a Canadian experience during the same humanitarian mission. In March 1993, sixteen-year-old Shidane Arone was caught inside the Canadian base at Belet Huen. Suspected of attempting to steal supplies, he was tortured and murdered by Commandos from the Canadian Airborne Regiment, who also took souvenir photos. As with the Abu Ghraib scandal later in Iraq, these photos would prove damning.

After the scandal broke, the head of Canada's military resigned and the Canadian Airborne Regiment was disbanded. A series of inquiries exposed a culture of racism and brutality, and called for sweeping reforms. According to the *Washington Post*, 'the Somalia revelations of 1994 and 1995 anguished the nation and traumatized the Canadian military'.[2]

According to John Caligari, the credit for the Australians alongside causing no harm to their international reputation can be put down to something more than leadership. 'It is a bit of a cliché. We talk ourselves up all the time, but the soldiers are suited to dealing with locals because they are egalitarian.' Brigadier Mick Moon remembers 'young soldiers stepping up to the mark. We saw a pattern. They could not stand to see women and children hard done by and old men beaten with sticks. We would see a tiny Aussie intercede with large groups of men to stop it happening. They will kill when they have to, but they won't like it.'

Bram Connolly might very well have been there with Mick Moon. He tells me of his group's number one rifleman walking into the crowd with them 'scattering in all directions . . . We had a couple of close calls in Somalia. I don't think I give it the credit the trip deserves, perhaps because I was too young and naive.'

At the beginning in Somalia, these young Australian soldiers were full of good intentions. By the end, Troy Simmonds found 'enthusiasm was somewhat jaded and I personally felt that it had been a hard ask for us to help people who made no effort to help themselves'.

For John Caligari, Somalia was a foundation experience. 'We learned a lot. When Mick Moon and I became battalion commanders in East Timor, we followed the Somalia model.' And like

Somalia, East Timor would build experience and confidence for another marathon mission ahead.

By 1997 Bram Connolly had two stripes, had completed Commando training and had gained selection to 4RAR (CDO). Still in his twenties by the time he arrived in East Timor as a section commander in 2001, and with yet another stripe on his sleeve, he had been in the Army for ten years.

While he saw special qualities in the Australian soldier at this stage, he did not see the supermen he observed while on a six month military exchange program in 1997 with the Royal Marines in the United Kingdom. 'What struck me about them was their amazing toughness. Most of them came from low socio-economic backgrounds or inner city-type projects. On the whole, they were much tougher than the guys I had worked with in our Army. They could carry huge weights and walk long distances very fast right from the first day they enlisted, and they always wanted to fight—each other and anyone who got in their way.'

Many prospective officers resist the commission not only because it entails a different set of responsibilities, but also because it reduces the opportunities for getting into the fight. Troy Simmonds did not want to make the jump. Bram Connolly, though conflicted, took a chance.

Now wearing three pips instead of three stripes, Captain Connolly joined Rotation VII in 2008, which in turn joined with the Royal Marines in the Mirabad badlands. Connolly was the Special Operations Task Group's (SOTG's) liaison officer. Fighting with some of the same men he had trained with eleven years earlier, Bram took part in clearance operations, which served to reinforce his high opinion of the Brits.

But now he detected something he had not before appreciated: the Australians had flexibility in command and decision making. While officers gave orders much the same as in any other army, he noticed a difference in the way orders were implemented down the chain. Fresh layers of thinking and initiative seemed to organically interpose.

Connolly came to regard what is sometimes described as Anzac spirit as being less mystical than identifiable, conditioned group behaviour. No matter how difficult the job or how inadequate the equipment, he saw his diggers wanting to 'have a crack'. Rising through the ranks, he was able to scan from top to bottom a mutual acceptance of responsibility, and so see that lesser rank did not mean divestment of accountability. At its peak an Australian combat unit was like a racehorse that did not need to be ridden; it could see the line.

Just as the paths of old comrades seem destined to cross, something else can also occur as careers move in parallel, unseen to one another, like trains in separate tunnels. Bram Connolly and Troy Simmonds joined in the same year, were both posted to 1RAR, and were deployed to Somalia in 1993 and now to Afghanistan in 2008. But they had never been in the same platoon, so they saw little of each other. Now they were united by Rotation VII, but also divided: Troy in the Special Air Service Regiment (SASR) and Bram with the Commandos. And although in separate corners of the battlefield, the fate of one would impact on the fate of the other.

As detailed in Chapter 8, on 2 September Troy Simmonds came within a centimetre of losing his life. Indeed, his entire patrol came close to being wiped out as it fought off a rolling ambush at Ana Kalay in Khas Uruzgan.

While Force Element (FE) Alpha was under siege, at the other end of the area of operations, FE Bravo, which was situated on the fringe of Kajaki, was about to go into action in Helmand in support of a NATO project to install a large turbine at the Kajaki Dam. FE Bravo was to conduct a dismounted clearance operation of the *karez* systems used to resupply the Taliban, a continuation of its mission to draw the insurgency away from the dam operation. As radio traffic alerted Connolly to the ambush in the north, and incoming reports of mounting casualties consumed the attention of the task group, he made the call to hold back.

Connolly was not able to talk to the SOTG Commander due to the FE Alpha crises. Nearing the time for FE Bravo to step off on its assault of the *karez* system, he made the decision to call Major M, advising him not to proceed due to the lack of casualty evacuation resources and air support. 'I think at the time he thought that the order had come from the CO, I didn't care as much as the SOCCE was too busy to discuss the reasons why.'

Soldiers have known and will know to eternity that the orders they give cost lives. Harder to measure are command decisions that do the opposite. The young Captain recognised the insurgents had simple but effective means of communicating the movement of the International Security Assistance Force (ISAF) such as the take-off time of the helicopters. They knew the operating reach of the aircraft, and Connolly knew aeromedical capability would be stretched. 'The insurgency as a whole understood a large amount of where we could and couldn't operate, or move freely to,' he explained.

Rarely are medals handed out for not stepping off; even so, Bram Connolly counts this as one of his better decisions.

I think of one of Bram's comrades, trigger finger curling when he sights a man in robes carrying a radio and an AK47. He says he did not shoot because a bunch of kids then gathered and he did not want to kill a man in front of children, perhaps his own. Having conducted many interviews with soldiers determinedly avoiding discussing what they do on the battlefield, I can't help noting their contrasting willingness to talk of what they don't do.

Of all the FEs, the Commandos come across as the most warrior like—their company totems depict a spartan, a viking, a wolf and a death's head—and like the forward pack in a rugby team, they provide the grunt to drive ahead. Connolly found comradeship even more intense than in the battalions, but he told me, 'In most cases it was the tactical restraint of the Commandos that impressed me the most.'

Like everyone in Special Forces, Bram was always heading off somewhere. And, like most, by his early thirties there was also a new family to consider. When asked how he balanced work and home life, Bram is classical soldier matter of fact: 'There is no such thing as balancing. It is a way of life. Having the right partner is the key. I met Jacky at the lowest time in my life. She persevered with me and tolerated much. She had to put up with not only me but the Army and its demands of us. I never heard her complain once.'

In June 2010 Connolly returned to Afghanistan as Yankee Platoon Commander with Delta Company, the death's head lot. The operational deployment, leading men in combat, is what drives every Infantry officer. 'Your worst day in the field is better than your best day in Canberra,' one tells me. So all the courses, the shit postings, the training duty penance, the crap head bosses, the cancelled leave is endured for the sake of this. For most of the past twenty years Bram Connolly had trained himself for this, the one shot at the grand final. His would be played at Shah Wali Kot.

When Delta Company deployed for Rotation XIII, it had just done Tactical Assault Group (TAG) duty in Australia. The constant, intensive counter-terrorism conditioning that honed skills in applying accurate surgical fire would prove important. So, too, would the enhanced thoroughness of TAG mission planning.

One member of Connolly's platoon exemplified a nascent generation of soldier with skills shaped to the new battle space. Private Simon, softly spoken and thoughtful, was not one of the more boisterous Type A personalities within FE Bravo. At 22 and on his third Afghanistan tour, he was Rotation XIII's youngest member. A former Wollongong boy, Simon paid methodical attention to learning Pashto and developing his medical skills, and he related well to the Afghans, who in turn trusted him.

Connolly saw Simon as being one of the soldiers to best embrace the 'white space', non-violent initiatives. 'He was able to switch from the soft humanitarian tasks to kinetic combat roles within seconds. Simon would place as much emphasis on learning the technical aspects of the application of fire and close combat as the language and medical training.'

Among the soldiers, counter-insurgency (COIN) doctrines have a mixed following. Some despise them, others apply them without enthusiasm and still others, such as in Simon's case, are devotees. Simon would say, 'I don't even call it COIN. I call it common sense. If you want to get to the Taliban you get to the people, because that is where the Taliban are.'

For some time the Gumbad Valley in Shah Wali Kot had been a no-go zone for the ISAF. Underground springs turned the lusher valleys into fields of gold, generating two opium crops a year.

The hidden trackless gorges and ravines surrounding the valley provided excellent cover for the insurgency to feel safe and take its R and R. For years it had been a lay-up area for strikes on Route Bear between Kandahar and Tarin Kowt.

On 19 July 2010, 112 Commandos in company strength headed south in CH47s and Blackhawks on a major clearance operation. They were returning to a different corner of the region where one month earlier Ben Roberts-Smith earned his Victoria Cross. It was mid summer, stinking hot, 47°C when you could bear to look. Water resupply would be one of the many serious problems confronting the five day operation.

Not long in theatre, Rotation XIII had yet to become acclimatised. The Commandos inserted on high ground late at night, when their night-vision goggles afforded an advantage. In the early morning, a spotter was sighted and engaged. Warrant Officer H inflicted the first casualty in what would be a protracted battle.

At 0730 on 20 July the clearance operation began. The Commandos had come to stick around, but so too had their opponents. The Officer Commanding, Major Brett, knew he would be up against an experienced insurgent commander and this was immediately evident.

The Gumbad and Tarawa fighters had prepared bunker and early warning systems, as well as casualty collection points and a makeshift regimental aid post. They knew the moment the helicopters left Tarin Kowt 60 kilometres away, and they were ready. Commandos moving to dominate the higher ground watched fighters dressed as women running to the bunkers and discarding their clothing as they arrived in position. Over the ICOM, commanders could be heard giving coded directions.

The insurgents in this valley seemed of a higher order than others so far encountered in the Shah Wali Kot actions. It was as if they were fighting in a more conventional war using Western-type defences.

Concern mounted as the various Australian insertion teams took accurate and determined fire. The insurgent commander seemed to know the limits of ISAF firepower and technology. As FE Bravo's ammunition ran low, its troopers saw children with wheelbarrows surrounded by goats rushing to resupply insurgent fighters.

The Afghan Provincial Response Company (PRC) team was soon in trouble, trapped between enemy forces. The Apaches were called in to make a strafing run, but the welling heat reflecting from the rocky ground made the gunships' thermal imaging less effective. Commandos watched the helicopters pass, but rarely heard the ripping of the 25 mm chain guns. The insurgents became more brazen.

There were Australian wounded at both ends of the battle space. The company soon called for casualty evacuation and fast air support. Around a dozen 500-pound bombs struck the enemy bunkers, but only a direct hit would eliminate them. The shooting continued, insurgents counter attacking compounds now held by FE Bravo. The Commandos could hear the enemy calling for more fighters to join them from an outpost in another valley.

On and off, the battle surged. It swelled and ebbed and swelled again. Four days in, Captain Bram Connolly began to fear the entire company might be lost. It had been resupplied only once, before a dust storm swept in and isolated it for most of the operation. 'We ran low on ammunition and food, but worst of all we had no batteries left for our strategic and operational communications.' Warrant Officer H's experience of the summer fighting had proved invaluable, ensuring additional water supplies were already in place.

On 23 June, Captain Connolly's own platoon operating in the green belt was in the thick of it. Outnumbered and isolated, his soldiers had taken cover in a former Dutch outpost, which meant the insurgents had some practice finding its range, pouring in walloping rocket-propelled grenade (RPG) and machine-gun fire from five directions.

Exposed on the side of the hill and unable to locate enemy positions, Captain Connolly ran between the teams he could not contact via radio. As he reached them, he urged a focus of fire where it mattered and for them not to be distracted by feint attacks. 'A couple of times my signaller and I found ourselves under direct attack and had to leopard crawl between rocks and through holes in the walls to avoid the RPG that would surely follow. Signaller Matthew was calm and controlled, never questioning me once as to why we were moving hundreds of metres between the four positions. It was only at the end of the fight I realised waving above him, like an indelible pointer, was the large antenna.'

They talk about the critical point of a battle as the hinge factor: will it swing your way, or their way? Major Brett and Warrant Officer H knew they could not leave the outcome to chance. Some forces were moved to block advancing enemy reinforcements and others moved to the aid of Bram's besieged soldiers. The Taliban counter attack was defeated. Major Brett was later awarded a Distinguished Service Medal for getting right some critical tactical decisions.

However, there was something else that contributed to FE Bravo eventually prevailing in the Gumbad Valley. It was something not so readily attributed to how a commander allocates force or even to those years of finessing fire and manoeuvre techniques.

Bram Connolly admits he was forced to overcome suspicion of the fighting capability of the newer generation with their 'trendy clothes' and regard for physical fitness as something to abide rather than worship. He soon found proof that the X factor was undeniably alive in Generation Y.

At one point when the battle hung in the balance Private Simon saw something was needed. Carrying a heavy MAG58 machine gun, he climbed onto the roof of a vacant compound and, according to someone who was there, 'he fired it until it broke'. Exposed to an enemy angry it could not hit him as it returned less accurate fire, Private Simon silenced three of six enemy machine guns.

With the fighting over, the company trekked out in separate groups heading for a prearranged extraction point 10 kilometres distant. Bad weather delayed the arrival of the CH47 for yet another day, which meant the company had to lie up for the night. To avoid exposure in open country, Warrant Officer H commandeered a compound. It turned out to be occupied by a group of enemy fighters also making their way out of the valley. Some of the wounded were given medical treatment and evacuated on the CH47s along with Delta Company, only to have an RPG explode just behind one of the helicopters.

Locals also began to appear from hiding. They were not a friendly crowd, having long been on the Taliban payroll. During the fighting, patrols noticed farmers turning on generators as they moved through vegetation to indicate by noise the location of the attackers' lines.

The PRC also brought in a group of men they believed had not long earlier been shooting at them. The fighting age males (FAMs) were tested for gunshot residue and biometrically enrolled, their identities listed on a database, and four of them later returned to Tarin Kowt.

The next hinge swing was towards the friendly stuff, what the Americans call the 'fighter–hugger' transition. A *shura* was conducted with elders and a medical clinic provided for locals.

Battles are often war-gamed, fought over and over, and in Shah Wali Kot the fighting was far from done. Around mid October another mission began to form. The target area, east of Gumbad and close to Tizak, was the scene of intense fighting by FE Alpha in June. This time FE Bravo would insert in smaller numbers. Captain Connolly's platoon would travel light, via Blackhawk.

On these counter-leadership missions, more commonly executed by the SASR, a proven technique was to first insert blocking forces by Blackhawk then buzz the target with an Apache, thus precipitating a 'squirt'. With intelligence indicating the presence of possibly five medium-value targets, Bram Connolly chose to forgo the warning and drop straight on top of the insurgents to limit the prospect of them squirting in all directions. Considering the long haul from Tarin Kowt, the US Blackhawks would stay outside audible range but close enough to assist with casualty evacuation if needed.

It was another hot day when FE Bravo arrived at the ramp on 18 October. The loadmaster required weight to be reduced, so Connolly decided to leave behind two interpreters, one member of the PRC and a trooper from each of his teams.

The four-bird packet of Blackhawks swept in to the hamlet of Zabat Kalay early in the afternoon, landing further distant from one another than planned. The insurgents, taken by surprise, scattered leaving shoes, prayer mats and ammunition as they sprinted for the cover of an orchard. The sound of fire from the door gunners on the US Blackhawks joined a torrent of shooting from the ground.

Yankee Platoon managed to trap a large force of Tier One Taliban fighters who were protecting a judge or 'commissioner' from the Taliban shadow government. The judge, his deputy and entourage had travelled from Pakistan to arbitrate the allocation of weapons and cash to insurgent cells throughout Kandahar. They were at the beginning of a planned extensive circuit. The bad luck for the attacking force was that this 'jackpot' was heavily guarded and they only numbered twelve.

Sergeant Dave saw two FAMs with weapons running and PKM fire spitting from a compound window. He felt rounds striking close to his head and saw them passing right through the chopper. All of the Blackhawks were hit, but held on until Bram Connolly's teams were off and running. The choppers roared away, the guns still firing, muzzle smoke merging in their slipstream.

Sergeant Dave's team, dropped right in the middle, had to run 80 metres across open ground and up hill towards a compound from which concentrated fire returned. They ran, pumping high explosives towards the compound to provide cover. The Sergeant's first magazine change occurred three paces after he left the Blackhawk.

In a compound further to the north, struggling to stay on top of the melee, it was more the noise that informed Captain Connolly of how the battle progressed. The roar of the enemy's PKMs and AK47s was unmistakeable and loud. Intermingled with those sounds he would occasionally pick up the double tap of a suppressed M4, the thud of a 40 mm grenade and an Apache above intermittently tearing the canvas sky. The Commandos and the PRC had only their lighter weapons, so in the early stages, on the weight of sound alone, Connolly feared the enemy was winning.

Noise also overwhelmed the comms. All teams were under fire, and within five minutes enough could be deduced to recognise the Australians were taking casualties. Team leader Lance Corporal Tim was shot twice in the arm, his weapon also hit. He was quickly losing blood; the Provincial Response Team soldiers he was mentoring were rattled and in danger of succumbing to shock and inertia.

Another team moved as quickly as possible to assist. In doing so, it crashed straight into the middle of the insurgents about to overwhelm Lance Corporal Tim.

By now most of the insurgent fighters and their leaders had found better cover within two compounds. Down to only eight men on the ground, the Commandos went after them. Private Simon used a 66 mm rocket to blast in one door.

Helmet camera imagery featured on ABC-TV's *Hungry Beast* shows a different corner of the battlefield as another team approaches to breach another compound. The soldiers cling to the walls. The enemy is close. Through the camera, an AK47 appears around the building edge then pulls back.[3]

Trying to co-ordinate the battle from hundreds of metres away, Captain Connolly urged his men to take the compound. They were taking too much fire from it and, besides, they needed to get to cover.

There was no time to reflect, when another sound drowned everything. The 25 mm cannons of an Apache gunship made a strafing run directly above the teams interlocked with the insurgents. Connolly figured someone in desperate straits had called it in. In the wake of the pass two insurgents lay dead, but the 'danger close' strafing run meant four of five members of Team Two were also wounded.

Bram called for the Blackhawks to return to collect the growing number of casualties, at the same time requesting a situation report from the Team Two leader. Sergeant Matthew came on the radio, explaining his men were down but leaving out the detail that a large section of his own scalp had been blown away.

Connolly radioed Lance Corporal Tim to move as quickly as possible to the extraction point. One side of his uniform soaked in blood and under constant fire, the wounded Commando would deem it the hardest walk of his life.

After conventional assault methods failed and knowing that some of his comrades had been 'shot to pieces', Sergeant Dave understood 'this had to end now'. Fire was coming from the doors and windows, so he pushed forward with a grenade. On his third tour, and having been on Rotation VIII when two comrades were charged over the similar use of a grenade, he tossed it and wondered, 'Is this going to be an investigation?'

The firing continued. Another grenade was thrown and yet more fire streamed from the *quala*. Sergeant Dave knew he had to get in, but the alleyway was too tight for the Team Four commander to get through with his rifle. Signalling the others to cover him and brandishing his pistol, he broke in only to reel back, having been met by a burst of PKM fire from less than 5 metres away. As he spun he fired, killing the machine gunner.

The Blackhawks were low on fuel when they returned and, battle scarred from the initial insertion, their pilots could have been forgiven for a show of hesitation. But there was none. Captain Connolly saw 'the first bird come in at an amazing rate of knots and slam hard into the LZ [landing zone]. As fast as it came it was gone, with the wounded on board. I have worked with helicopters my whole career and have never seen such commitment.'

The Blackhawk then lily pad hopped to the other edge of the fighting to recover Sergeant Matthew, whose skull was fractured and exposed.

Those who were there describe the minutes inside the compounds as astonishing, like a real-life version of the TAG training back at Holsworthy. Another compound was breached, with teams simultaneously entering two doors. Connolly could now hear the angry bursts of PKM and AK47s interspersed with the more methodical tap, tap of the M4s, the latter sound in time dominating the former.

The soldiers entering from two directions saw insurgents fighting back using civilians as shields; two Commando teams raced to get between them. From between 5 and 25 metres and on the move, they shot around the civilians. The twelve months of counter-terrorism conditioning that preceded this tour helped them return fire with practised discrimination.

That was the battle inside. On the outside the enemy still had the ascendency, although its numbers were fast shrinking. As at Gumbad, something was needed to sway the hinge in favour of Yankee Platoon. And as at Gumbad, the same soldier stepped up. Private Simon climbed an incline and, in full view of the enemy, took them on with his M4 and grenade launcher. According to Bram Connolly, 'He moved alone and positioned himself forty metres above the main compound, drawing the bulk of PKM fire. He returned fire with controlled double taps, dropping the insurgents, who were becoming more frantic in an effort to break out and make a run for the green belt.'

The 22-year-old private saved two teams as he accounted for one front on his own, his actions protecting the others as they overwhelmed the compounds. 'A frigging idiot or a frigging legend,' is how another soldier who was there described him. Private Simon had fought the action with one elbow bleeding and swollen from a fragmentation strike.

In the eastern compound it was quiet; all the Taliban there were dead. Those to the west, following the sound of the battle and noting the silence, dropped their weapons and webbing and moved among the civilians. One wounded insurgent pursued by the Commandos was seen ducking behind sheltering women and children. He was taken alive.

In the immediate aftermath, as the Blackhawks winged back to collect Yankee Platoon, thirteen dead insurgents were counted, one of them a main fixer-cum-judge for Taliban leader Mullah Omar and another his deputy, both high-value targets. Also dead were seven more medium-value targets from Pakistan, four members of the protection team and Taliban commanders from Kandahar and neighbouring provinces.

Most of the victims had fallen to head shots; blood trails could also be seen leading to the hills. Thirteen PKMs, 24 AK47s and three pistols were recovered. Coalition soldiers came across further caches of equipment, ammunition, battle brass and radios which, being too heavy to retrieve, were destroyed. Among the nine detainees were more medium-value targets.

Generally, it is obvious if locals are killed. Tellingly, the people of Zabat Kalay demonstrated no sympathy for the slain fighters and detainees; the Pashto speakers in FE Bravo heard them say the Talibs had come from outside and were not welcome. The women wanted the soldiers to destroy a Toyota HiLux and motorbikes, the vehicles they believed the insurgents had arrived in. The locals did not want the vehicles or their occupants back.

Cams ripped and the floor covered in blood, Yankee Platoon

headed back to Tarin Kowt aboard the Blackhawks. Americans from 'another government agency' soon arrived to take stock of the result. Yankee Platoon had hit the mother lode.

With every rotation the SOTG improved its approach to targeting and the conduct of operations. Concern among some Special Forces soldiers that as the war progressed they were more often fighting teenagers and farmers did not apply this time. The enemy at Zabat Kalay was experienced and resilient and the outcome had definable strategic benefit.

Private Simon, already a veteran of many battles, saw Zabat Kalay as important, although not as frightening as other battles where the Taliban came closer to victory. As for fighting adolescents, he said he, too, had been a teenage soldier. Later promoted to Lance Corporal, Private Simon was nominated for a Victoria Cross and awarded a Star of Gallantry. Sergeant Dave would receive a Medal for Gallantry.

An action that lasted barely two hours produced in all five Australian gallantry awards. According to one soldier who was there, 'Medals are not generally won as the result of a well-executed plan. If we had the full pull picture we would have done it differently. And if we had not landed we would not have achieved an extraordinary result.' With regard to the medals, 'There should have been more.'

After twelve months of treatment Sergeant Matthew recovered fitness and, along with Lance Corporal Simon and Sergeant Dave, would line up for another tour when Delta Company of 2 Commando rotated back in 2012.

In December 2010 Captain Bram Connolly returned to Australia. For helping make it work when fate dictated otherwise, he was awarded a Distinguished Service Medal and promoted to Major. At the age of 38, he resigned from the Army. 'I decided to leave, knowing that any jobs I take in the future would not compare to the thrill of leadership that I had in combat.'

CHAPTER 16
GETTING OUT

This book has followed two paths. One is to the modern Australian soldier, exploring their world with an aim of giving shape to their lives and colour to their character and personality. The other path is to their alternative world of Afghanistan. The public accounting of this story is so constricted, I long ago came to the view Australians are more familiar with the digger drawn from history than they are with the ones doing the killing and dying in the here and now.

For the deficiencies in my own narrative I seek tolerance and understanding. The record of the Australian government and the Department of Defence in sharing what they know with the Australian public is poor. I am not surprised they have so many enemies in the media and difficulties with public opinion. They have a way of creating them. Between Parliament House on one side of Lake Burley Griffin and the Australian War Memorial and Defence Headquarters on the other, something important is being lost. This crucial middle ground is overgrown with neglect.

It is from the great middle that Australia's strong citizenship values have been tapped to flow on into voluntary military service. Since Federation, this country's political and military classes have kept a distance as well as a healthy eye on one another. Anzac Day has a valuable place in the way it honours military service while also providing a cautionary allegory of loss and suffering. Australia's strong military heritage has not given rise to a militarist people. As Thucydides is supposed to have observed: 'The nation that makes a great distinction between its warriors will have its thinking done by cowards and its fighting done by fools.'

In Afghanistan I met few if any Australian soldiers I would consider fools. I understand the view that it is foolish to be there, as equally I hope those who express it understand the operating environment is no place for fools. All the inquiries into negative Defence culture at home could pay some attention to the positive culture demonstrated abroad.

While you might not want to take all of these soldiers home to meet your mother, you would more than likely be content with their company in difficult circumstances. Major General John Cantwell, who commanded the Afghanistan mission in 2010, noticed the same. He saw something in the way they behaved abroad, with assured tact, consideration and professionalism to indicate they understood they were representing the values of their nation. He told me: 'There is something about the Australian character that is suited to things soldiers are asked to do.'

Since Somalia, there have been many challenging peacekeeping missions and no nation-shaking scandal brought to light. In contrast, at home the scandals have come thick and fast. The persistent episodes of sexism, racism and bullying are not to be excused, nor should they come as a massive shock. The Army is 90 per cent male; its soldiers behave much the same way as in other institutions dominated by men. Human Rights Commissioner Elizabeth Broderick's review into the treatment of women in the Australian Defence Force identifies a shrinking talent pool in making a case for urgent change.[1]

Increasing female representation is but one challenge. Australia's new multicultural norm is underrepresented, and the traditional source of recruitment of sons and daughters and friends of former service personnel is also shrinking. The narrowing recruitment base and growing disengagement threatens the replacement of a proud culture with a disaffected subculture.

There is something about the way the Army goes on a war footing that seems to bring forth the Alpha personality. And I can see why soldiers would wish to be left alone to do what they do, because they are so good at it. I can see why they don't want women in combat roles, and most of the female soldiers I spoke with see it too. It would be very hard for a woman to command combat troops she could not keep up with. But nothing in this argument, or for that matter in Afghanistan, is simple. While women are withheld from the front line, the front line is not withheld from them.

And there is clearly not just room for flexibility, but also benefit. The women soldiers I saw brought something valuable to Afghanistan. I think of Clare O'Neill being able to go into the maternity wing at Tarin Kowt, and in doing so opening up another important front. I think of Rachel Ingram being able to manage and calm local women terrified at the prospect of being searched by foreigners. I think of the magnificent Captain Sam out on voodoo patrols for Special Forces, saving the lives of locals, a force multiplier all on her own.

I can also see why they don't want journalists hanging around. In a total war that is fine, because the threat and horror is mutual. But if it is a controversial war where a coherent narrative is not formed, that attitude should change. Ever since Vietnam there has been deep mistrust of the virtue of letting the public in on what limited war actually looks like.

The military mindset is hard to conquer: soldiers fight wars, not publicity campaigns. The military see the media not getting it right, having a spurious agenda and more often than not causing trouble, a belief that has held all the time the battle for public opinion was being so comprehensively lost. Defence media continues to drive its 1980s model of media management, servicing the home towners and failing to connect where it mainly matters.

I am still astonished that no official correspondent has ever been in place in Tarin Kowt reporting directly to the public, although Defence should not take all the blame. The news industry has been otherwise preoccupied with its own battle for survival. It is a pity, though, that some of those bright Commanding Officers who have an excellent understanding of the mission could not have appeared more regularly in the nightly news explaining what is going on.

Also astonishing is how a clear, credible strategy and objective was never properly articulated and shared with the Australian public. While disengagement might have been the easier course it was wrong, both ethically and practically.

The Afghanistan mission has been too difficult for the soldiers alone to manage. It has called for full engagement, not just in provision of aid and reconstruction but in good ideas. Just as there is propinquity in mateship so, too, is there profit in absorbing a spectrum of intelligence from the community. When General John Monash helped break the deadlock on the Western Front in

1918, he did so using skills developed as a civil engineer back in Melbourne.

This brings to mind the Army Reserve. The Regulars won't agree, but it seems to me the chocos have been under utilised. They were scorned for not having the fighting skills of the Australian Regular Army, but as everyone knows it is not all about fighting.

I think of Force Element Charlie during Rotation XI. Their other lives as teachers, police officers, nurses, garage proprietors and window cleaners maybe helped them better trust the non-kinetic initiatives. Seeing half the battle in Afghanistan was with public ignorance, they would take audio visual aids into the field to help educate the population on Coalition objectives. On his own initiative, one Reservist came up with a scheme for providing a School of the Air such as the one operating throughout the outback.

In my view, a few of the Reserves got a very dirty deal. The manslaughter charges brought against the two members of 1 Commando still feel like scapegoating. I very much doubt the civilian deaths at the hands of Australians in Afghanistan were the first or even the worst. My sympathy for Sergeant John and Lance Corporal Dave is not at the expense of empathy for the civilian victims; the death of innocents is never easily excused.

The trial process took years to arbitrate judgement that took seconds to make. It was simply undone at the bitter end when Defence barrister David McLure made clear what should have been apparent from the start: the prosecutor had never contended that injuries to civilians were intentional. An assertion that the soldiers had taken insufficient care could have had meaning if the injuries were caused in a workplace or on a public road. But this was a battlefield; what happened was horrible and reckless, but only in so far as war is horrible and reckless.

Some of the soldiers who were there are still angry at having 'been let down by everyone'. One father of four will carry for life the memory of a little boy dying in his arms. Another who was charged will never be able to vanquish the memory. Yet another has had a range of ongoing problems.

Many of these Commandos see that the lesser clout of the Army Reserve meant ranks did not form to protect them. Instead of trying to explain to the public the reality of the chaotic and immoral operating environment, Defence had blamed the defenceless.

Demonising the Director of Military Prosecutions for the tortuous and counter-productive attempt to demonstrate justice and transparency is about as profitless as blaming the soldiers. This type of rolling disaster seems to happen too often in the labyrinthine corridors of Defence, where process overwhelms good sense. Former Chief of Army Peter Leahy calls it the 800 metre rule, 'the cost of doing business in Russell'. Somewhere between the military, the ministry and the bureaucracy, the faculty for good judgement and decisiveness that diggers take pride in goes missing in action.

It has happened so often to me in writing this book: the personnel you deal with in the Russell offices are intelligent and co-operative but progress requires the patience of a saint, and getting a decision out of them is too often a lost cause. 'Harden up,' they tell their own. 'Get used to it,' they tell each other. 'The Army does not love you back,' I am told by so many when they get out. There is little attempt to keep even the best.

Major Tony Gilchrist DSM had been in for nineteen years. When he returned from Iraq, nerves stretched after a brutal bomb disposal tour, he wanted some time in Townsville with his family. 'I had bought a block of land. The wife had a job and the kids were settled at school. I had never said no to a posting. I had done the right thing by them and thought they would do the right thing by me.' He was posted to Canberra, and resigned soon after.

Just before he left, Major Bram Connolly DSM received a twenty year service rosette. It was left in his drawer; there was no ceremony, not even morning tea. Connolly has had to adjust to suddenly being on his own after spending his professional life learning how to be a leader. It is not so much the giving of orders he misses as the comradeship.

The 2012 Human Rights Commission review identifies investment in personnel at between $580,000 and $680,000, with the high-value officer category climbing to $2 million. The cost of recruiting new members through television advertising and the like has tripled from $7000 per enlistment to almost $22,000,[2] but they let them go. Little of the cleverness you see up front in the forming of the soldier is found at the back end when they get out.

I think Bram Connolly made a good choice. The soldiers fight for the sake of coming home. Majors and Sergeants in particular can attain a kind of ceiling rank where the goals have all been reached—you will see some of them hanging on past their used by date, the 'POMs' ('passed over Majors') and non-commissioned officers of the deepest green, institutionalised beyond all prospect of recovery.

Having joined in the same year, Sergeant Troy Simmonds also got out around the time Bram Connolly did. Not that they are likely to say too much, but both will have much to tell any grandchildren. Troy Simmonds, still carrying a bullet lodged in his hip, said he never thought he would stay so long and see so much action: 'But that's how it goes. I had a wonderful adventure but it's definitely out of my system now, and I look forward to a future filled with gentler pursuits.'

There are plenty of habits the diggers will never leave behind. They will be inclined to be up earlier, dressed and waiting ahead of the rest of the family. They will be surprisingly handy with an iron. They will become impatient when friends take too long to make a choice from the menu. Partners will repeatedly remind them to slow down while eating. If sharing a holiday with an ex soldier, they will have the map the right way up, perfectly folded, and they will never get lost. When in a queue at the bank, bus stop or immigration control they will have everything ready, forms filled, the right change, the lot.

More negative conditioning also comes into play. Some will lapse into rage triggered by next to nothing, such as one of the kids failing to replace the toilet roll. Yearning for the comfort of belonging and hierarchy, others will fall into bad company, join bikie gangs and post abusive commentary on fringe websites. While walking or driving they will go on automatic, searching out the most likely locations where an enemy would hide its snipers and machine guns.

A lot of memories will be hard to leave behind. The torment can come from nowhere and strike at any time. Like others, psychologist Colonel Peter Murphy sees the peacekeeping era producing a newer, smarter soldier facing up to newer, confronting responsibilities.

While war trauma is hardly a new phenomenon, there is 'a shadowy history of stress reaction'. Murphy has found soldiers do not need to be in the front line to suffer post traumatic stress disorder; indeed, sometimes the condition more often presents with support soldiers. 'The perception of threat was enough.' And considering the number of soldiers in Afghanistan killed when securely inside the wire, that perception is also certainly reality.

The increase in green on blue killings said to me it was time for the mentoring teams to go. And I am not convinced the alliance with former warlord Matiullah Khan works. Australians will go into the field with his men, who have their own ideas about who is the enemy. Sometimes they refuse to fight; other times, the locals warn the Australians they have teamed up with thugs.

At the same time I understand we can't simply cut and run. The mission is at as dangerous a phase as ever it was. Efforts to ensure the Afghans provide their own security has seen a mass of weaponry enter the hands of people who do not easily give up their hatred for one another. As at Gallipoli, we need to be cleverer in the getting out than we were in the getting in.

I expect Special Forces will hang on for as long as it can. Its soldiers have proven themselves to be the world's best, and they have the Taliban terrified, but they also need to be rescued from themselves. Given a choice, too many of them would stay on indefinitely because this is the way we train them, to never give up. And there will be an ongoing case for keeping boots on the ground, if only to prevent the war morphing into a contest between suicide bombers and drones.

To me, Afghanistan has been like a century long war fought in a tenth of that span. Victory will never be claimed, but progress is clear. The tribal enemies will ultimately settle into a form of mutual accommodation within an environment somewhat advanced. For the Australian soldiers to get as far as they did in little over a decade earns them eternal admiration. My life is richer for knowing them.

Elvi Wood tries not to be bitter about the loss of her husband Brett to Afghanistan. 'It was not a plot. He was in the wrong place at the wrong time.' She misses him, and continues to struggle. 'He learned to manage my expectations. He never held grudges. He could forgive people easily. I tried to learn from him. He loved Australia. We planned to drive all the way around the coast.'

David Deitz stayed on, and is now a Corporal. He tells me the lack of freedom has not bothered him. 'I am happy to be told what to do and have not stepped over the line. I don't go against the system like some.'

Captain Aaron Cimbaljevic, hit by an improvised explosive device just in front of Deitzy, is also still in. During a Christmas holiday after he got back Cimba and I went walking in the bush, almost stepping on a death adder. He later emailed to say he is afflicted by 'post traumatic death adder disorder'.

Corporal Dan is now a Sergeant. His mates are already giving him a hard time about my depiction of him as a bit like an IT specialist. He accepts it with good humour.

I think of Private Rudi, who won a Medal for Gallantry following the action that killed his friend, Jason Marks. Rudi got out while maintaining a link through the Reserves. The experience of trying to keep his mates alive drove him to obtain a degree in paramedic practice. When I ask him to read me the citation for his Medal for Gallantry, he says he has never seen it.

I envy their comradeship, to a degree. The ones who have shared extreme experiences have a particular bond, not that I would wish the experiences. The sainted mantle of mateship I have some doubts about, not only because there are mates in all armies, but also because there are so many non-mates. I could not help notice how many disaffected soldiers there were, how much contempt they held for some, and how much rivalry existed between others.

What I mostly feel is that we should try to know them better. If we can't be a part of their past, perhaps we can be more involved in their future. They join for the sake of the rest of us; they go to Afghanistan at the behest of the rest of us. The pressure for reform is a load they should not bear all on their own.

SOME MERITORIOUS CONDUCT AWARDS FROM ME

I am grateful first to Peter Leahy the former Chief of Army. When bestowing senior rank, someone made an excellent choice; you tend to have productive discussions with Peter. That is what occurred back in 2006 when he was exploring the nine core values of the modern Australian soldier and we fell into conversation about the character and culture of the digger.

The soldier who would from that moment have the strongest shaping influence on this book was then Captain Brendan Maxwell. Brendan and I have had hundreds of similarly fruitful talks over subsequent years. They are marked in my mind by generosity, insight and good humour. More than anyone he helped me enter the mind of the modern soldier. We became friends. I know his family. He invited me to the wedding with gentle Remy and then he deployed overseas. Brendan is now a Lieutenant Colonel and a great asset to us all, as he is one of the few to speak the language of both the soldier and the media.

There are a great many of his colleagues who also helped, working through tensions and obstacles that come with the territory when you deal with Defence. If a Colonel makes an incomprehensible decision and wants to impose it on to me, it is often the duty of the young public relations officer to be the messenger. I came to know well the despairing look that conveyed something like, 'Yes, I know we publish it on our own website, but we don't want you to publish it.'

With chronology more than rank in mind I want to thank Captains Chris Linden, Maggie Nichols, Haydn Barlow, Alistair McPherson, Al Green, Simone Heyer, Campbell Spencer, Lieutenant Adrian Miller and Lieutenant Colonel Jason Logue. From Canberra's Russell offices I am particularly grateful to Tony Bradford, who often went the extra distance for me. My thanks also go to Tanya Cleary, Phuong Nguyen and Nishara Miles.

I learned early in the piece that I would make little distance without support from the top. It was fortuitous Air Chief Marshal Angus Houston was in charge for most of the time it took to write this book. Australia's trust in Angus is well placed. He is one of its great citizens.

Ken Gillespie, who succeeded Peter Leahy as Chief of Army, was another important ally as is current Chief, David Morrison. In the Special Forces Command I am grateful to Major General Gus Gilmour and Brigadier Mark Smethurst for extending rare trust.

I travelled to Afghanistan three times sharing memorable experiences with some talented filmmakers. Had I not been able to make a series of documentaries, I could not have gained the access, made the connections and acquired the knowledge that underpins the Afghanistan chapters. Cameraman Andy Taylor pioneered the way in 2007. Sound Recordist Shane Munro accompanied Andy and returned with me in 2010, this time with Neale Maude. Gathering pictures and words was only as important as gathering trust. They were all like my forward scouts, heading out and inch-by-inch breaking down reservation and suspicion that would otherwise have made those assignments next to useless.

Ash Sweeting was another talented and useful collaborator for the 2010 series, 'A Careful War'. Mat Marsic and Kim Butler from Channel Ten were my valued partners for the later programs on Special Forces, 'Tour of Duty, Australia's Secret War'. So too were Sergeant Brent Tero and Leading Aircraftsman Leigh Cameron.

Some early conversations with Lieutenant Colonel Jamie Cullens, Warrant Officer Kevin Woods and Brigadier Simone Wilkie helped bring a massive subject into sharper focus. Colonel Stuart Yeaman, who commanded RTF4, furnished details of the earlier reconstruction programs in Uruzgan.

Working principally with 6RAR and the 2 Commando Regiment has meant greater attention is directed at the conduct and operations of those regiments. This does not reflect a lack of regard for the work of all the other fine regiments. As I explained at the beginning, I can only write about what I know about.

I have had so many consultations with Defence barrister Lieutenant Colonel David McLure that he could reasonably bill me. David's patient intelligence, so evident in court, advanced my understanding of some difficult cases as well as casting light on the important role of the General Reserve soldier.

It follows that friendships have been forged, with Aaron Cimbaljevic, Jason Groat, David Deitz, Jason and Susan Blain and more. I hope Lieutenant Colonel Gerry, who commanded Special Forces Rotation XVI, will one day write his own book. It would read well. So too would one from his SASR comrade Major James.

If I am welcome I will enjoy having a beer on Anzac Day with many of their brothers and sisters in arms: Chook, Clint, Paul, John, Brett and so many others who might rather not be named.

Particular regard is reserved for Corporal Dan, Bram Connolly and Troy Simmonds, all with stories central to the *Uncommon Soldier* theme. These fine men, unaccustomed to attention, do not easily take to the stage. Thanks to all three for succumbing to my blandishments and for saving me the embarrassment of making more than the usual dill of myself when juggling military jargon, nomenclature and the like. In particular, Bram Connolly made many a save.

One objective of the book has been the sharing of experience of the Afghanistan conflict. This has particular resonance for the families to have born losses. By retracing the last steps of loved ones I have risked aggravating ongoing grief. It is a delicate path I have tried not to overstep. I am grateful to Elvi Wood, Felix Sher, Madeline Fussell and Sandy Moerland for taking some of these difficult steps with me.

Allen & Unwin's Rebecca Kaiser is more than an editor. Her force of personality and professionalism is on every page. I thank Rebecca for a prodigious everything, including teaching me how to spell draught horse.

You know by now that I am by and large an unapologetic admirer of the Australian soldier, mostly seeing soldiering as something this country gets right. It would not be so without the endeavour of partners and families who endure it all without signing on. For them there should be a special place in the nation's heart.

To my wife Tanya, who has also had too much asked of her, there is a permanent place in my heart.

Chris Masters

NOTES

A QUARREL WITH MYSELF

1 Lieutenant General Sir John Monash, *The Australian Victories in France in 1918*, Hutchinson and Co., 1920, p. 290.

2 Eric Bergerud, *Touched With Fire*, Penguin, 1996, p. 268.

CHAPTER 1 CORPORAL DAN

1 Corporal Cam was awarded a Medal for Gallantry for this action.

2 'Inquiry Officer's Report into the death of 8265028 Pte L.J. Worsley in Afghanistan on 23 Nov 2007', Department of Defence, 8/12/07.

CHAPTER 2 'I DON'T KNOW HOW TO EXPLAIN IT …'

1 As of 2009 the annual income for a starting single soldier was $30,709. In 2012 it could be as high as $42,170.

2 'Anzacs', *Four Corners*, ABC-TV, broadcast 16/10/06.

3 The Australian Military Community, www.ausmilitary.com/forums 17/3/10.

4 Robert Graves, *Goodbye To All That*, Penguin, 1957, p. 156.

CHAPTER 3 BIAS FOR ACTION

1 *Royal Military College Duntroon*, National Film and Sound Archive 9383, c. 1926.

2 Major General Neville Howse, as a Lieutenant in the New South Wales Medical Corps during the Boer War, was awarded Australia's first Victoria Cross.

3 Darren Moore, *Duntroon: The Royal Military College 1911–2001*, Australian Military History Publications, 2001, p. 291.

4 Bruce Moore, *A Lexicon of Cadet Language*, Australian National Dictionary Centre, ANU, 1993, pp. 79, 80.

5 General Peter Cosgrove, *My Story*, HarperCollins, 2006, p. 39.

CHAPTER 4 GOING GREEN

1 No precise figures are available. In the second half of 2012, Class III at RMC had an approximate 16 per cent component of former serving members.

2 Investigating Officer's Report into the death of 8299931 Pte Jeremy Paul Williams, Executive Summary, www.defence.gov.au/publications.

3 'Anzacs', *Four Corners*, ABC-TV, broadcast 16/10/06.

CHAPTER 5 MISSION DRIFT

1 Eric Blehm, *The Only Thing Worth Dying For*, HarperCollins, 2010, p. 297.

2 PBS, 'The Battle of Tarin Kowt', *Frontline.*

3 Rory Callinan, 'In the valley of death', *Time Magazine*, 30/5/05.

4 One of the soldiers who spoke to *Time Magazine* was later identified as signaller Geffrey Gregg. A concern had been raised at the time that Gregg had not been given the appropriate training for the 2002 mission. Gregg left the Army and, tragically, committed suicide. Ean Higgins, 'Botched mission led to soldier's suicide', *Weekend Australian*, 21–22/4/07, p. 5.

5 Karen Middleton, *An Unwinnable War*, Melbourne University Press, 2011, p. 300.

6 Lieutenant Colonel David Kilcullen, 'Fundamentals of Company-level Counterinsurgency', Joint Information Operations Centre, reprinted *Australian Army Journal*, Volume V, Number 2, Winter 2008.

7 Speech by the Governor General, 26/10/07.

8 Some Seal Team Six members who survived this mission went on to take part in their most famous assignment, the execution of Osama bin Laden in Pakistan on 1 May 2011. Some were also lost in the worst single incident of the war for the Americans. On 6 July 2011 an MH47 was again shot down by a RPG. Of those on board 38 were killed, including 22 Navy Seals.

CHAPTER 6 ANOTHER 20 YEARS AT LEAST

1 Ian McPhedran, 'Bloodiest battle since Vietnam', *Herald Sun*, 13/9/06.

2 Major Michael Scott, 'Rebuilding Afghanistan one mud-brick at a time', *Australian Army Journal*, Volume IV, Number 1, Autumn 2007, p. 58.

3 Chris Mason, Sharan Provincial Reconstruction Team, US Center for Advanced Defense Studies, correspondence with author, 1/11/07.

4 Warrant Officer Class One Kevin Woods, 'Leadership from a soldier's point of view', Australian Defence College survey, 2005–06.

5 1 RAR, The First Battalion Association newsletter, D Coy Op Slipper.

6 Earlier in 2002 Todd Langley was awarded a Commendation for Distinguished Service for operations in East Timor.

7 'Forward Base Afghanistan', *Four Corners*, ABC-TV, broadcast 2/7/07.

8 ibid.

9 ibid.

10 Ian McPhedran, 'Each soldier in Afghanistan costs taxpayers a million', *Daily Telegraph*, 18/1/12.

CHAPTER 7 OPERATION HOME FRONT

1 Adam Heemskirk later told me that upon return to Australia and after a good talk it was decided he would stay on.

2 The survey applies to all services, Navy and Air Force as well as Army. Department of Defence Census 2007, Public Report, February 2009, p. 8.

3 Australian Bureau of Statistics, March Quarter, 2012.

CHAPTER 8 MOWING THE GRASS

1 Aryn Baker, 'Afghan women and the return of the Taliban', *Time*, 9/8/2010.

2 The Liaison Office, 'Three years later: A socio-political assessment of Uruzgan Province from 2006 to 2009', 18/9/09, p. 20.

3 Lieutenant-Colonel I.D. Langford DSC, 'NATO Special Operations: Exploiting new structures in command, control and intelligence in order to transform NATO into *the* alliance of the 21st century', Joint Special Operations University, May 2010, p. 16.

4 The Liaison Office, 'Three years later …', p. 29.

5 Colonel D.K. Connolly, 'Inquiry Officer's Report into the death of Signaller S.P. McCarthy in Afghanistan on July 8 2008', p. 11.

6 Rob Maylor with Robert Macklin, *SAS Sniper*, Hachette Australia, 2010, p. 285.

7 Peter Pedersen, 'Recock and refigure. Trooper Mark Donaldson VC speaks', *Wartime*, Issue 46, Australian War Memorial, 2009.

8 ibid.

9 Rob Maylor with Robert Macklin, *SAS Sniper*, p. 301.

10 A US Special Forces soldier recovered Sarbi when he spotted the dog and noticed it responded to military commands.

CHAPTER 9 CIVCAS

1 Lachlan Grono would later become an officer, graduating RMC in June 2011.

2 *Afghanistan Handbook*, Joint Operations Intelligence Centre, Australia, p. 36.

3 Matthew Carney and Thom Cookes, 'In Their Sights', *Four Corners*, ABC-TV, 1/9/11.

4 Three years on, Bronson Horan spoke on behalf of the welfare initiative Soldier On, with Michael Fussell's parents in the audience. Major Horan revealed further traumatic costs of having been 'diminished to a point that he could not remember his children's names'. Soldier On launch, Canberra Services Club, 13/4/12.

5 A tribute to Private Greg Sher, the first Australian General Reserve soldier killed in Afghanistan, can be found at www.gregsher.com.

6 'ISAF forces kill key insurgent commander', ISAF press release, 11/1/09.

7 'Diggers kill Taliban leader in Afghanistan', *Australian* and Agence France Presse, 11/1/09.

8 Colonel S.E. Clingan, 'Inquiry Officer's report into an allegation that an indirect fire mission by Special Operations Task Group in Afghanistan on 5 January 2009 caused a number of unintended civilian Casualties', 20/2/09, p. 12.

9 The Regiment was renamed in June 2009.

10 Nick Leys, 'Honour Brett's memory', *Sunday Telegraph*, 27/9/09, p. 5.

11 'A Real Fighter', *Sixty Minutes*, Channel Nine, 12/8/10.

12 Department of Defence, media release, 'Australian troops in major battles with Taliban insurgents', 25/4/09.

13 Major Jim Hammett, 'We were soldiers once . . . the decline of the Royal Australian Infantry Corps', *Australian Army Journal*, Autumn 2008, p. 47.

14 Tim Lester, 'Still missing Benjamin', *Sydney Morning Herald*, 25/4/12.

CHAPTER 10 'WE DIDN'T GET DRESSED UP FOR NOTHING'

1 Ian McPhedran and Gary Ramage, Embedding Trial Report, September 2009.

2 Five soldiers faced administrative action over Mason Edwards' death. At the time of writing, 'at least two have been issued termination notices requiring them to show cause as to why they should not be

sacked'. Nick McKenzie and Richard Baker, 'Soldiers face sack over commando training death', *Sydney Morning Herald*, 14/7/12, p. 1.

3 It should be noted there are variations on interpreting the ISAF acronym, including 'I Saw Americans Fighting' and 'I Suck at Fighting'.

4 NATO/ISAF, *Commander's Counterinsurgency Guidance*, 2009–2010.

CHAPTER 11 SNOWY AND SMITHY

1 ISAF, *Commander's Counterinsurgency Guidance*, 2009–2010.

2 Major Ian Langford, 'Australian Special Forces in Afghanistan', *Australian Army Journal*, Autumn 2010, p. 32.

3 'Warlord, Inc., Extortion and Corruption Along the U.S. Supply Chain in Afghanistan', Report of the Majority Staff, June 2010, p. 25.

4 Ash Sweeting interview for 'A Careful War', part 2, *Four Corners*, ABC-TV, broadcast 12/7/2010.

5 Rajiv Chandrasekaran, 'U.S. eager to replicate villagers' successful revolt against Taliban', *Washington Post*, 21/6/10.

6 Major David McLure, counsel for Sergeant John of 1 Commando facing manslaughter charges would defend Private Steve.

7 Ash Sweeting conducted the Tarin Kowt interviews.

8 Dr Peter Pedersen, 'The falling leaves of Tizak', *Wartime*, Issue 57, Australian War Memorial, January 2012.

9 'A Careful War' part 1, *Four Corners*, ABC-TV, broadcast 5/7/2010.

10 Essential Research Survey, 21/6/10, http://www.essentialmedia.com.au/troops-in-afghanistan/#more-183.

CHAPTER 12 ANZAC DAY

1 John Curtin, 'Anzac Remembrance', *Westralian Worker*, 29/4/27.

2 'A Careful War', part 2, *Four Corners*, ABC-TV, broadcast 12/7/10.

CHAPTER 13 THE AFGHAN WAY

1 The quote varies slightly from the original, the fifteenth of 'Twenty Seven Articles' produced in 1917 to assist British soldiers working with Bedouin tribes.

2 Opening Statement, Air Chief Marshal Angus Houston, Media Roundtable, 13/9/10.

3 'A Careful War' part 1, *Four Corners*, ABC-TV, broadcast 5/7/10.

4 Royal Australian Regiment Association, 5th Battalion, 'A close call', *Tiger Tales*, Issue 28, August 2011.

5 Ian McPhedran, 'No way to treat a hero. Lazarus rises in anger at Defence', *Herald Sun*, 6/3/12.

6 Matthew Carney, Thom Cookes, Shoab Sharifi, 'In Their Sights', *Four Corners*, ABC-TV, broadcast 5/9/11. (My last report for *Four Corners* was the 'A careful war' series in 2010.)

7 Nathan Mullins, *Keep Your Head Down*, Allen & Unwin, 2011, p. 138.

8 Tim Lester, 'The Fallen', part 2, Brett Wood, *The Age*, 2/5/12.

9 Statement on behalf of the family of Sapper Rowan Robinson, 'Vale Sapper Rowan Robinson', Department of Defence, www.defence.gov.au, June 2011.

10 ISAF colour coded key participants: Red Force, the enemy; Blue Force, the Coalition; Green Force ANA/ANP; and White Force GIRoA.

11 Department of Defence, Inquiry Officer Inquiry Into the Facts and Circumstances Associated With an Incident That Resulted in the Death of Lance Corporal Andrew Gordon Jones in Afghanistan on 30 May 2011, p. 33, 2/3/12.

CHAPTER 14 CAMP RUSSELL

1 Dan Oakes, 'Defence head backs warlord: Generous Afghan an important ally', *The Age*, 30/10/10.

2 'Tour of Duty. Australia's Secret War', Network Ten, broadcast 28/11/11 and 5/12/11.

CHAPTER 15 MAJOR BRAM

1 Bob Breen and Greg McCauley, *The World Looking Over Their Shoulder*, Land Warfare Studies Centre, Canberra, 2008, p. 31.

2 Charles Truehart, 'Canada can't shake Somali scandal', *Washington Post*, 29/12/96.

3 www.abc.net.au/tv/hungrybeast/stories/extended-helmet-cam-footage/index.html

CHAPTER 16 GETTING OUT

1 Australian Human Rights Commission, 'Review into the Treatment of Women in the Australian Defence Force', Phase 2, 2012, www.humanrights.gov.au/defencereview.

2 ibid., pp. 43, 52.

INDEX

Chris Masters is Australia's foremost investigative reporter, and the author of the bestselling *Jonestown* (2006). In 1985, he won Australia's most prestigious award in journalism, the Gold Walkley, for his *Four Corners* report on the sinking of the *Rainbow Warrior*. His reports 'The Big League' and 'The Moonlight State' both led to royal commissions that helped transform the nation.

Praise for *Jonestown*

'Tough and impassioned . . . this is a finely written and sparkling book.' — Bridget Griffen-Foley, *Sydney Morning Herald*

'Masters unveils a richly detailed and surprisingly rounded portrait of Jones . . . the account of how Jones wields and abuses his power as a broadcaster makes for profoundly disturbing reading.' — Matthew Ricketson, *The Age*

'. . . a textbook example of how to write a biography of a public figure and a fascinating, compulsively readable account of not just a man but also a city.' — *Herald Sun*

'Masters' account of the abuse of political power is startling.' — Mike Carlton, *Sydney Morning Herald*

'Chris Masters had done extensive research and the result is a compelling story of the rise and rise of Alan Jones.' — *Newcastle Herald*

'. . . an extraordinarily well-written, well-research biography.' — *Illawarra Mercury*